GLOBAL DEVELOPMENT AND HUMAN SECURITY

GLOBAL DEVELOPMENT AND HUMAN SECURITY

ROBERT PICCIOTTO
FUNMI OLONISAKIN
MICHAEL CLARKE

FOREWORD BY SIR LAWRENCE FREEDMAN

TRANSACTION PUBLISHERS
NEW BRUNSWICK (U.S.A.) AND LONDON (U.K.)

JZ5588 .P53 2007
0134111245152
Picciotto, Robert.

Global development and
human security
c2007.

2008 12 15

Copyright © 2007 by Transaction Publishers, New Brunswick, New Jersey.

All rights reserved under International and Pan-American Copyright Conventions. No part of this book may be reproduced or transmitted in any form or by any means, electronic or mechanical, including photocopy, recording, or any information storage and retrieval system, without prior permission in writing from the publisher. All inquiries should be addressed to Transaction Publishers, Rutgers—The State University, 35 Berrue Circle, Piscataway, New Jersey 08854-8042. www.transactionpub.com

This book is printed on acid-free paper that meets the American National Standard for Permanence of Paper for Printed Library Materials.

Library of Congress Catalog Number: 2006044673
ISBN: 978-0-7658-0374-0
Printed in the United States of America

Library of Congress Cataloging-in-Publication Data

Picciotto, Robert.
  Global development and human security : towards a policy agenda / Robert Picciotto, Funmi Olonisakin, Michael Clarke ; foreword by Sir Lawrence Freedman.
     p. cm.
  Includes bibliographical references and index.
    Contents: The challenges of partnership—Towards a more secure global development agenda—The new security landscape—Rethinking development cooperation—Improving conflict-handling mechanisms—Development cooperation and human security.
     ISBN 0-7658-0374-7 (alk. paper)
     1. International cooperation—Social aspects. 2. Globalization—Social aspects. I. Olonisakin, 'Funmi. II. Clarke, Michael. III. Title.

JZ1318.P49 2007

2006044673

Contents

Foreword by Sir Lawrence Freedman	xi
Introduction	1
1. The Challenges of Partnership	7
A. The Context: Poverty, Violence, Uncertainty	9
B. Global Development: A Shared Responsibility	27
C. Common Objectives: Human Security	31
D. Distinct Accountabilities: The Imperative of Coherence	45
E. Reciprocal Obligations: Human Rights	49
F. Conclusions	52
Appendix: Survey of Policy Coherence Practices	57
2. Towards a More Secure Global Development Agenda	65
A. Policy Coherence and Security	65
B. Managing Globalization	74
C. The Transmission Belts of Globalization Need Adjustment	84
D. Missing Goals?	98
E. Conclusions	100
3. The New Security Landscape	105
A. The Antecedents and Trends of Violent Conflict	105
B. Intra-State Wars Resist Classification	114
C. Terrorism Can be Tackled through Democratic Means	122
D. Weapons Proliferation Should be Reversed	128
E. Implications for Security Policy	132
F. Conclusions	141

4. Rethinking Development Cooperation — 147
   - A. Changing Conceptions of Development Cooperation — 147
   - B. State Fragility and Conflict — 154
   - C. New Policy Directions — 173
   - D. Reforming Aid — 185
   - E. Conclusions — 197

5. Improving Conflict-Handling Mechanisms — 203
   - A. Conceptual Underpinnings and Policy Responses — 204
   - B. From Policy to Practice: Gaps in the Field — 209
   - C. Addressing the Conflict-to-Development Gap — 221
   - D. The Prevention Deficit: Where Wars are Waiting to Happen — 231
   - E. Reliance on Regional Actors for Conflict Management — 233
   - F. Conclusions — 236

6. Development Cooperation and Human Security — 241
   - A. The Rationale for Change — 241
   - B. The Global Governance Environment — 244
   - C. Trends in Global Risk — 250
   - D. The Anatomy of Global Risks — 252
   - E. Towards a New Country Engagement Framework — 255
   - F. Human Security Priorities — 260

References — 271

Index — 281

Tables

Table 1. Human Security and Categories of Human Rights — 51

Table 2. Share of Developing Countries with Favorable or Unfavorable Endowments Achieving Security or Development — 171

Table 3. Share of Fragile and Not Fragile Developing Countries Achieving Security or Development — 171

Table 4. Impact of Capacity and Resilience on Security and Development — 172

Table 5. The Vulnerability-Exposure Nexus — 258

Acronyms

ASEAN	Association of East Asian Nations
CPIA	country policy and institutional assessment
DAC	Development Assistance Committee of the OECD
DDR	disarmament, demobilization, and reintegration
DNA	deoxyribonucleic acid
DPKO	United Nations Department of Peacekeeping Operations
DRC	Democratic Republic of Congo
DFID	United Kingdom Department for International Development
ECOMOG	Armed Monitoring Group of the Economic Community of West African States
ECOWAS	Economic Community of West African States
EGDI	Expert Group on Development Issues
ENP	European Neighborhood Policy
EU	European Union
EU-15	the 15 countries that formed the European Union until the end of April 2004
EU-25	the current 25 member countries of the European Union
FDI	foreign direct investment
G8	Canada, France, Germany, Italy, Japan, Russia, United Kingdom, and United States
GBP	British pounds
GDP	gross domestic product
HIV/AIDS	human immuno-deficiency virus/acquired immune deficiency syndrome
IAEA	International Atomic Energy Agency
IFAD	International Fund for Agricultural Development
LICUS	low-income countries under stress
MDGs	Millennium Development Goals
NAFTA	North American Free Trade Association
NATO	North Atlantic Treaty Organization
NGO	nongovernmental organization
NPT	Nuclear Non-proliferation Treaty
ODA	official development assistance
OECD	Organization for Economic Cooperation and Development

OSCE	Organization for Security and Cooperation in Europe
PCD	policy coherence for development
PSA	public service agreement
QIPS	quick impact projects
SARS	sudden acute respiratory syndrome
SIDA	Swedish International Development Cooperation Agency
SIPRI	Stockholm International Peace Research Institute
SRSG	special representative of the Secretary-General
SSR	security sector reform
TRIMS	Agreement on Trade-related Investment Measures
TRIPS	Agreement on Trade-related Intellectual Property Rights
UK	United Kingdom
UN	United Nations
UNAMSIL	United Nations Mission to Sierra Leone
UNICEF	United Nations Children's Fund
UNCTAD	United Nations Conference on Trade and Development
UNDP	United Nations Development Program
US	United States
USAID	United States Agency for International Development
USD	United States dollars
WMD	weapons of mass destruction
WHO	World Health Organization
WTO	World Trade Organization

Foreword

This millennium began in an optimistic mood, which even extended to the adoption of ambitious goals for development. Fuelling the optimism was heady economic growth, driven forward by the information revolution, low commodity prices, and enthusiastic consumption. The conclusion of the Cold War at the end of the 1980s removed the specter of a nuclear conflict among the great powers, and the subsequent decade opened up the prospect of the peaceful resolution of yet more damaging conflicts. The *apartheid* regime in South Africa conceded defeat just as the East European communist regimes had done, and the Oslo process offered hope of an eventual deal between Israel and the Palestinians. The break-up of the former Yugoslavia and a series of vicious civil wars in Africa and elsewhere suggested a less promising prospect, but by the end of the 1990s it could be argued that Western countries were coming to accept a responsibility to aid the weak and distressed, even with armed force. Humanitarian intervention was patchy and led to demanding long-term commitments to reconstruct shattered societies, but discussion in the UN and elsewhere focused on how to do them better rather on than how to walk away.

The optimism did not last long. The failure of the Camp David talks involving Yasser Arafat and Ehud Barak, convened by President Clinton in the summer of 2000, helped spark the second Palestinian *intifada*. The bubble in technology stocks burst and big corporate names, such as Enron, tuned out to have depended more on fraud than productivity. Joining the Japanese economy, which had still failed to revive from the torpor into which it sank after the bumper years of the 1980s, was Europe's. Whatever advantage was gained by a common European currency was lost without at the same time engaging in structural reforms. The American economy kept going by tolerating deficits and trade imbalances that foreshadowed an eventual reckoning, and that past Republican administrations would have considered downright irresponsible. Although the remarkable advance of China and India was an overall plus for the international economy, it added to the sense of unease in countries that felt unable to compete with these low-cost giants.

A particular source of gloom was the growing incidence of Islamist terrorism, most dramatically in the suicide attacks of September 11, 2001. These events created a unique sense of vulnerability in Western countries, and set in motion a series of responses that have had major domestic and international consequences. One explanation for President Bush's Iraqi adventure was to keep oil prices down. If so it was a failure in this as well as other respects. By 2005 prices were high and supplies were tight, becoming even more so when the U.S. Gulf coast was hit by the successive hurricanes Katrina and Rita.

This is not the easiest context in which to encourage states to turn away from narrow, short-term concerns and opt for enlightened self interest in a pursuit of internationalist goals. But Sweden's sponsorship of this book and its unswerving commitment to these goals encouraged the authors to present a set of propositions on how best to address the interconnected issues of development and security. The analysis offered in the following pages is unsparing in its criticism of past failures in policy implementation and it is not negligent of the continuing barriers to progress. But it is infused with optimism and a conviction that much can be usefully and realistically be done. By drawing on the best thinking on these issues of recent years, and providing a coherent synthesis of policy options, the volume points a way forward. Taking up its proposals might not eradicate all the world's ills but would help to alleviate many of the worst effects.

At a time of diminishing expectations it is important not to succumb to fatalism. As the authors note, it is not the case that aid measures invariably fail or that international organizations always screw up, or that external interventions invariably make things worse rather than better, or that nothing has been learned from recent experience. Among these experiences, that in Iraq has inevitably undermined assumptions that complex problems can be solved at a stroke through bold and decisive military moves, or that the tough exercise of hard power is more reliable than the more cautious and compromised exercise of soft power. In the U.S. it has created wariness about future military operations, and greater sensitivity to the need to find partners and work through multilateral organizations. The lessons are relevant to all forceful interventions: the sort of force that might topple a regime and occupy a country is quite different in composition and demeanor from the sort that can maintain law and order and address, through economic and political reconstruction, the everyday concerns of ordinary people.

If such lessons are learned, it is all to the good, although problems of a different sort could result if the U.S. decided that it had better stay clear of all future foreign entanglements. Negative experiences do not necessarily create enthusiasm for fresh initiatives. One reason why a degree of engagement might be sustained is the presumed link, hard though it is to pin down, between fragile and failed states and terrorism. Fragile states are those that can barely cope with the social, economic, and political demands that are placed upon them. Failed states are those that fail to cope; they are usefully seen as those that can no longer monopolize organized violence within their own borders. In this sense strong states may still fail against such criteria as eradicating poverty and improving welfare, let along introducing democracy, but the strength of such states can be illusory. When really tested, they prove to be quite brittle. Such states are not uncommon in the developing world. They might be, in their own terms, very efficient but their inherent lack of legitimacy and their inattention to constitutional proprieties when dealing with their own people can lead them to decay from within.

When states do fail, and become full of conflict, they generate much anger and bitterness. Largely this is directed inwards, which is why these countries are so difficult to "stabilize" after a civil war, yet it can also be generated outwards, against those who are believed to have supported their oppressors, either actively or tacitly. This is why it can result in international terrorism. One line of argument, evident among some Islamist groups, is to link together a number of otherwise disparate conflicts as evidence of a wider conspiracy. For example, to many Islamists, the varying forms of external engagement in Chechnya, East Timor, Kashmir, and Kosovo as well as Afghanistan, Iraq, and Palestine do not result from the exercise of discretion, guided by prudence as much as conscience, but instead follow a pattern of action designed to undermine Islam.

This is one reason why leaving well alone does not necessarily avoid difficult consequences. Further, the more this inclination is followed the more difficult any later intervention will prove to be if the risks of continued passivity also start to seem unacceptable. Common sense suggests that the most effective approach is to get involved earlier rather than later, before the rot has set in, to stop quarrels within and between countries before they become deadly and descend into long-term violence, to go for early prevention rather than belated cure.

This seems so obvious that it is worth considering why it doesn't happen more. Part of the problem is diagnosis. When the symptoms are ambiguous a bad diagnosis might lead to a faulty prognosis. Vicious conflicts may look inevitable in retrospect, but as the conflicts develop the participants may be in deep denial, and discourage offers of external help. Moreover, public opinion in donor countries only starts to take note when situations are desperate; governments tend to respond to crises as they peak rather than as they develop. That said, it is important to note that many disputes have been called and then barely heard of again because quiet diplomacy has done the trick. This volume argues that addressing the circumstances of poverty, disease, and repression that lead states to become fragile, and some eventually to fail, makes conflict less likely to happen, and should, in the process, improve the human condition.

Human security requires a functioning state. Some states are undoubtedly causes of great insecurity for their people and others, but there are still no better agencies for ensuring security, so the challenge is to help develop the sort of state that can cope. Ideally, the only security policies of relevance will be to support police work to deal with low-level criminality and rowdy behavior. To this end, effective development and security policies ought to reinforce each other, by building up states in the third world that are capable of coping with the multiple challenges they face, and through which international support can be channeled. When outsiders have to provide the state functions, dependence on them grows and they become responsible for all that goes wrong. They will not find their exit strategy until they have been able to transfer power to the local communities.

This process is more state building than nation building, although a sense of nationhood can create an identity and generate loyalty to state institutions that might otherwise be lacking. This is why a holistic approach is needed, which recognizes that it is vital to build up the capacity for self government, even while attending to immediate needs. Underlying this approach is recognition that promoting security and development is a highly political activity and must be understood in these terms, but also that they must be brought together. In too many discussions of such problems as core poverty, infant mortality, or the incidence of HIV/AIDS, as well as human security, they are assumed to be quite different types of issues best considered in quite separate institutional settings.

An unsentimental analysis of strategic risk points to the need to engage with the multiple problems of the developing world because in the end chronic instability has consequences for the whole international community. Yet altruism is also important. As shown by the build-up to the July 2005 Gleneagles summit of the Group of Eight industrialized nations, there are vast wellsprings of idealism waiting to be tapped. There is also a readiness to engage in a serious debate about whether the transfer of resources from rich to poor can ever be enough unless attention is also paid to issues of governance and security. Idealism is not enough; but it is not a bad start.

During the 1990s it was believed that progress could be almost effortless, with trade barriers coming down and investors searching for promising emerging countries. We now know that progress requires coordinated action across a number of fronts, and that actors in one area must think through the consequences for other areas. This approach is both more demanding and more realistic. It is why *Global Development and Human Security* is particularly timely.

Sir Lawrence Freedman
Vice Principal
Kings College, London

Introduction

"The lesson for the twenty-first century is that the fight for security, prosperity and justice can no longer be won on any one nation's ground...It requires agreement on values. It is predicated on an acknowledgment of interdependence...It requires courage and leadership." –Will Hutton

The idea for this book originated in conversations with Ruth Jacoby, Director General, Development, of the Swedish Ministry for Foreign Affairs, and Torgny Holmgren, head of the Ministry's Expert Group on Development Issues. The upshot was a request addressed to King's College, London to examine a range of policy questions that had arisen when the bill that now governs Sweden's development cooperation was debated by its Parliament.

Sweden's Shared Responsibility bill addresses peace, security, opportunity, environmental conservation, human rights, and democracy.[1] It stresses ownership of these goals by all Sweden's development partners. No other rich country's government has made so explicit a link between global poverty reduction and the full range of policy links that connect rich and poor countries. Putting such an ambitious policy stance into practice constitutes a momentous challenge, internally as well as externally. Long standing obstacles to 'joined up' government and divergent perceptions about the role of development cooperation among OECD partners have to be overcome.

Knowledge gaps about the "footprint" of rich countries' policies on poor countries have to be filled. While development researchers have made considerable efforts to identify policies and processes for equitable and sustainable growth in poor countries, they have barely begun to examine the impact of rich countries' policies on global poverty reduction. In particular, the complex intersection between security and development policies has not been adequately mapped or explored

The reasons for this state of affairs are well known. There has been too little commerce between defense studies and development economics.

Policy research is fragmented. Trespassing across disciplinary boundaries is frowned upon. Even so, decision makers are under pressure to achieve policy coherence. To guard against the excesses induced by fear among the electorates of the industrial democracies, public concerns must be balanced by accurate information and thoughtful debate. Objective analysis is needed to help improve the public discourse, relate segregated fields of inquiry, and discredit misguided policy proposals.

The current mood of uncertainty contrasts with the widespread optimism that prevailed at the turn of the millennium when all heads of states gathered in New York under United Nations auspices. The Millennium Declaration that they endorsed in 2000 marked the culmination of decades of efforts by the world body.[2] Despite major differences in interests and perspectives, all UN member countries pledged to address the root causes of global poverty, conflict, ignorance, disease, malnutrition, gender inequity, environmental degradation, and other chronic "problems without passports" that have consigned vast zones of the world to stagnation and despair. For the first time in UN history, specific development goals were agreed, along with a battery of performance indicators designed to track the outcomes of a comprehensive approach to human development. Reflecting universal aspirations and grounded in the deliberations of numerous international conferences, the Millennium Development Goals (MDGs) secured substantial public support and enhanced the legitimacy of development assistance.[3]

But it did not take long for disillusion to set in. By now it is clear that a majority of developing countries will not achieve the Millennium Development Goals. Inadequate resources have been mobilized. Doubts have surfaced about the capacity of the multilateral system to reform and deliver. Probing questions have been raised about the fairness of the compact between rich and poor countries that had generated such high expectations at the Financing for Development Conference in Monterrey (Mexico) in 2002.

Under a new global "partnership for development," poor countries had accepted the responsibility to improve their governance and reform their policies. Since then, most have complied with the obligation to prepare poverty reduction papers for review by international financial institutions—a prerequisite of debt reduction and increased aid. But rich countries, for their part, have offered only a broad acknowledgment of the need to level the playing field of the international economy. The eighth Millennium Development Goal merely notes the shared responsibility of rich countries for poverty reduction. Time-bound undertakings or performance indicators for this goal were not agreed. Thus, no major change in the rules of the game that govern the global market is on the horizon, and most of the performance indicators selected to track progress towards the Millennium Development Goals point south.

Also lacking are agreed goals and indicators for global security and conflict prevention. This gap is significant for three reasons. First, the core mandate of the United Nations Charter is the protection of international peace and the enhancement of collective security. Second, the Millennium Declaration was explicit about the need to combine security and development efforts. Third, the holiday from history of the post-Cold War era has come to an abrupt end.

On 9/11 the turmoil of the periphery reached the shores of the world's lone superpower. By now, the dark side of globalization has been revealed. The spreading chaos of an insecure world has dimmed the appeal of the global market integration project that the dissolution of the Soviet Union had made feasible. The same characteristics of open societies that facilitate the global reach of multinational companies have induced rising inequalities, social tensions, and natural resource depletion—which the Millennium Development Goals sought to tackle—as well as a rise in violent conflict, weapons proliferation, international crime, and transnational terrorism—which they did not.

While the overarching goal of connecting all countries to the global economy remains critically important, it is now evident that complementary measures are needed to defuse the social tensions and manage the security risks that result from exposure to a turbulent international system. The legitimate security concerns of electorates can no longer be subordinated to the dictates of orthodox economic management. An explosion of illicit transactions, fuelled by globalization, is overstretching the regulatory and enforcement capacities of the international system.

Against this background of turmoil and anxiety, the protocols and practices of the aid industry appear ill adapted to the challenges and threats faced by the international community. Aid allocations penalize frail and failing states that lack sound market and security institutions. Fragile states are the weak links of an interconnected world, and yet the aid allocation principles agreed under the aegis of the Development Assistance Committee of the Organization for Economic Cooperation and Development (OECD/DAC) discourage engagement with "difficult partners" and hinder interaction with the security community.

Thus, OECD policymakers face a difficult transition as they seek to revitalize the aid enterprise to address emerging security threats. They face stiff resistance not only within aid agencies but also in the civil society. Humanitarian and development advocates harbor legitimate fears that the aid business could be "taken over" or undermined by a defense establishment partial to military solutions and committed to state-centric security doctrines. To adapt the development cooperation business to the new challenges of security (while remaining true to the ideals of the aid enterprise), new concepts, new tools, and new practices will have to be forged. Similarly, doctrinal shifts towards strategies that combine "soft" and "hard" power will have to take place within tradition-bound defense establishments.

What paradigm should supplant the development consensus that was forged at the turn of the century? What meta-narrative can unify security and development policies? What does the "securitization" of development imply for poverty reduction? Should corollary steps be taken to "developmentalize" security? To address these and related queries, the authors undertook a stocktaking. We screened the recent literature through the prism of Sweden's Shared Responsibility bill and consulted with scholars and practitioners.

The resulting document is geared to the adaptation of operational strategies to new realities. It does not seek to blaze new academic trails or to drill down into arcane areas of security and development research. Instead, it brings together lessons of experience currently scattered in the public domain. Foreign policy dilemmas are very diverse and require context-specific approaches. But access to past experience can help to shape global, regional, and country strategies in response to specific challenges.

Thus, the book is aimed mostly at practitioners who need up-to-date knowledge about security and development issues. But it can also serve as an introductory text for security specialists with little knowledge of development and for development specialists with limited knowledge of security. It lays out novel ways of thinking about development cooperation and sketches new policy emphases for the international development community.

Each chapter is self-contained and, where applicable, includes specific policy findings and recommendations. Chapter 1 examines the challenges of partnership in the current international context. Chapter 2 identifies the main adjustments to rich countries' policies that global poverty reduction requires. Chapter 3 outlines emerging security threats and their policy implications. Chapter 4 proposes new directions for development cooperation. Chapter 5 does the same for conflict management. Chapter 6 concludes with policy recommendations.

Notes

1. *Shared Responsibility – Sweden's Policy for Global Development.* Government Bill 2002/03: 122; Act of Parliament 2003/04: UU3.
2. At the Millennium Summit 147 monarchs, presidents, and prime ministers committed their nations to creating an international system in which poor nations would assume responsibility for enhancing the well being of their poor citizens and rich nations would accept the obligation to help in the achievement of specific and measurable reductions in poverty, malnutrition, illiteracy, disease, gender discrimination, and environmental stress by the year 2015. Subsequently, under the terms of the compact endorsed at the United Nations Financing for Development Conference in Monterrey in 2002, rich countries undertook to enhance the quantity and quality of their aid and to adjust the rules of the game of the global economy.
3. The eight goals are: (1) eradicate extreme poverty and hunger; (2) achieve universal primary education; (3) promote gender equality and empower women; (4) reduce child mortality; (5) improve maternal health; (6) combat HIV/AIDS, malaria, and other diseases; (7) ensure environmental sustainability; (8) develop a global partnership for development. The MDGs reflect universal aspirations but are not widely known. Sweden stands out as the European country with the highest awareness of the Millennium Development Goals (MDGs). But this only means that 27 percent of the Swedish public (compared to 22 percent for the EU-15 group as a whole, and 10 percent for the new EU member states) are acquainted with the MDGs (Eurobarometer, 2005).

1

The Challenges of Partnership

"The point of politics is to change things."—Javier Solana

The business of development—Adam Smith's "progress towards opulence and improvement"—has undergone major transformations. From its original focus on national well being, measured by the growth of per capita income, it has evolved towards the satisfaction of basic needs, the achievement of social and environmental sustainability, the elimination of poverty, and, most recently, the pursuit of self-fulfillment for all: development as freedom. Similarly, the meaning of security has become more diverse and complex. Turmoil at the periphery has supplanted the East-West balance of terror that marked the Cold War era.

Security concerns are shared by rich and poor countries alike but the major threats to human survival have migrated towards the developing world, where more than four fifths of the world's people (and most of the world's absolute poor) live. In these zones of turmoil and change, the need for protection extends well beyond the risks of violence to people's lives; poverty, ignorance, malnutrition, and disease are the greatest killers. Some of these threats—health pandemics, international crime, illegal trafficking, and trans-national terrorism—spill over towards rich countries, where they create a climate of insecurity.

The policy implications are far reaching. Given public opinion, and the advocacy of human rights by an ascending global civil society, governments' legitimacy and survival will increasingly depend on their capacity and willingness to guarantee the safety, basic needs, and essential freedoms of individual citizens and groups. The unit of account has gradually shifted from the state to the individual. The concept of security has broadened and it is now intertwined with ethical concerns that transcend national security considerations. In the public mind if not yet in government and academic establishments, freedom from want and freedom from fear have become inseparable.

This is why coherence has become an overarching imperative of competent public policymaking and why decision makers have begun to break free from the narrow strictures of their professional silos. In the industrial democracies the public is now demanding results that require joined up, mutually reinforcing policies and programs that combine all major international relations instruments: defense, diplomacy, and development cooperation. Within the development community, two broad policy propositions have gained ground: (i) development should be "securitized" to create a safe enabling environment for poverty reduction; and (ii) security should be "developmentalized" to deal with the root causes of conflict.

These are the contextual factors that have favored the advent of a more comprehensive *human security* paradigm. Just as it is no longer relevant to limit the security discourse to the military realm, it makes little sense to adopt a "soft" definition of human security that ignores such "hard" threats as trans-national terrorism or weapons proliferation. On the other hand, it would be self-defeating to conflate all possible threats to life, liberty, and the pursuit of happiness under the human security umbrella. This would devalue the term and destroy its usefulness. For a new paradigm to take root, it must facilitate effective public action, bring together scattered ideas, mobilize dormant energies, and facilitate joint endeavors.

Prior attempts to promote human security did not elicit broadly based support. They were not backed up by a logic that allowed the setting of priorities and the assignment of accountabilities. Properly defined, human security enhances policymaking by bringing the discipline of policy coherence and the rigor of risk management to bear on strategic choices and on resource allocation. Specifically, the revamped human security framework for development cooperation that is the subject of this book embraces rights-based approaches, emphasizes clear allocations of responsibilities to duty bearers, and proposes a mix of analytical tools to assess and rank policy options.

Once tested and adopted, such a framework would help to define new policy emphases and allow the use of risk management techniques to evaluate policy options across the security and development domains. It would distinguish between threats to human survival (the core meaning of security) on the basis of the probability, variance, and predictability of adverse events and the extent of damage they are likely to cause to life and livelihoods. Collective action theory and policy coherence concepts would be brought to bear. Freed from the strictures of blueprint models, policymakers would address explicitly the public yearning for protection against rising threats and challenges.

To lay the foundations for such a human security agenda, this chapter begins by outlining the context for policymaking and then (in Section B) emphasizes the need for rich countries to acknowledge their share of the responsibility for global poverty reduction. Next, Section C outlines the proposed human security paradigm and identifies opportunities and means for its practical application. This is followed by a four-way typology of policy coherence for development (Section D) that extends beyond aid. In turn, Section E shows how human rights can provide a unifying conceptual framework in support of the human security agenda. Section F concludes.

A. The Context: Poverty, Violence, Uncertainty

In the changed landscape of the post-Cold War era, the international community is groping for ways to bring security and development closer together. In an era of interdependence and rapid change, what goes on outside borders affects what happens inside. The converse is also true: the problems of others have become our own. To be sure, security and development policies seek independently worthy goals. Poverty reduction is a noble objective in its own right and citizens' safety is the central purpose of the state. While poverty does not cause conflict (the causality runs in the other direction), both poverty and violence are connected to state frailty and failure. Accordingly, assessing threats, managing risks, and building the capacity of vulnerable states have become policy priorities for security as well as for development.

This is where the human security agenda comes in. Its design responds to five characteristics of the operating context that are described below. They reflect the interaction between security and development imperatives and confirm the need for coherent policy solutions: (i) poverty reduction is lagging: the Millennium Development Goals appear out of reach for a majority of developing countries; (ii) security concerns dominate public opinion; (iii) the center of gravity of violence has shifted towards the developing world; (iv) the rules of the game in the global market economy are unbalanced; and (v) a new global compact between

Europe, the United States, and developing countries is imperative if results are to be achieved.

Poverty Reduction is Lagging

Across the developing world, poverty inflicts massive damage. One third of all human deaths (18 million annually) are poverty-related. Some 2.7 billion people, or 44 percent of the world's population, subsist on less than USD 2 a day. They use only about 1.3 percent of the global product while the 955 million citizens of high-income countries, or 15 percent of the world's population, consume 81 percent. This means that a targeted and permanent shift of only 1.2 percent of rich countries' incomes towards the poor of the world would make poverty history (Pogge, 2005).

The Millennium Development Goals have more modest aims: to halve the share of the population living on less than one dollar a day by 2015 and to appreciably reduce the ill health, illiteracy, malnutrition, and enslavement caused by poverty. These goals and the associated indicators are grounded in conclusions reached by several United Nations conferences. They have gathered unmistakable public support. But progress towards them has been disappointing.

With less than a decade left to reach the 2015 milestone, a huge challenge looms. Every hour, 1,200 children under five die from preventable diseases and we already know that most regions will fall short of the reduced child mortality goal. Some 115 million children are still not in school and three out of six regions are unlikely to reach the goal of universal primary school completion over the next decade. Nor will gender disparities in education decline as planned in half of the regions. In Sub-Saharan Africa alone, HIV/AIDS kills two million people every year. When a major international cooperation effort was launched against the pandemic a turnaround was expected, but this has yet to happen.

The reduction of income poverty has been somewhat more encouraging, but with major regional differences. Globally, according to the World Bank, the number of people with per capita income of less than a dollar a day declined from 1,482 million in 1981 to 1,093 million in 2001 (Chen and Ravallion, 2004). East Asia has already achieved the 2015 target and South Asia is on track. But in Sub-Saharan Africa, overall poverty rates have risen and most countries will fall short of the goal.

As a share of the population of developing countries, the number of people in absolute poverty has declined from 40 percent to 21 percent, measured by the one dollar a day benchmark, and from 67 percent to 53 percent by the two dollar a day benchmark. The estimated improvement is entirely due to China's unique growth record, however, and there are doubts about the quality of Chinese survey data for the early years of the period. Outside China, increases in the number of the absolute poor have exceeded the reductions. Using the still frugal two dollar a day benchmark, the number of poor people worldwide has *risen*—from 2,450 million in 1981 to 2,736 million in 2001.

Huge inequities underlie the current world order. Since the end of the Cold War, the ratio of average income in the richest countries to that in the very poorest has risen. The gap in per capita annual income between rich and poor countries has grown from about USD 17,000 to USD 24,000.[1,2] A person picked at random in the richest country (Norway) is seventy-three times as wealthy as a person chosen at random in the poorest (Sierra Leone). If the world's richest ten people invested their aggregate wealth (USD 217 billion) so as to secure a 5 percent return, they would earn as much as the entire population of Tanzania (35 million people).

The distributive implications depend on how income inequality is measured (World Bank, 2005a). There is strong evidence that within countries, income inequality has increased. Inequality has also risen among countries, especially since the 1980s. But globally, if *individuals* rather than countries are the unit of observation, inequality has been reduced, largely because of the remarkable income growth and poverty reduction recorded by the large and populous countries of Asia.

Wide inequalities in income are associated with a small middle class, a weak civil society, and a lack of government responsiveness. In East Asia, land reform, human capital formation, smallholder development, and export-oriented industrialization helped to create a middle class that demanded government accountability. This is not what happened in other parts of the developing world, where history has weighed heavily on the poor. All too often, inequitable distribution of land and economic dependence on natural resources have perpetuated a lopsided concentration of wealth, limited access to education, weak social services, and elitist governments.

Insecurity Dominates Public Opinion

The development agenda has always been shaped by the great issues of the day. In the 1950s it addressed post-war reconstruction; in the 1960s, decolonization; in the 1970s, the energy crisis; in the 1980s, the debt crisis; and in the 1990s, following the implosion of the Soviet empire, the creation of a global market. Thus it is not surprising that since 9/11 the spotlight has shifted towards security concerns.

Security issues now loom large in public perceptions and a wide range of challenges and threats permeate the development discourse. World Bank consultations that gave voice to 20,000 poor people in twenty-three developing countries showed that a majority of those interviewed perceive that economic opportunities are fewer and insecurity greater than in the past.[3]

According to a worldwide poll taken in 2002,[4] opinion leaders believe that fighting poverty is critical to achieving world peace and lowering global tensions. This sentiment is especially strong in Sub-Saharan Africa (91 percent), South Asia (87 percent), and the Middle East and North Africa (79 percent). Support for the same proposition is also high within rich countries, where seven in ten opinion leaders believe that fighting poverty is the path to peace. Equally, among 43,000 people who were recently surveyed by Gallup International in 51 countries,[5] most think that prosperity cannot be attained without security. Revealingly, perceptions that economic performance is poor have a disproportionately negative effect on perceptions of security.

It is not that "everything changed" as a result of 9/11. Well before, there was full awareness that our planet was getting smaller, that the diverse peoples of the world were living a single history, and that the unprecedented growth in consumption was generating extraordinary environmental stress. In particular, the public was well aware that the greatest security risks of our times—natural disasters, violent conflict, international crime, illegal trafficking, infectious diseases, and environmental threats—do not recognize national boundaries. But 9/11 crystallized the public mood and accelerated the adoption of policies that had only been incipient.

After the Soviet Union collapsed, the United States became the uncontested world military power and the ideological rationale for intervening in the affairs of other states vanished. For some time, the U.S. moderated its "exceptionalist"[6] posture under the diplomatic cover of a multilaterally inclined and commercially focused Clinton administration. It remained on the sidelines of intra-state conflicts and did little to counter international terrorism. Lacking a clear-cut national interest in becoming involved, the U.S. did not intervene in Rwanda and it did not stay the course in Somalia. Its lone superpower status predisposed it to proceed without United Nations sanction in Kosovo, but it did so only because repeated and flagrant civil rights violations at the heart of Europe had galvanized domestic public opinion in favor of intervention. Otherwise, from 1989 to 2001, the country enjoyed a "holiday from history" (Will, 2001).

By 2001, the number of major conflicts in the world was declining. While there were indications that international crime and terrorist activities were on the rise and that many of the post-Cold War conflicts had merely been frozen rather than resolved, the warnings of anti-terrorist specialists were ignored. Only when the vulnerability of the homeland came to light did the American public call for retaliation. The proven threat led to a sharp policy turnaround towards interventionism: the 2002 United States security doctrine (U.S. Government, 2002) set a new course that was reaffirmed in 2006 (U.S. Government, 2006b). Both documents acknowledge the threat that state weakness in poor and troubled countries poses for international stability. Both justify preemptive action on grounds of self-defense.

9/11 was only an opening salvo. Subsequently, terrorists hit Jakarta, Bali (twice), Istanbul, Madrid, London, Islamabad, New Delhi, Moscow, Nairobi, Dar el Salaam, Casablanca, Tunis, Riyadh, Sharm-el-Sheikh, and Amman. These outrages have shifted global perceptions of risk. They have brought into focus the vulnerability of the integrated and open system of economic relations that underpins globalization. As a result, Western security doctrines now conflate two previously separate threats: international terrorism and turbulence in the developing world.

A small band of terrorists trained in an isolated and poor country caused massive civilian casualties in the world's most powerful country, paralyzed international air traffic for days, depressed major global industries (tourism, insurance, and energy), and triggered a worldwide recession. The very policies of openness that had permitted Western corporations to extend their reach across borders had provided terrorists with the mobility and secrecy they needed to achieve their horrific feats.

In turn, the unilateral military response of the United States had unintended consequences. The failure to discover any weapons of mass destruction in Iraq discredited Western intelligence services and shifted the balance of international public opinion against the United States and its coalition allies. A tipping point was reached as anti-war anger, cultural resentment, and fear of additional military actions coalesced. Resentment of intrusive power has become the leading reason for unfavorable opinions of the United States around the world, according to surveys by the Pew Research Center for the People and the Press.

Underlying the deterioration of America's image abroad is the perception that the U.S. is now even more prone than before to act internationally without taking account of other nations' interests. But neither is there much enthusiasm for any other country becoming as powerful as the United States. Therefore, diplomats on both sides of the Atlantic are seeking to restore mutual understanding and accommodation. Recently, following a period of relative tranquility on the domestic terror front, the United States has shown a more balanced posture that combines vigilance, restraint, and consultation with allies.[7]

The United States has increased its aid outlays. It is making more use of multilateral institutions, for example in sponsoring United Nations resolutions to block finance for terrorists and to stop the illegal trade in materials and technology for weapons of mass destruction (Bailes, 2005). It has yielded to multilateral efforts in response to the serious nuclear proliferation threats of North Korea and Iran and the humanitarian crisis in Darfur. It has complied with requests to intervene in Haiti and Liberia and has done so in close consultation with its allies, withdrawing its forces as soon as practicable. Obviously, not all European efforts to engage the United States in principled debates about international policy priorities will succeed, but the effort is well worth making, given the enormous weight of the United States on the international scene.

The Center of Gravity of Violence has Shifted Towards the Developing World

Following two devastating world wars in Europe and a Cold War characterized by a fear of mutual destruction, the dominant threats to international security have moved to the periphery and become embedded within states.

However, inter-state security issues have not vanished. The long-standing Kashmir dispute, the Gulf War, and the Ethiopia-Eritrea conflict are reminders that inter-state rivalry continues to threaten world peace, while the Afghanistan and Iraq wars show that Western military intervention remains a chronic feature of the international security environment. Though war is now obsolete within the territories of the "rich country club," elsewhere regional rivalries, inter-state tensions, and competing economic interests continue to dominate relations among states. Most states are thus "modern" rather than "pre-modern" or "post-modern."[8]

Foreign policy "realists" who dominated foreign policy establishments during the Cold War and post-Cold War eras viewed the nation state as the basic unit of power. They favored the status quo and espoused principles of sovereignty and non-intervention. Their "balance of power" calculations gave scant weight to small nations, minority groups, or individuals. In the United States, with the ascendancy of the more assertive "idealist" approach associated with neo-conservative thinking, containment has given way to proactive prevention.

Thus, the United States *2006 Quadrennial Defense Review* describes the shift in thinking of senior civilian and military leaders in the Department of Defense as follows: "(i) from conducting war against nations—to conducting war in countries we are not at war with (safe havens); (ii) from responding after a crisis (reactive)—to preventive actions so problems do not become crises (proactive); (iii) from crisis response to shaping the future…." (U.S. Government, 2006a).

Traditional inter-state conflicts (such as the Iran-Iraq war or the festering border dispute between Ethiopia and Eritrea) remain highly destructive. Furthermore, potential confrontations involving regional nuclear powers now involve the risk of catastrophic warfare (such as between North and South Korea, between India and Pakistan, and perhaps some day between Israel and Iran). In addition, a new source of violence has become internal to weak states unable to protect the cohesion of their societies or to maintain control over their territories (for example in Nepal, where a Maoist insurgency and a reversal of democratization are inducing large-scale unrest and violence). Rather than the expansion of nations, it is the breaking of nations (former Soviet Union, Yugoslavia) that has emerged as a dominant security threat.

The September 2002 security strategy of the United States announced that weak states "can pose as great a danger to national security as strong states" (U.S. Government, 2002). To be sure, in some instances, the neighborhood effects of localized intra-state conflicts are circumscribed and allow mainstream economic activity to continue (as in Myanmar, Sri Lanka, Uganda, for example) but in others they spill over national borders. Accordingly, the "let it fight it out among themselves" posture has gradually lost its allure now that widespread human rights violations, refugee flows, and the spread of diseases have destabilized entire regions and sub-regions (as in the Democratic Republic of Congo,

Rwanda, or Sudan). The spectacular use of Afghanistan as a platform for international terrorism has made the strategic risk associated with failing states even more salient.

Non-state actors have become a major source of instability and state weakness has supplanted state strength as a major security threat. The United States *2006 Quadrennial Defense Review* notes that threats from nation-states are giving way to decentralized network threats from non-state enemies, so that the peacetime tempo of the post-Cold War era is being replaced by a wartime sense of urgency. A "long war" against Islamic extremism has once again been declared, even as the *Review* acknowledges that terrorists cannot be defeated solely through military force and lays stress on the "orchestration of all elements of national and international power" in a contest that is "both a battle of arms and a battle of ideas." Military means nonetheless still dominate the United States strategy, albeit with a new emphasis on integrated forces and on mobile, expeditionary operations geared to multiple asymmetric challenges.

Dissatisfaction with foreign policy doctrines grounded in multilateralism (which it perceived as inadequately focused and ineffectual) induced the Bush administration to adopt a strategy of unilateral intervention and democracy promotion. But out of the Iraq quagmire a more cautious foreign policy stance shows signs of emerging, with ad hoc coalitions of strong states as the instrument of choice. It has become plain that no nation is powerful enough to impose its will unilaterally.[9] Indeed, among the operational lessons learnt and highlighted by the U.S. *Quadrennial Review* is the imperative of working with and through others and of acquiring authority for flexible funding to build the capacity of partners.

The United States has yet to endorse a collective approach that respects international law under United Nations auspices. But the idea that conflict prevention involves assisting weak states and helping them to build up their institutions and their economies has gained ground. Most security specialists believe that poverty breeds lethargy more than it breeds violence. However, they recognize that widespread poverty, despair, and social disintegration can culminate in state failure and international instability. While the risks that intra-state wars now pose to global stability cannot be precisely measured, security strategists favor proactive and preventive engagement with weak states, in preference to the benign neglect of prior years.[10] This helps to explain why security and development policies have begun to converge.

Another reason why security doctrines are evolving has to do with changing perceptions of catastrophic risk. Under the current home security regime, some specialists (including Allison, 2004) rate the likelihood of a nuclear terrorist attack on America as more than 50 percent in the next decade and as virtually certain if one lengthens the time frame. Other analysts consider such catastrophes less likely but agree that the consequences would be so disastrous that new policies should be designed to address them.[11]

Jihadist leaders have affirmed their intent to procure weapons of mass destruction and many intelligence reports (never confirmed) have warned about Al Qaeda's imminent access to weapons-grade nuclear materials. There are 130 nuclear research reactors in 40 countries. In Russia, 10,000 nuclear warheads and fissile material for 30,000 weapons are vulnerable to theft. The illicit network set up by Pakistan's nuclear scientist A.Q. Khan is reputed to have sold comprehensive "nuclear starter kits" along with personal consulting services on the black market.

If terrorists with appropriate skills bought a complete weapon they could set it off immediately. If they secured fissile material, they might be able to assemble a device within a year. A relatively small (10 kiloton) nuclear device exploding in New York's Times Square would destroy the theater district, Madison Square Garden, the Empire State Building, Grand Central Station, Carnegie Hall, and probably the United Nations complex. On a weekday, at least half a million people would die.

Only 5 percent of the trucks, rail cars, and ships that deliver 50,000 containers of freight daily to the United States are screened, and current screening methods may not detect fissile material. The United States once relied on the threat of mutually assured destruction to deter the Soviet Union from launching a nuclear strike. But in today's fragmented world, a new strategy is needed, especially with nuclear material vulnerable to theft or sale through black-market channels.

Thus a potentially disastrous confluence of threats (state fragility, international terrorism, and weapons proliferation) characterizes the current security equation. Mounting effective strategies to counter the looming threats is imperative: the emerging dangers cannot simply be wished away, nor can they be effectively addressed without international cooperation and collective security arrangements.

Already, intricate combinations of context-specific inter-state and intra-state security risks are testing the skills of defense strategists. From a risk management perspective, it may have been a tragic mistake to devote enormous resources to a conventional war to tackle the peripheral threat posed by Iraq. Using the blunt instrument of technologically advanced might while neglecting to implement the lessons of successful counter-insurgency campaigns has proved to be counterproductive. The unilateral intervention has not resolved the problem. It has also disrupted the Atlantic Alliance, and created a groundswell of support for extremism throughout the Islamic world.

Simply put, the protracted "wars after the war" in Afghanistan and Iraq show that traditional wars carried out without adequate planning for post-war stability and reconstruction do not work, given the capacity of the weak to use suicide bombing and other asymmetric means of resistance to keep domestic insurgencies alive. It is virtually impossible to capture enemy combatants and protect civilians against foes who can blend into the population.[12] Equally, limits on the "compellence"[13] of peacekeeping forces have become self-evident in situations where elusive non-state actors (for example in Sierra Leone, Liberia, and the Democratic Republic of Congo) use profitable natural resources to finance their purchase of illegal arms and sustain violent attacks on civilians and government forces.

In sum, the new security equation has multiple variables and no uniform solution. To respond to a complex mixture of traditional threats and unprecedented challenges, OECD countries must reform their defense doctrines and explore new ways to coordinate coercive military intervention with civilian peacekeeping and development cooperation. In particular, the transition to and from hostilities has become a prominent issue of security and development strategy formulation.

"Joined-up" units combining development assistance planning with diplomacy, policing, and military force are being set up in the United Kingdom and the United States to facilitate reconstruction and state building tasks in post-conflict countries. Proposals to set up human security response forces combining civilian and military personnel are in the works in the European Union. These are critical areas of security policy where creativity and innovation will be in growing demand.

The Rules of the Game of the Global Market Economy have had Unintended Effects

Globalization is the compression of time and space induced by an unprecedented revolution in information and communications technology. One of its consequences has been the advent of a global civil society that promotes international law, human rights, and development cooperation. Paradoxically, the voluntary organizations that owe much of their influence to the interconnectedness of email communication and the Internet have been highly critical of globalization.[14]

But radical criticism of global market integration dismisses the conclusive evidence of a vast body of research: in the aggregate, economic growth and improvements in living standards have been sustained, notwithstanding limitations in natural resources and the unprecedented growth of the world's population. Technological progress and the creativity of private enterprise have helped the world avert a Malthusian crisis.[15]

New technology has triggered the integration of national economies. Shipping costs are only 30 percent, air fares 16 percent, and telephone charges only 1 percent of what they were 80 years ago. More open trade, mobile capital, and mass travel have yielded considerable welfare gains. The skewed distribution of the benefits is due not to technological change or to market opening but to major differences in the institutional capacities of nations.

Globalization has expanded economic opportunities, but the nations that benefit are mostly those with the institutions and the human resources needed to compete in the global marketplace. In the United States, for example, the combination of shrinking distances and lower trade barriers has raised annual incomes by USD 10,000 per household (Hufbauer and Grieco, 2005).

Nor has globalization prevented competent states from charting their own economic and social course. In combination with good domestic policies, globalization has helped some poor countries, including the two Asian giants, China and India, to achieve major gains in poverty reduction. Export-oriented industries have improved the livelihoods of millions of workers. There are exceptions, of course, but wherever foreign investors have set up manufacturing facilities in poor countries, aggregate working conditions have improved. In sum, more than other factors, it is the expansion of the market economy and the innovations of technology that have made recent welfare gains possible.

The uneven playing field is less the result of globalization per se than the legacy of history—especially the fragility of institutions in poor states—and the structure of the international system—including the rules of the game that govern the global marketplace. What underlies these rules is not natural forces but the accumulation of policy choices by rich countries. Other policy choices could have been made and they are still possible.

International public opinion acknowledges the unfairness of the global economic system: it favors a smaller world but expresses concern about the impact of rich countries' policies on the poor.[16] These concerns, expressed in public opinion polls, do not always translate into decisions by politicians and their electorates. If policies are not being reformed, despite the huge potential benefits that would accrue in the aggregate, it is because the gains from trade are widely dispersed among large and powerless groups while the much smaller losses are concentrated among small and powerful groups who have a disproportionate impact on policymaking.

Inequities persist because the progressive taxation, regulatory frameworks, and social safety nets that industrial countries have gradually built to overcome market failures at the national level do not exist at the global level. Under the rules of the international system, capital is more mobile than labor. This partial integration has tipped the scales against poor countries.

In parallel, fiscal competition among countries has reduced the capacity of states to raise resources for redistribution. A further obstacle to poverty reduction has been in the trade area, where the rules of the game have remained heavily biased against poor countries. Much effort has gone into international trade negotiations, but the obduracy of vested interests has eroded the development credentials of the Doha round, and its frequently revised timetables have not been met.[17]

Global inequality has risen inexorably. The U.S., Europe, and Japan are currently 100 times richer than Ethiopia, Haiti, and Nepal, whereas the gap across countries was only 9 to 1 at the dawn of the twentieth century. The increasing reach of global markets has encouraged inequality among and within countries by rewarding those with access to capital, skills, and entrepreneurship. Sharp rises in the returns to education have meant that countries well endowed with human capital and reliant on skill-intensive production have fared far better than those plagued by illiteracy and highly dependent on primary commodity exports (Birdsall, 2005).

An unintended consequence of globalization has been the erosion of official controls over international exchanges. This has been a boon for smugglers and criminals. Since the 1990s, illicit trade has boomed. As government constraints on cross-border transfers have receded, the new technologies have enlarged the market for smuggled goods, services, and persons, decreased the risks of engaging in illicit behavior, and vastly increased its rewards.

Illegal trafficking in people, drugs, arms, intellectual property, and money has become big business.[18] It is corrupting all branches of government, including the judiciary and the police, especially in developing countries, in countries in transition, and in the border areas of rich countries. Criminal networks have adopted flexible and decentralized management techniques, flourishing by shrewdly adapting to the realities of an interconnected world. They now have the tools and enjoy the opportunities of operating on a global scale while escaping detection, concealing their wealth, and diversifying their assets. Increasingly, they are finding ways to intrude into politics in order to consolidate their operations and escape capture (Naim, 2005).

Unfortunately, a severe global governance gap and splintered approaches to law enforcement have hindered an effective international response. Illicit trade cannot be curbed by one government agency or even one country acting on its own. Global problems require global solutions: international cooperation is needed in law making, enforcement, policing, and intelligence gathering. New technologies must be developed and deployed. "Whole of government" approaches are essential, as is the involvement of citizens.

Furthermore, mistaken resource allocation decisions and unrealistic policy aims should be corrected. It is not rational to spend USD 8-9 billion a year on missile defense while under-budgeting for port security and development assistance. Equally, it is self defeating to deploy vast resources to fight drug wars by spraying the fields of poor farmers in poor countries while letting the workings of illegal drug markets of rich countries proceed undisturbed. Nor, given budget constraints, can a repressive strategy be implemented at all stages of the drug supply chain. The stakes of the illegal drug trade are such that, in cost-benefit terms, legalization should be considered as a serious policy option.

Despite the obvious links between domestic and foreign policies in an interconnected world, popular advocacy has barely begun to convince the electorates of industrial democracies of the responsibility that rich countries bear towards the poor countries where 85 percent of the world's population lives. Aid has been inadequate in both quantity and quality. Official development assistance reached USD 78.6 billion in 2004. Though this implies an annual rise in real terms of almost 4.5 percent from the 2002 level, aid is still only 0.25 percent of the gross national income of OECD countries, compared to the 0.7 percent level repeatedly endorsed by United Nations conferences.[19] Furthermore, some of the aid currently delivered is "phantom aid": misdirected and burdened by prohibitive transaction costs—and, for about half the volume of aid, saddled with rules on reserved procurement ("tied aid") that reduce its value.

Despite frequent commitments by donors to streamline and standardize their practices, harmonization remains an aspiration rather than a reality. The aid delivery structure is fragmented and its cumbersome processes burden the frail administrative capacities of poor countries. Equally, rich countries' intellectual property and migration policies have been detrimental to poor countries, and their environmental practices are endangering the global commons. The delivery of global public goods is lagging and, as a result, HIV/AIDS, tuberculosis, and other infectious diseases are spreading their tentacles within Africa and towards other poor and vulnerable regions. Finally, the international community has yet to mount a credible response to the looming challenge of global warming, which is expected to have a disproportionate impact on poor countries.

No wonder then that the heady optimism about globalization that prevailed in the 1980s has evaporated. Looking ahead, human security hinges, in part, on adjustments in the policies of rich countries that shape the global economy. This will require intense and sustained public advocacy for development cooperation in all OECD countries, since these countries bear a share of responsibility for the current state of affairs.

Once the electorates of rich countries see that the policies of their governments are a major reason why international crime is spreading and global poverty is not being tackled, they will demand action to strengthen global institutions and to make equitable and secure development easier to achieve. Just as national governments in OECD countries created strong judiciary systems, income redistribution mechanisms, and social safety nets for disadvantaged citizens, in time a global social contract will have to be forged to address the legacy of inadequate security, health, and education for the poor of the world.

Policy Harmonization is Imperative

In the 1980s scholars had visualized a decline in United States power (Kennedy, 1987). Then suddenly, the talk was of American hegemony.

The dissolution of the Soviet Union transformed the international system, reconfigured the geopolitical landscape, and ushered in a uni-polar security order centered on the United States. The demise of the centrally planned economic model expanded the reach of the global market and gave rise to a "new economy" in which private capital roamed freely and knowledge was at a premium. The implosion of communism accelerated the spread of neo-liberal economic doctrines.

Throughout the 1990s the United States economy was boosted by a robust business expansion facilitated by sound budgets and open trade policies. These were also the years when a rival capitalist model, "made in Japan," stumbled. The *dirigiste* policies of Japan Inc. proved ill-adapted to the challenges of a tumultuous global market, and Japan's technological edge was blunted. Europe's productivity lagged as the huge costs of unification ensnared the growth of the German economy, and as political energies focused inwards to manage the expansion of the European Union. Even the dislocation of Yugoslavia did not elicit a cohesive European response; the United States had to intervene and the peace deal for Bosnia was brokered in Dayton, Ohio.

With the disintegration of the Soviet Union, the United States satisfied its urge to assert absolute military superiority over all other powers. It strengthened the efforts that began in the 1970s to reduce the heavy reliance of the West on the nuclear threat for its security. By the turn of the century, the United States had more military clout, greater economic strength, and more political influence than any other country. Today it is still the solitary military superpower. It has displayed its absolute technological dominance during the Gulf war, the NATO-sponsored intervention in Kosovo, and more recently in Afghanistan and Iraq.

Heavy military spending and state of the art technologies have given the United States a massive strategic advantage in conducting traditional battlefield operations and deploying advanced weapons systems. High-tech weaponry, overhead surveillance, global mapping, "precision" bombing, and interactive information systems have greatly increased the mobility and flexibility of the U.S. military. But the transformation has been achieved at the cost of force numbers. Rather than cutting-age technologies, the "human-centric" wars of the twenty-first century require large numbers of skilled professionals with area and language expertise and "on the ground" capacities in counter-insurgency operations, policing, and nation building tasks.

The U.S. *2006 Quadrennial Defense Review* (U.S. Government, 2006a) recognizes the importance of inter-agency cooperation, language and cultural skills, and in-depth regional expertise. But this lesson has been secured at extraordinary cost. The 2006 budget includes USD 160 billion for the Afghanistan and Iraq wars, bringing their total direct estimated cost to USD 440 billion. The cost of the Iraq war now approaches that of the Korean war (USD 330 billion) while the total cost of the "long war" on terrorism, at about half a trillion dollars, will soon exceed that of the Vietnam war.[20]

Aimed at a domestic audience, the demonstration of United States military prowess may have healed scars in the national psyche inflicted by the Vietnam conflict and 9/11. But disillusion has begun to set in. In Afghanistan, tribal warlords still control the countryside and the Taliban remains a credible fighting force well supplied with money, weapons, and fighters within the border areas to which it has retreated. In Iraq's devastated society, the protracted insurgency has attracted thousands of new *jihadist* recruits from around the world, caused large-scale fatalities, and hindered economic reconstruction plans that now face severe budget cutbacks.

The Iraq war has also depleted international good will towards the United States. Unsanctioned by the United Nations Security Council, it fractured the Atlantic alliance.[21] Stringent homeland security measures and the rough and possibly illegal treatment of enemy combatants have generated concerns about the ability of the U.S. democracy to wage its war on terrorism without impinging on the freedoms of individuals and groups. Only slowly are trust and dialogue being restored among the Atlantic nations. Resentment about an overbearing America is mingled with concern that the Iraq difficulties might induce a hasty withdrawal into isolationism that would not be in the international interest.

United States economic policy has been hardly more judicious. The U.S. economy has continued to expand but it is experiencing enormous budget deficits. The dollar has lost a third of its value against the euro since 2001. The U.S. current account deficit at more than 6 percent of GDP compares with a prior peak of about 3.5 percent and is larger than Indonesia's or Argentina's prior to their financial crises. Paradoxically, developing countries in search of financial security in a volatile global economy[22] have accumulated more than USD 335 billion in reserves—while the United States faces a large budget imbalance (projected at USD 400 billion for fiscal year 2006) combined with a large and growing current account imbalance (USD 785 billion in 2005, or 6.5 percent of GDP).

The U.S. aggregate domestic product has fallen below that of enlarged Europe, despite Europe's sluggish growth, high unemployment, and fiscal pressures. In parallel, the remarkable advances in industry and technology in Asia's modernizing economies have begun to transform the geopolitical and security landscape. In particular, China and India have achieved very rapid and sustained growth as well as international clout. China provides a platform for highly competitive manufacturing networks that bring together modern technologies, cheap labor, and global capital. India is becoming a global knowledge hub and a shunting yard for information and services.

The United States has more scope for maneuver than other nations, given its size and strength.[23] While it has been sobered by the Iraq quagmire,[24] it remains oriented towards global change, the expansion of democracy, and the promotion of liberal market policies. But its financial situation is stressed, its military forces are stretched, and it needs alliances in order to prevail. "Transformational diplomacy," the hallmark of the American Secretary of State, Condoleezza Rice, is consistent with the shift from the Cold War stance of containment to an open, proactive posture that does not take the world as given but rather aims to change it.

Thus, the reactive "war on terrorism" first metamorphosed into a "war on extremist violence" and next into a "long war against global terrorist networks." The pursuit of this new war requires unconventional and indirect military approaches and seeks to combine persuasion with the promotion of democracy rather with the exercise of military might. Under current administration policies, the United States is likely to sustain the military thrust of its foreign policy while deploying foreign policy tools that put more weight on political suasion, economic incentives, and cultural values.

This opens a narrow window of opportunity for Europe to lay the foundations of a common transatlantic agenda that in a changed geopolitical environment may help to respond to the aspirations of peoples everywhere. To make the most of this opportunity, Europe would have to recover its own cohesion, adopt outward-oriented policies, and implement a coherent approach to aid and diplomacy consistent with its values and interests. Recent overtures by the United States towards a stronger transatlantic partnership offer scope for a dialogue focused on fairer policies towards developing countries.

Following the rejection of a proposed EU constitution by French and Dutch voters and the ensuing budget gridlock, new coalitions will have to be forged to overcome the combined opposition of anti-globalization activists and anti-immigration nationalists. Though a pause in the momentum of Europe's outward expansion seems likely, further broadening of the European Union could resume if the doctrinal disputes that pit liberal against socialist conceptions of Europe are set aside. Pragmatic compromises are possible with respect to fiscal policy, agriculture, structural funds, trade in services, and security cooperation. Equally, a wider menu of membership options would help build a consensus in support of further enlargement. This would not undermine the prospects for a common and proactive foreign policy, provided a rapprochement with the United States is achieved.

The opportunity would be missed if Europe were to turn inwards. Beleaguered forces of moderation in Turkey would suffer a serious setback. Conflicts that are currently held in check by the prospect of joining the European Union might be reignited, for example in the Balkans. Nor could a "fortress Europe" model be sustained, given globalization. Hence, it is critical to channel the yearning of all European citizens for security and prosperity towards a continued widening of EU membership in the near abroad, combined with a forward-looking development cooperation policy. A reinvigorated relationship with the United States would greatly facilitate this evolution and help to deal with the imbalances that threaten the global economy.

It is Europe's proud tradition to emphasize multilateral approaches to global development, the promotion of democracy, and the international rule of law. Under any scenario, Europe will need to keep its international relations focused on peacemaking and to strengthen its capacity to project power to help maintain stability in its own neighborhood. This will require the combined build-up of military and civilian assets geared to peacekeeping. But the security shield of the United States will retain its relevance for many years to come, and Europe's comparative advantage in the concert of nations will continue to lie in its "soft power" and the potential for continuous EU enlargement and/or new forms of association.

Hence, Europe should keep bridges of communication open across the Atlantic, adopt domestic policies that will nurture public support for further EU enlargement, and keep focused on the long-term goals of constructing a global collective security system that is respectful of the international rule of law and supportive of developing countries' economic and social aspirations.

B. Global Development: A Shared Responsibility

Though all European Union countries are part of a comprehensive security and development community, unique national characteristics and distinctive histories mean that each country plays a distinctive role on the global scene. Thus, the commitment to development of individual European countries varies widely. Out of twenty-one OECD member countries ranked for the development friendliness of their policies by the Center for Global Development in 2005, Denmark stands at the very top of the list while Greece ranks next to last (in twentieth place, just above Japan) (Roodman, 2004b).

In trade policy with respect to developing countries, the European Union lags behind New Zealand, the United States, Canada, and Australia. The tariffs imposed by the EU-15 with respect to low-income countries average 6.5 percent[25], compared to 2.3 percent in the United States, 4 percent in Australia, 5 percent in New Zealand, and a whopping 40 percent in Japan. Compared with the tariffs of the United States, EU barriers are about three times as high in agriculture, and twice as high overall. Non EU members such as Norway and Switzerland have erected even higher trade barriers against developing countries (Roodman, 2005).

The EU-15 countries as a group perform better in aid than in trade. They commit aid of USD 11 per poor person in developing countries, compared to USD 5 committed by the United States and USD 2 by Japan. But the average European performance conceals considerable variation among countries. Denmark leads the EU-15 in terms of aid as a share of gross national income (0.85 percent)[26], followed by Luxembourg (0.85 percent), Sweden (0.78 percent), the Netherlands (0.73 percent), Portugal (0.63 percent), France and Belgium (0.41 percent), Ireland (0.39 percent), the United Kingdom (0.36 percent), Finland (0.35 percent), Germany (0.28 percent), Spain (0.24 percent), and Austria and Greece (0.23 percent). The lowest rank is held by Italy, with a performance (0.15 percent) even poorer than that of Japan (0.19 percent) or the United States (0.17 percent).

With respect to investment, the rankings of European countries also vary widely. The worst performers are Ireland (which does not provide political risk insurance and does little to prevent double taxation) and Austria (which severely restricts pension fund investments in developing countries). The United Kingdom is the best performer, because it does better on all counts and has participated energetically in international arrangements to control corruption, such as the Kimberley Process to track and eliminate trade in "blood diamonds" used to finance warlords in countries such as Angola and Sierra Leone. The U.S. ranks sixth and Japan ranks fifteenth.

The development friendliness of migration policies is ranked in terms of openness to migrants and students from poor countries. Austria and Switzerland tie for first place in importing the most labor for their size, especially unskilled labor. At the very bottom is Japan. Sweden is in sixth place and the United States, famed for its openness to immigrants, ranks a mediocre twelfth because illegal migrants are not counted in the index and 9/11 has led to tougher immigration restrictions.

Britain and Germany lead in the environment rankings: they have cut their greenhouse gas emissions by 10 percent during 1993–2003 through high gasoline taxes and strong support for wind and other renewable energy sources. Japan is in last place because it is a heavy subsidizer of industrial fishing and a big importer of tropical timber. It is also the only major holdout among OECD countries against a UN agreement aiming to limit over-fishing in international waters. The U.S. ranks next to last because it did not ratify the Kyoto Protocol.

In the Center for Global Development index, support for humanitarian interventions is rated as a positive feature of security policy. By contrast, exports of arms and weapons to countries with poor governance pull country rankings down. The index also rewards countries that base naval fleets where they can secure sea lanes vital to international trade. Australia and Norway share the top spot on security—Australia for its UN-approved action in 1999 to stop Indonesian oppression of East Timor, and Norway for steady contributions to peacekeeping operations in the former Yugoslavia and the Middle East.

The standings of France, the Netherlands, the U.K., and the U.S. are boosted by their role in patrolling sea lanes. Since the Iraq war does not feature in the index, the U.S. scores above average overall, given its dominant military muscle near sea lanes, while losing some points for its record as a leading supplier of arms to dictatorships. Japan earns a high score on arms exports to developing countries (it has none) but it lags otherwise, because of its minimal international military profile.

No OECD country does spectacularly better than its peers on policies affecting intellectual property. The index rewards policies that support the creation and dissemination of innovations of value to developing countries, including subsidies for research and development, although spending on military R&D is discounted by half. The U.S. loses points for pushing for compulsory licensing bans and the Europeans are penalized for allowing the copyrighting of databases containing data assembled with public funds. Greece and Ireland lag overall because of their low government subsidies for R&D. The first place is shared by Finland, which spends a substantial 1 percent of GDP on government R&D, and Canada, whose policies on intellectual property rights are least restrictive.

Some countries' patent laws go too far in advancing the interests of those who produce innovations at the expense of the poor countries that use them. Other countries use their leverage to negotiate trade agreements with individual developing countries that extend certain intellectual property rights beyond the international norms in the General Agreement on Tariffs and Trade. U.S. negotiators, for example, have pushed for developing countries to agree never to force the immediate licensing of a patent even when that would serve a compelling public interest, as a drug for HIV/AIDS might if produced by low-cost local manufacturers.

Sweden's Shared Responsibility Bill Points the Way

The Shared Responsibility bill approved by the Swedish parliament in December 2003 conforms to a comprehensive conception of development as a social transformation process. The bill is fully consistent with the emerging human security paradigm: well beyond the economic sphere, it equates development with the expansion of human freedoms. It supports the Millennium Development Goals and recognizes that peace and development are indivisible. Thus, it incorporates peace, security, poverty alleviation, environmental conservation, human rights, and democracy within the remit of the development enterprise.

The explicit inclusion of defense within the purview of the bill is notable. Going beyond aid, the bill recognizes that failed and fragile states require special attention, and gives salience to conflict management and conflict prevention. Since the end of the Cold War, Sweden's defense policy has emphasized modernization, mobility, and flexibility, and the realignment of security policy towards global peacemaking. Therefore, there was substantial readiness to integrate security and development policy when the Swedish Parliament passed the landmark bill.

The bill has put a stamp of legitimacy on the principles of policy coherence for development and has opened the way for a unique experiment in joined up government. Under the leadership of the Director General, Development Policy, of the Ministry for Foreign Affairs, every major government ministry contributed to the formulation of the strategic goals that make up the bill. Thus, conflict prevention and management, international peacemaking efforts, strengthening of international law, and promotion of transparency and accountability with respect to the arms trade have become integral to the official mission of the Ministry of Defense and Armed Forces.

The Shared Responsibility bill acknowledges reciprocal obligations between rich and poor countries in the pursuit of global development that were first articulated in the Millennium Declaration of 2000. Emphasizing the distinct responsibilities of rich countries, Sweden's bill looks to all donors to pull in the same direction towards protecting the physical environment, leveling the playing field of international trade and finance, and alleviating heavy debt burdens. Such a reshaping of the rules of the game that govern international economic transactions cannot be taken for granted: the international community has agreed on the ends but not yet the means of global development.

Policy coherence for development needs to be promoted within the European Union and in multilateral forums. To allocate accountabilities among partners would require political will and harmonization of concepts, strategies, and practices across all donors and all policies. Chapters 2, 3, 4, and 5 below elaborate on the demanding policy changes that would be needed to improve global security and development.

The Development Assistance Committee principles of effective development cooperation rely on developing countries' ownership of policies and processes designed to reduce poverty through reforms of governance. But the ownership principle does not address the dilemma posed by fragile states, for reasons elaborated in chapter 4. These states are home to one third of the poor. Few have the capacity and/or the commitment to implement the reforms needed to achieve equitable and sustainable development. A coordinated program of development cooperation in a cross-section of fragile states is needed. Innovative approaches must be piloted since general principles of development cooperation are of little help in achieving good results in difficult environments.[27]

Donors have shifted away from blunt aid conditionality, which had proved ineffective. In its place, they have introduced demanding criteria for aid allocations and required recipient countries to prepare poverty reduction strategy papers as a condition of debt relief. While these new approaches have encouraged aid coordination, they can be just as intrusive as the prior system, especially where additional and often onerous conditions are imposed on a project-by-project basis. For their part, some partner countries in the developing world perceive the convergence of the policy stance among rich countries and multilateral agencies as "ganging up"—ignoring their felt development needs and burdening their fragile governance processes.

Unless the new approach to aid is managed with care and sensitivity, and backed up with assistance for capacity building, it could erode the sovereignty and weaken the very states that aid is supposed to bolster. Once again, the unintended by-product could be a penalty on countries that do not meet prevailing performance-based criteria for aid allocation or that lack the wherewithal to prepare poverty reduction strategy papers that can pass muster in the aid community. Donors might become even more reluctant to take risks for peace and invest resources in troubled countries—an undesirable outcome given the human costs and the risks involved in isolating these countries. As highlighted in chapter 4, the current evidence is that fragile states as a group are substantially under-aided. The development community should urgently address the "aid orphan" issue.[28]

Last, the pursuit of consistency among defense and development policy instruments through "whole of government" approaches could have the perverse effect of subjecting aid to the imperatives of defense and diplomacy, and facilitating a shift in security doctrines away from the "soft power" instruments of diplomacy and development that ought to be emphasized. This is where European values and principles come in. Practice of these principles should limit the risks of aid capture by narrow defense interests. They point to a gradual shift away from statism and nationalism and towards a new conception of internationalism that stresses human security, political equality for all human beings, the rule of law, social justice, and responsible stewardship of the environment.

C. Common Objectives: Human Security

As Immanuel Kant pointed out two centuries ago, we are "unavoidably side by side." Today more than ever, the international community is struggling with dilemmas of collective action. Severe imbalances in the world economy, the violent insurgency in Iraq, the ongoing tragedy of Darfur, and the myriad of conflicts that prevail over vast zones of the developing world suggest a need for strong leadership and more intense international cooperation. Poor countries are plagued by insecurity problems that rich countries have ample capacities to help resolve, for example by promoting regional security arrangements. Equally, global poverty reduction is severely hindered by obstacles that rich countries could help eliminate, through selective policy adjustments that would also be in their national interest.

Beyond achieving policy coherence among states, the growing role of non-state actors must be reckoned with. Globalization has eased the ascent of the private sector as a major influence on the global policy stage and a major participant in security operations through outsourcing. Temporarily weakened by corporate scandals, the private sector has adopted tougher standards of corporate governance along with corporate social responsibility principles that are conducive to establishing public-private partnerships geared to global development.

Globalization has also accelerated the growth of a far-flung system of voluntary organizations set up to monitor the progress of human freedom and to deliver humanitarian services. Recently, the NGO movement has become more fragmented as anti-capitalist activists, globalization reformers, and peace activists vie for control. In response to more intense public scrutiny, NGOs are seeking to satisfy more demanding financial sponsors about issues of legitimacy, transparency, and results orientation. To this end many of them are crafting pragmatic partnerships with the business sector.

Both the voluntary and the private sector have become heavily involved in formulating norms and standards, including "dos" and "don'ts" for work in conflict-prone and conflict-affected areas, to facilitate coherence in social and environmental policies. These initiatives deserve nurturing and support since they facilitate policy convergence. Just as international networks of government officials increasingly exchange information, coordinate their activities, and share good practice in order to deal more effectively with global problems (Slaughter, 2004), vertical interaction needs to be strengthened to connect individuals, local communities, civil society organizations, and the private sector.

Human Security Should Shape Development Cooperation

Human security has to do with the well being of individuals rather than the protection of states. The concept is emblematic of a post-Cold War world in which the threat of mutual destruction has been supplanted by a cosmopolitan concern with the ability of people everywhere to enjoy safe, healthy, and fulfilling lives (Duffield, 2006). The precise meaning of the term human security remains contested but it has achieved growing prominence in academic and development circles.[29] It has also evoked fears that rich countries' preoccupations regarding homeland security and international stability ("hard" security) could tip the balance of the development project away from its humanitarian, rights based, poverty focus ("soft" security).

For Amartya Sen (UN, 2005a):

> The idea of human development… is far too upbeat to focus on rearguard actions needed to secure what has to be safeguarded. This is where the notion of human security becomes particularly relevant. Human security as an idea fruitfully supplements the expansionist perspective of human development by directly paying attention to what are sometimes called downside risks.

As Sen's formulation makes clear, the concept of human security modifies rather than displaces that of human development. It emphasizes prudence and due diligence. It stresses quality in the delivery of development assistance. And it emphasizes social capital creation and community cohesion.

An agreed working definition of human security—backed up by objective assessments of risks and rewards—would help set the policy directions for development in a businesslike manner. It would have the additional merit of treating protection against the threat of violence, whether local or external, as an integral part of the analysis—instead of an exogenous factor immune from policy influence.

A first definition of human security was articulated by the UNDP. It emphasizes freedom from want and concentrates on protection against threats to human survival, the safety of daily life, and the natural dignity of men and women. A Commission on Human Security co-chaired by Sadako Ogata and Amartya Sen further elaborated the concept, reporting to the United Nations Secretary-General on May 1, 2003. The Commission report (UN, 2003a) addresses economic security, health, education, knowledge, and migration. It also includes chapters about the safety of people caught up in violent conflict and the recovery of human communities following a conflict. The government of Japan, which sponsored the Commission, has now set up a Human Security Fund to fund community-level projects designed to deliver social services and promote empowerment and solidarity at the local level in poor countries.

Canada has championed a second strand of the human security agenda: freedom from fear. This conception of human security posits that a state can best maintain its security by ensuring the security of others. It puts people—their rights, their safety, and their lives—first. It aims to build a world where universal humanitarian standards and the rule of law protect all people; where those who violate these standards are held accountable; and where international institutions are equipped to defend and enforce those standards. It is committed to the advent of a global civil society, supports the "responsibility to protect" principle, and endorses multilateralism as the way to keep the world a safe place. [30]

This review seeks to combine both concepts into a single paradigm sharply focused on threats to human survival. This new paradigm differs from prior conceptions of security and development in fundamental ways: (i) its scope extends well beyond the threat of violence since it encompasses all major threats to human survival and well being; (ii) it addresses development risks systematically; (iii) it puts military, policing, and diplomatic functions at the service of development; (iv) it puts the individual rather than the state at the center of the policy; (v) it brings development policy concerns to bear on conflict management since human insecurity is most threatened by conflict; and (vi) it implies vastly different resource allocation patterns.

To put this paradigm into practice when choosing policies requires the use of a rigorous approach based on the systematic application of the principle of policy coherence for development, risk analysis, and institutional economics, as elaborated later in this section of the volume. These and related techniques would guide trade-offs and priority setting within the expanded security domain. According to Kofi Annan, human security has three dimensions: "freedom from want, freedom from fear, and the freedom of future generations to inherit a healthy natural environment" (UN, 2003a).

There are tensions among these objectives—for example, military expenditures designed to address freedom from fear may divert resources from achieving freedom from want; equally, environmental conservation geared to the rights of future generations may require slower economic growth and reduce the prosperity of current generations, while the sustained development measures that are needed to improve the lot of the many may yield insecurities for some, e.g. through the "creative destruction" that arises from free market competition. To strike the right trade-offs, risk management should play a prominent role in development policy.

Thus the human security paradigm calls on security and development professionals to work together. These two communities have long operated at arm's length; each group has looked at the world through its own lenses and used language intelligible only to its members. But the conflicts in goals and approaches that exist between the security community and the development community need to be overcome to discover practical methods of encouraging policy convergence.[31]

The stakes are considerable. Both poverty and insecurity have become matters of international as well as local concern. United Nations Secretary-General Kofi Annan, in his report to the 2000 General Assembly, challenged the international community to forge a consensus around the issues of principle and process involved in humanitarian intervention. To respond to that challenge, an independent International Commission on Intervention and State Sovereignty was established by the Government of Canada in September 2000. The Commission's report (ICISS, 2001) is the culmination of twelve months of intensive research, worldwide consultations, and deliberation.

The Barcelona Study Group on Europe's Security Capabilities drew on human security concepts to design a doctrine, adapted to European values and principles, to guide intervention in intra-state conflicts. The Group's proposals rest on seven principles: (i) primacy of human rights; (ii) clear political authority; (iii) multilateralism; (iv) a bottom-up approach; (v) a regional focus; (vi) use of legal instruments; and (vii) appropriate use of force (Study Group on Europe's Security Capabilities, 2004). Other intellectual investments designed to lay the foundations of a human security order range from those of the Ogata-Sen Commission on Human Security and the Worldwatch annual reports (Worldwatch Institute, 2005 and 2006) to the "harder" focus of the University of British Columbia Human Security Center.

To achieve consensus, a new definition should be broad enough to embrace the diverse concerns of different countries and narrow enough to have technical credibility as an analytical framework. Serious obstacles stand in the way of reaching agreement on a single definition. Additional academic and civil society initiatives will have to be mobilized to achieve a full convergence of views.[32]

Europe is well placed to promote the development of a global consensus centered on a revamped conception of human security. Most EU members support the notion of global public goods, including physical security and stability, political participation, an enforceable human rights legal order, an open and inclusive economic order, and social well being. The European Security Strategy acknowledges that marginalization and exclusion help to explain conflict. It champions the concept of effective multilateralism under which the individual is the point of reference (Biscop, 2005).

Individual governments acting alone cannot tackle the diffuse multidimensional threats to human security. These include the threats that international terrorists pose for open societies and market democracies. Equally, the HIV/AIDS pandemic was recognized as a security threat by the United Nations Security Council because it is emblematic of serious health risks that cross borders and threaten the fabric of the societies they plague. Another existential security threat is caused by the huge and growing volume of carbon emissions.

Stronger collective security agreements are needed to manage intrastate conflicts, reduce the risks of inter-state wars, reverse the proliferation of deadly weapons, and confront the challenge of catastrophic terrorism. In an interconnected world, governments must work together. In the process they must also involve the civil society and the private sector. Just as threats to peace and prosperity involve non-state actors, so should the responses to them. For example, the maintenance of international financial stability requires the coordination of economic policies among governments as well as the willing participation of the private banking sector. Similarly, the management of violent conflict in poor countries requires proactive and effective engagement of governments, business, and the international civil society.

Risk Management is Critical to Human Security

Risk has to do with the uncertainty and unpredictability that induce welfare losses and create poverty. Since the capacity to withstand risk varies among individuals and groups, risk management strategies must be geared to their specific circumstances. The poor are the most vulnerable, being exposed to more risks and having fewer means of withstanding them. Accordingly, managing risk for development is the essence of human security and risk management instruments constitute essential components of the human security toolkit.[33]

Risk management involves *prevention*—reducing the probability of downside risks; *mitigation*—reducing the adverse consequences that may result from downside risks; and (iii *coping*—relieving the impact after the risk has materialized. It aims at (i) minimizing the maximum welfare loss associated with an event; (ii) reducing the probability of a welfare loss below a given threshold; or (iii) maximizing the return on resources given the variability of outcomes associated with alternative resource allocations.

The first of these goals is especially relevant for the very poor, for whom the maximum loss may involve utter destitution or death. The second is in line with the preferences of people of limited means, including people close to the poverty line, who are best served by savings instruments. The third applies to people in the higher income groups and is best met through portfolio diversification.

Individuals, households, communities, and states are exposed to multiple risks from natural sources (such as earthquakes, floods, droughts) or man-made sources (such as economic mismanagement, violent conflict). As development proceeds, new risks emerge and traditional, informal, exchange-based risk sharing mechanisms (for example through extended families, charitable donations, mutual gift giving, crop sharing) tend to break down. Hence in industrialized, urban environments, more formal social protection arrangements are needed to reduce vulnerability and improve social equity (Holzmann and Jorgensen, 2000).

Violent conflict affects welfare not only through its direct effects on individuals and communities but also through the damage it causes to social protection arrangements, whether informal, market-based, or state-based. The macro risks associated with violent conflict are characterized by low frequency, severe or catastrophic consequences, and high covariance for individuals. This is why the informal and market-based (insurance) instruments designed for idiosyncratic (micro) risks are not effective for managing the risks of war.

Risks are weighed differently depending on who bears them. In public affairs, the perception of risks matters more than their actuality. Highly visible risks such as those of airplane hijacking arouse greater fear than silent and dispersed risks such as the health risks associated with lack of clean water and sanitation. Risks voluntarily incurred (for example from tobacco smoking, careless driving, unsafe sex) do not elicit the same public outcry for state protection as do involuntary risks (for example from an earthquake).

For nations as for individuals, risk perceptions vary. Risks incurred "out there" matter less to voters than risks faced "right here." In particular, voters in rich countries are more sensitive to the catastrophic risks posed by weapons proliferation and international terrorism than to economic risks, while citizens in poor countries are more concerned with the daily risks imposed on them by poverty. When available statistical knowledge is poorly disseminated, individual citizens, groups, organizations, or nations may single out some risks as worthy of policy attention while ignoring others that may be more deadly.

A shared perception of risks is critical to policy coherence as well as effective risk management. To achieve this requires evidence, professional analysis, principled dialogue, and "give and take"—it will not happen on its own. Leadership is required first at the analytical level and next at the operational level.

From an analytical perspective, inadequately weighing the probability of the costs and benefits associated with alternative scenarios may lead to mistaken policy choices, excessive caution, or excessive regulation. Strict application of the precautionary principle has such consequences, by assuming the worst even if there is no hard evidence that the worst might come to pass; under such a policy regime mobile phones or artificial sweeteners would be banned. Clearly, total risk avoidance is a recipe for policy paralysis. In development cooperation, policies and programs that seek to generate changes are the norm rather than the exception, and most such changes carry some risks. The opposition to even a prudent use of genetically modified foods in Africa illustrates the pitfalls of policies that seek to ban change if the downside risks are a possibility rather than a probability and the status quo is likely to generate major welfare losses (more severe malnutrition).

Strict application of the precautionary principle ignores the prohibitive opportunity costs of inaction. Its popularity rests on the fascination that worst-case scenarios exert on the media and on the irrational salience of spectacular risks in the public imagination, even for events of extremely low probability. Cost benefit analysis based on the best available evidence, combined with democratic deliberation (informed by surveys of the public willingness to pay for risk protection), is the best remedy against irrational and populist applications of the precautionary principle (Sunstein, 2005).

From an operational perspective, once professional cost benefit risk assessments have been carried out, agreement must be reached on shared goals, reciprocal obligations, coordination protocols, and good practices in order to share and mitigate risks. The stakes are high since the "securitization"[34] of any public policy issue raises it to the top of the political agenda. Labeling a topic as critical to national or international security evokes an appeal to higher authority, implies priority in resource allocation, and may even connote a state of emergency that justifies the suspension of normal decision making rules (Buzan and others, 1998).

Obviously, not every issue that affects human welfare justifies a security label, or else the concept loses its meaning. This is why policy analysts are on firm ground when they resist attempts to incorporate all possible development concerns into the human security agenda. On the other hand, confining security to the military is not the correct approach when the nature of risks requires the use of policy instruments other than the military.

The Economics of Human Security

In an era of volatility and anxiety, a new security and development logic can set priorities and induce cooperation within the expanded range of the human security domain. The conceptual building blocks exist (Treverton and Klitgaard, 2005). Risk management theory is equipped to rank threats whether they originate from conflict, infectious diseases, natural disasters, or other threats to human welfare. Cost benefit analyses combined with probability theory can be used to evaluate alternative responses to identified threats. Under certain conditions, game theory and systems analysis can test the resilience of chosen responses to the countervailing strategies of adversaries. Finally, institutional economics can be put to work to resolve collective action dilemmas and design incentives for cooperation.

Though the risk assessment criteria of the human security agenda differ from those that are currently used by the aid and defense establishments, they are no less demanding. Just as health policy researchers apply a single metric (such as the impact on mortality rates) to compare policy actions, policy coherence principles can be applied so that all relevant stakeholders participate and outcomes are Pareto-efficient ("first, do no harm"). This approach would also provide an appropriate framework for striking the necessary trade-offs.

Good governance means accountability to the public. But because citizens may misjudge risks or fall prey to risk panics, professional risk assessments and sober reflection are needed to inform public debate. Security and development priorities are only legitimate if they are set following principled deliberations and protected by the safeguards of checks and balances. At the national level, the deliberations should involve citizens, their representatives, and the independent judiciary.

At the international level, human security strategies should involve all countries, rich and poor, in equitable measure. All partners should share the objectives selected. Reciprocal obligations should be clearly specified. This implies professional policy design, a multilateral decision framework, and engagement strategies that generate country ownership.

Especially complex are the institutional arrangements that ensure peace and security. To design them, institutional economics offers useful analytical tools (Kaul and others, 2003). In theory, peace is a pure public good: its enjoyment by one party does not diminish its availability to other parties (non-rivalry) and the benefits are available to all (non-excludability). The market cannot price public goods efficiently and ownership rights cannot be defined for them. Therefore, peace has traditionally been supplied by the state, which holds the monopoly of violence. Some public goods can be given the characteristics of private goods since, in practice, "publicness" is a social construct. It is the institutional framework (the rules of the game that are actually enforced) that defines the nature of goods.

For example, intellectual property legislation has turned knowledge products into private goods. Similarly, in an insecure neighborhood, protection rackets turn peace into a private good. Crime syndicates forcibly exclude those who do not pay, and deny peace to their potential rivals. Gated communities turn peace into a toll good by providing protection to those who can afford the purchase price, and excluding those that cannot. Community policing helps to manage excludability through neighborhood cooperation (common pool good), and so on. This confirms that peace is socially determined and that peace, a public good, is a policy choice.

A weak army that can protect some border areas but not others will induce crowding in areas that it can secure, confirming that public goods are chronically undersupplied. The same feature of public goods explains why small countries flanked by hostile neighbors are less secure: they have trouble funding a strong enough military to supply the needed level of security. On the other hand, economies of scale will ease the under-provision in larger states. Strong incentives to compensate for free riding behavior exist in collective security regimes where the weakest link determines the level of aggregate security. The more powerful member will usually compensate for the shortfall, since not doing so would decrease the level of security to close to zero for every alliance partner.

Incentives are critical to the design of appropriate security arrangements. Peacekeeping yields benefits to the conflict-ridden nation as well as to its neighbors, provided they devote enough resources to ensure that they do not turn into the weakest link, incur the wrath of the security guarantor, or bear the costs of resumed conflict on their territory as well as the opprobrium of the international community. The international recognition given to security-supplying nations (for example the United Kingdom in Sierra Leone) provides additional benefits.

Institutional economics also explains why defense technology matters to collective security arrangements: non-conventional weapons that require large investments (as in nuclear capability) are best-shot public goods—either they are supplied or not. Such discrete public goods will tend to have few suppliers whereas conventional forces will attract more suppliers, since even a second-best force contributes to the overall security level. Similarly, institutional economics explains the emergence of private security services as facilitating the efficient allocation of resources, by matching the level of security to the capacity to deliver the service and the capacity to pay.

Market mechanisms undersupply public goods—including peace. What then are the economist's prescriptions for peacemaking (Brauer, 2004)? First, free riding can be minimized through forming alliances that impose selective incentives on members. This is the logic of collective security under which peace becomes a club (or a toll) good. Second, the notion of property rights, a prerequisite of well functioning markets, can be used to produce credible guarantees of enforcement. Without them, the incentives to observe peace contracts are weak.[35]

In turn, the contracting parties should be legitimate for a contract to be self-enforcing; an agreement coerced by an external force does not meet this test. Social sanctioning of the contracting parties who share power under a peace agreement requires democratic validation. However, recourse to a higher authority that has the power to enforce the peace agreement is still needed to avoid defection and the resumption of hostilities. Hence there is a need for peacekeeping forces in transitions.

Markets fail when there is little competition, information is plentiful, and there are no externalities. A pluralistic society is more conducive to the emergence of genuine peace since it favors the creation of coalitions.

Transparency also favors peace by making clear in advance the likely costs of a conflict. To internalize the costs of war for parties who initiate violent conflict requires an external authority to impose sanctions and reparations.

Collective action theory points to the need to introduce incentive frameworks that favor cooperation (for example by controlling the warring parties' access to arms and resources); that create vested interests for peace through development (facilitating the reintegration of former combatants in the peace economy); that encourage reciprocity in behavior through training and facilitation (as is being done by International Alert and other voluntary organizations); that afford easy access to conflict resolution mechanisms; that reduce uncertainty through self-monitoring and independent oversight; that enforce "subsidiarity," by conducting conflict resolution at the lowest level necessary to achieve a positive outcome; and that tap economies of scope and scale, by combining peacekeeping functions that have high fixed costs under a single umbrella organization.

The Governance of Human Security

Insecurity in the developing world is largely the result of historical weaknesses in governance that have been sustained by a pattern of subordination to (and dependence on) rich and powerful countries (Moore, 2005). Many governments of poor countries do not exercise effective control over a significant share of their national territory. In part, this is explained by the patchy and centralized features of state institutions inherited from the colonial era. It is also the result of the international recognition granted to post-colonial states even where central authorities have exercised less than full control over the national territory.

Exclusive and absolute state sovereignty is not always compatible with human security. In many instances, authoritarian regimes have been sustained by fiscal reliance on rents made possible by exports of natural resources. This circumvents the need for domestic taxation (and eliminates the obligation to guarantee the safety and welfare of citizens) while laying the state open to external political and economic control. Imports of modern weaponry facilitate coercive control of the population; they make political bargaining with the citizenry redundant and the legitimacy that flows from providing public services unnecessary for maintaining the regime.

State dependence on external factors and independence from the citizenry leads to vulnerability over the long run by creating incentives for domestic conflict, unless citizens have peaceful and democratic means for challenging the regime. Here again a pattern of dependency on extrinsic factors materializes. Insurgency movements export primary products and import arms, just like the regimes they are trying to topple. Typically, rebel forces rely on revenues from illegal exports, whether of drugs, timber, or diamonds, and secure their weapons from the flourishing and unregulated arms trade.

At the *country level*, the policy implications of this destructive pattern of international relations are straightforward. All instruments of engagement with misgoverned poor countries should focus on economic diversification, fiscal transparency, public expenditure management, security system reform, and development of democracy.

Strengthening the state is not synonymous with helping to perpetuate authoritarian regimes. Human security evokes a society in which each individual has an intrinsic value and each state is conceived as a collective enterprise that protects the freedom of individuals. This means that state sovereignty is only legitimate if it protects human rights and facilitates economic and social development.

The promotion of peace, prosperity, and freedom also requires *regional and global* action. First, the interactions of dependency are not limited to the connections between developing countries and OECD countries: regional hegemonic powers (such as China, India, Russia, South Africa) exercise similar influences on their smaller and weaker neighbors. Second, neighborhood effects matter: security trends in one country can have major consequences across national boundaries. Failed states can often lead to failed sub-regions. Third, global norms and standards have important effects on the dependency relations that perpetuate poor governance.

The idea that international institutions should be able to provide security dates back to the League of Nations. It went into abeyance following the crises of the 1930s but resurfaced after World War II in the United Nations Charter, which envisages regional agencies acting as partners in peace. The role of regional bodies gradually expanded because of frequent gridlocks at the Security Council during the Cold War. As a result, regional and sub-regional organizations achieved considerable autonomy and sidestepped the world organization in numerous instances. Regional action has many advantages: proximity, knowledge of local conditions, and nimbler decision making. Regional organizations have shown a capacity to act where the United Nations has been unable to do so.

Coalitions of the willing have proven more cohesive and effective when rooted in regional security structures. And as a practical matter, without regional initiatives, the sheer number and range of external interventions undertaken since the end of the Cold War would have overwhelmed the capacities of the United Nations. Calculated ambiguity about the relationship between the UN and the regional organizations favors a flexible allocation of responsibilities based on the principle of subsidiarity (devolution of responsibility to the lowest competent level) (Pugh and Sidhu, 2003).

Beyond the North Atlantic Treaty Organization and the Commonwealth of Independent States—which embody respectively the hegemonic power of the United States and Russia—the Islamic Conference, the Organization for Security and Cooperation in Europe, the Organization of American States, the Association of Southeast Asian Nations (ASEAN), the Caribbean Community, the South African Development Community, the Economic Community of West African States (ECOWAS), and the African Union have all played a role in regional peace and security initiatives.

Over the past fifteen years, Europe has been involved as a regional actor in Africa, the Balkans, South Eastern Europe, the Caucasus, Central Asia, and the Middle East, while the North Atlantic Treaty Organization (NATO) has promoted capacity development at the European periphery and beyond. Both the EU and NATO are developing new quick-response military capacities while civilian crisis management is acquiring a higher profile in the EU as a complement to regional development assistance and diplomatic efforts.

In West Africa, peace operations have benefited from the mutual security initiatives of ECOWAS. In Southeast Asia, ASEAN has focused on conflict prevention while ceding the initiative to Australia and the United Nations in East Timor. The lack of effective regional mechanisms in the Middle East has been sorely felt in the wake of the unilateral intervention of the United States and its allies and its costly aftermath.

International structures, functions, and processes have only begun to adapt to the challenges of human security (Knight, 2005). The traditional multilateral model derives from state-centric security and development principles; through the deliberations of the Security Council and the General Assembly it aims at achieving better coordination of national policies and at equitable solutions. The system is under severe stress and often leads to gridlock.

More flexible arrangements are needed given the uni-polarity of the world's military order, the diffuse multi-polarity of its economic order, and the concentration of political power among a limited number of hegemonic powers. The advent of a global civil society, the growing influence of private multinationals, and the increased security threats emanating from non-state actors also call for more open and innovative organizational solutions.

Hierarchical systems are increasingly giving way to coalitions and networks formed to focus on specific goals. These organizations bring together the public, private, and voluntary sectors and facilitate cooperation within highly decentralized decision-making frameworks. Some of them are geared to delivering public goods, including security services. Others focus on developing common principles, cooperation protocols, behavioral norms, or codes of conduct.

In the field of peace and security, increased coordination between the United Nations and the European Union illustrates the trend towards pragmatic coalitions in such fields as conflict prevention and the civilian and military aspects of crisis management, and towards such regions as the Balkans, the Middle East, the African Great Lakes Region, the Horn of Africa, and West Africa. Coordination and compatibility of mission planning is governed by a joint declaration and steering committee.

Governance for human security needs to transcend traditional governmental processes and practices. It involves a wide range of public, private, and voluntary actors. It takes place at all levels—the neighborhood, the municipality, the province, the nation, the region, or the world. It facilitates orderly and transparent market processes while promoting broadly based, sustainable development through norms and standards designed to protect individual freedoms, empower the weak, and redress social inequities.

From this perspective, the current multilateral security and development architecture will eventually have to be reshaped. In time, the bureaucratic and state-centric structures may evolve towards deliberative and democratic rule making bodies connected to regional bodies and specialized networks that would provide platforms for public-private initiatives, testing grounds for policy experiments, and transmission belts for ideas and knowledge.

D. Distinct Accountabilities: The Imperative of Coherence

Coordination within donor countries' governments has proven elusive even when dealing with economic aspects such as trade or migration. Some promising "joined up" government initiatives that combine security and development have been launched. But they are very new and concentrated in a few OECD countries, and their replication cannot be taken for granted. The challenge of introducing security objectives into the development landscape of the post-Cold War era will be even more demanding.

The limits of policy coherence are confirmed by the fledgling theory of policy coherence. The "here" in policy coherence is necessarily elusive (Winters, 2001). A top-down approach to policy coherence that responds to the interests of donor countries (understandably concerned with the security and economic interests of their own citizens) may not coincide with the policy outcomes that would result from a bottom-up process responsive to the agenda of developing countries and geared to achieving poverty reduction "on the ground." Kenneth Arrow (1963) has proven that consistent outcomes cannot be achieved when more than one preference function need to be aggregated.

Theory also shows that agenda setting and sequencing of decision making are critical to the determination of outcomes when decision making is complex and involves a wide range of participants (McLean, 1987). On the other hand, unnecessary incoherence (that is, policy options that work at cross-purposes and make both donor countries and partner countries worse off) should not be tolerated. Consequently, realistic and worthwhile goals for the agenda of policy coherence for development are: (i) to do no harm; (ii) to ensure that policy synergies are sought where feasible; and (iii) to take account of global poverty reduction objectives when rich countries' policies are formulated and implemented.

Also relevant are the results of an opinion survey through which the authors surveyed donor policy coherence practices. Replies to a structured questionnaire were received from officials familiar with policy coherence issues in Belgium, Canada, France, Italy, Japan, Sweden, Switzerland, the United Kingdom, and the United States. Most respondents stressed the importance of policy coherence for enhanced global security and for aid effectiveness in fragile states, and substantial support was evinced (especially from European countries and Japan) for greater reliance on multilateral bodies. For more details of the responses, see the appendix to this chapter.

Definitions of Policy Coherence

The *Poverty Guidelines* of the OECD Development Assistance Committee define policy coherence as "the systematic promotion of mutually reinforcing policies across government departments and agencies, creating synergies towards achieving the defined objective" (OECD, 2001). The DAC *Journal of Development Cooperation* uses a different formulation: "Policy coherence means different policy communities working together in ways that result in more powerful tools and products for all concerned. It means looking for synergies and complementarities and filling gaps among different policy areas so as to meet common and shared objectives" (Hilker, 2004).

The first definition allows unambiguous assessment of results. The second requires prior negotiation of goals among the parties in order to define an explicit objective function against which to assess results. In the world of practice, the second definition trumps the first, because pluralistic societies thrive on judicious trade-offs among policy objectives and because political feasibility requires a balance between the demands of development and the interests of domestic constituencies in donor countries. It follows that policy coherence for development is best understood as a process that aims at transparency rather than at predetermined outcomes.

From this perspective, policy coherence for development is a process designed to minimize the risks of either unintended or unnecessary incoherence—that is, of policy solutions that make both rich and poor countries worse off. It seeks synergies in policymaking, but first and foremost, it helps to prevent policy decisions that benefit vested interests at the expense of the common welfare (Picciotto and Weaving, 2004). Conversely, in certain circumstances, intended incoherence (that is, the adoption of second-best solutions) may be necessary to achieve a principled compromise while still avoiding doing harm.

Robust progress towards policy coherence for development is in the interest of rich and poor countries alike, given the interconnectedness of national economies that globalization has brought about. For example, developing countries absorb a third of the export sales of OECD countries and half of their oil supplies. Conversely, developing countries' exports generate more than thirty times more revenue per capita than aid, and twelve times in the case of the least developed countries. Remittances from migrants are about twice as large as aid flows and they are growing. Inflows of direct foreign investment to developing countries stood at USD 156 billion in 2002 (and USD 172 million in 2003), compared with aid flows of about USD 58 billion.[36]

Policy coherence for development has four dimensions (Picciotto, 2004). They are interrelated and complementary and they all contribute to the effectiveness of development cooperation:

(i) *internal*: the consistency among the ends, the means, and the resources that a donor country allocates to the implementation of development objectives, whether through aid or non-aid policy instruments;
(ii) *"whole of government"*: the consistency between the aid and non-aid policies of a donor country;
(iii) *harmonization*: the consistency of aid and non-aid policies across donor countries; and
(iv) *alignment*: the consistency between the policies and practices of one or more donor countries and its developing country partner(s).

Type (i), or internal, coherence for aid operations has been the traditional focus of development policy and evaluation. To achieve development effectiveness, a seamless relationship is sought between the inputs, outputs, outcomes, and impacts of policy. This implies the use of results-based management systems and logical frameworks in the oversight of aid programs and projects. DAC has focused on Type (i) coherence ever since its inception. Under its aegis, donors have reached agreement on principles of aid effectiveness, performance monitoring, and independent evaluation.

Much less attention has been given to Type (ii) coherence—the consistency between aid and non-aid policies.[37] Yet this area is equally critical. Given the capacity and policy constraints of difficult environments, non-aid policies significantly influence donor countries' relations with developing countries, especially those countries that are fragile and conflict-ridden. In particular, robust and sustained political and diplomatic action can help fragile states prevent, resolve, and recover from violent conflict. Hence in difficult environments a "whole of government" approach is a sine qua non of effective donor engagement. Fortunately, the peer review process of the DAC helps to track the progress that individual donor countries are making towards this aspect of policy coherence (Nicod, 2004).

Type (iii) coherence has shared objectives, distinct accountabilities, and reciprocal obligations of external actors as its main ingredients. This dimension of coherence is of major importance since developing countries, and especially fragile states, must contend with a bewildering number of external bilateral, multilateral, and non-state actors.

Therefore, if donor countries' engagement strategies are to be consistent and complementary, Type (iii) incoherence issues must be tackled in parallel with those of Type (ii). On the operational plane of development cooperation, DAC has taken steps to codify the simplification and harmonization of aid practices and coordination of aid activities (the Rome agenda)[38], but non-aid policies remain hostage to economic competition and geopolitical imperatives.

Type (iv) coherence is enshrined in the DAC Principles of Development Cooperation under the ownership and partnership labels. Of all four aspects of coherence, this is the most neglected in practice.

E. Reciprocal Obligations: Human Rights

Both in security and in development the focus has shifted from "needs" to "rights." The new people-centered approach is reflected in the mainstreaming of concern for human rights throughout the United Nations system. In the security domain, the growing recognition of a "responsibility to protect" reflects a distinct shift in the locus of accountability: "victims" are becoming "rights-holders" while domestic governments and international agencies are becoming "duty-bearers." Similarly, in development, the concepts of empowerment and participation have supplanted references to "beneficiaries" and "target groups." The adoption of social and environmental safeguard policies by international financial institutions (and by some multinational companies) reflects the same evolution.

A vast array of human rights initiatives and agreements in the civil, political, and development domains are now in place, ranging from the United Nations Charter, the Universal Declaration of Human Rights, and the International Covenants on Economic, Social, and Cultural Rights to conventions on the status of refugees, the political rights of women and the elimination of all forms of discrimination against women, the status of stateless persons, the abolition of slavery and forced labor, the elimination of racial discrimination, the suppression of apartheid, and the rights of the child—as well as conventions that govern the environment and the use of natural resources.

Civil rights protect the right to life, liberty, and personal security; the rule of law; the right to worship; and the freedom of the individual from state-sanctioned interference or violence. Political rights guarantee freedom to be involved in public affairs and affairs of state. Civil and political rights have been termed negative rights since they are upheld simply if they are not violated. By contrast, social, economic, and cultural rights are "aspirational" and programmatic: governments are enjoined to provide citizens with these positive rights, which cannot be guaranteed without adequate capacity and fiscal resources. Finally, solidarity should address rights to public goods (including peace, development, and the environment), and this has trans-national implications.

Strengthening the legal machinery to enforce existing rights at the global and regional levels is an unfinished task. In particular, much remains to be done to adapt the international legal framework to emerging issues of war and peace.

Agreements on the use of weapons and the practice of torture are embedded in conventions, treaties, and customary international law. However, the bulk of the violence currently visited upon poor countries results not from declared wars among states but from wars *within* states. Hence international law needs to extend to the role of individuals. This need is acknowledged in the establishment of the International Criminal Court.[39] Yet, whereas the rules of warfare provide for immunity of noncombatants, the advanced technologies of warfare create considerable collateral damage that is not forbidden under international law.

Frequently, violent coercion by state and non-state actors involves flagrant human rights violations (for example systematic rape and ethnic cleansing) that lead to massive refugee movements. On a smaller scale, development projects (dams, mines, roads) may involve involuntary resettlement and other negative social and environmental consequences for local communities or indigenous peoples. Human rights advocates' exposure of abuse combined with a constructive and cooperative search for sustainable solutions, helps to ensure that the environment is protected and that mitigation options are fully explored and that affected communities are offered adequate compensation.

The gradual convergence between the security and development agendas coincides with a vigorous debate about the compatibility of their respective principles, goals, and methods. Conflict prevention strategies in particular call for harmonization of objectives and practices. Here too human rights concepts and rules can help induce coherence by clarifying the roles and responsibilities of duty bearers. Whereas humanitarian work typically has a short-term focus on protecting human welfare and/or alleviating the consequences of conflict or socially unsound investments, security and development activities tend to address root causes over the medium and long term.

Thus, the human rights framework fully supports the human security agenda (Table 1).

Table 1
Human Security and Categories of Human Rights

	Positive (provision of benefits through resources, policies, etc.)	Negative (protection against practices that violate rights)
Civil and political	Good governance, judicial reform, democracy development, etc.	Protection vs. violence, arbitrary detention, torture, disenfranchisement, unfair trial, etc.
Economic, social, cultural	Access to health, education, social protection etc.	Prevention vs. ethnic and gender discrimination in employment, social services, etc.
Solidarity	Conflict prevention, biodiversity, clean air and water, development aid, debt reduction, etc.	Environmental pollution, unfair trade, etc.

Source: Landman, 2005.

Politicization, co-option by political actors, and incompatibility of goals or means constitute major risks in the "securitization" of development. The safety of aid personnel may require protection by one party to a conflict and undermine the impartiality of development activities. Typically, development practitioners seek to steer clear of political engagement to maintain their integrity and their credibility among all those who may benefit from their work. Yet they must take account of the governance context in planning their interventions. The line is hard to draw precisely and it does not always coincide with security imperatives.

The principles of neutrality, impartiality, and independence associated with needs-based development activities can clash with security policy considerations. It is not possible to generalize about appropriate ways of resolving these dilemmas. Punishment for past human rights violations may have to be forsaken, for example to facilitate a peace settlement, promote reconciliation, and accelerate economic recovery. In other cases, maintaining development activities in circumstances of blatant state-sponsored human rights violations may be perceived as legitimizing repression.

The means used to enforce law and order or to combat an insurgency so that reconstruction can proceed may not comply with the human rights principles evoked above. On the other hand, rights-based approaches that allow legitimacy considerations to come into play may make it easier to harmonize security and development approaches. In general, the search for synergy between security and development activities is greatly helped by human rights approaches that specify the obligations of duty bearers and enhance the legitimacy of both types of interventions.

At their September 2005 UN Summit, world leaders agreed to double the budget of the Officer of the High Commissioner for Human Rights over the next five years and also agreed in principle that the discredited Commission on Human Rights (where governments that abused human rights were able to block condemnation of their practices) should be replaced by a Human Rights Council. The responsibility to set up the new body was deferred to the General Assembly. The President of the General Assembly negotiated the mandate, modalities, functions, size, composition, membership, working methods, and procedures of the Council.

The Council endorsed by the General Assembly is a distinct improvement over the Commission. Members would be elected directly and individually by secret ballot without reference to regional slates. Those elected would be expected to abide by Council rules and their human rights record would be assessed. Poor performers could be suspended. Thus, notorious human rights violators may not be able to shield themselves from scrutiny through Council membership as they previously did through membership of the Commission.

F. Conclusions

Though human security faces tough challenges, some silver linings can be discerned. The number of conflicts in the world has declined, partly as a result of conciliation and peacemaking efforts. The limits of military coercion are now better appreciated. The "overstretch" of United States military power caused by the Iraq insurgency has favored the advent of a more positive approach to international diplomacy and development cooperation. Transatlantic relations have begun to improve.

Public opinion supports the convergence of security and development efforts. There is evidence of a momentum toward building a closer link between security and development. Academics, policymakers, and civil society activists alike are championing efforts to bring the two fields closer together in policy and action.[40] Additionally, the report of the

Secretary-General's High-level Panel (UN, 2004) underscores the natural connection between the two fields so that the adoption of its recommendations would take the UN a step closer to achieving the much needed convergence between these endeavors.

A change in leadership at the World Trade Organization—along with recent proposals by the United States to reduce agricultural subsidies provided the European Union reduces its tariffs on food and agriculture products—are raising faint hopes for progress in trade talks.[41] Aid volumes are trending up and debt reduction has made substantial headway. Donors have begun to consider more active engagement with fragile states. Finally, based on the outcome of the September 2005 Summit, the United Nations is considering ways and means to strengthen its peacebuilding and human rights machinery.

Shared responsibility implies results-oriented partnerships

To translate the human security agenda into operationally useful results, policy needs to support three goals:

(i) adherence to policy coherence for development principles;
(ii) advocacy of a rules-based international order in support of human rights;
(iii) stronger multilateral machinery to promote aid quality and implement human rights approaches. These approaches should be promoted globally and in the context of the European Neighborhood Policy.

This will require a sharpened strategic focus directed towards shared objectives (a revamped notion of human security), distinct accountabilities within a coherent policy framework, and reciprocal obligations embedded in human rights based approaches to security and development.

First, policy coherence is needed for peace and prosperity, because international crime and terrorism thrive on social tensions and inequities and because a global policy environment that is more supportive of sustainable and equitable development would improve security for all. Hence rich countries should be encouraged to implement the agenda of policy coherence for development, if only to serve their own long-term interests. Engagement with developing countries, especially fragile states, will require a coherent combination of aid and non-aid policies.

The coherence of rich countries' policies should be monitored just as rigorously as the efforts of developing countries to reach the Millennium Development Goals. Tracking the progress of rich countries towards specific indicators with respect to trade, aid, debt reduction, foreign direct investment, migration, intellectual property, international security, and the environment would require strengthening the Eighth Millennium Goal and unbundling it by specifying the performance indicators that rich countries' efforts ought to be judged by.

Second, progress towards a rule-based international order would help in the implementation, mainstreaming, and sustainability of human rights approaches. A key trend, explored in chapters 3 and 4 below, is that 9/11 has re-confirmed the critical role of the state. But it has also given rise to repressive measures and a roll back of civil liberties in the name of security (including intrusive surveillance, lack of due process for terrorist suspects, and brutal treatment of detainees). The spread of human rights values means that the legitimacy of the state now rests on its capacity and willingness to protect basic freedoms. Thus, while states still retain a vital role in assuring the security and welfare of their citizens, stronger international laws and more effective monitoring and enforcement are essential components of the policy convergence challenge. This is why the United Nations decision of March 2006 to create a new Human Rights Council is significant. The agreed provisions will strengthen the authority of the Human Rights Commission; they will make it harder for notorious human rights abusers to win seats, and they will provide for regular reviews of the humanitarian record of all countries.[42]

Third, faster reform of the international security and development system is desirable. For a start, increased aid and reform of the aid industry are vital credibility tests for the international community. It is high time for the aid business to implement basic reforms regarding tied aid, the harmonization of aid practices, the coordination of donor programs, and the alignment of aid objectives and delivery with developing countries' own budgetary and planning processes. Decisions could be guided by the United Nations' recent review of progress towards the Millennium Development Goals (Sachs, 2005). The *In Larger Freedom* proposals of the Secretary-General (UN Secretary-General, 2005) to all United Nations members were not universally endorsed but they remain highly relevant to the design of collaborative policies that respond symmetrically to the felt needs of rich and poor countries alike.

The global and country-level strategies of engagement recommended in this volume would be consistent with the regional approach taken by the European Neighborhood Policy. The new borders of the European Union have created new opportunities as well as new threats. Europe may have to sustain its efforts towards further enlargement, even if this means offering more restrictive forms of membership to its neighbors, as the most effective way of creating a protective belt of friendly and well-governed countries at its periphery. In the meantime, the EU's foreign policy will have to respond to the diverse mix of problems faced by individual neighbors. To this end, concerted action is critical and so is the ability to achieve harmony among policy instruments: policy coherence is as fundamental for the European Neighborhood Policy as it is for development cooperation with distant countries.

The Prospects for a New Policy Compact have Improved

Cooperation is often easier to secure after a catastrophic event or when ominous dangers loom. Thus, the Indian Ocean *tsunami* of December 2004 elicited unprecedented private and public donations. Conversely, the climate of anxiety generated by the troubled aftermath of 9/11 has generated a pent-up public demand for strong international leadership aimed at peacebuilding and economic prosperity.

Yet the advent of terrorism as a trans-national insurgency tactic has transformed the security and development equation in unexpected ways and with destabilizing consequences (Overseas Development Institute, 2003). Instead of generating intensified advocacy in support of global peace and security and triggering an open dialogue among nations, 9/11 has divided international opinion. It has provoked a blunt, coercive, and ultimately counterproductive response by the United States. Mired in conventional war thinking, the American security establishment has so far proved incapable of combining the military, civilian, and developmental assets needed to counter the Iraq insurgency. Paradoxically, the sobering effect of this prolonged setback may have improved the prospects of a diplomatic effort designed to achieve a greater measure of harmony in the international community.

Are we approaching a turnaround in the prospects for international cooperation? Globally, tentative agreements have been reached for the United Nations to strengthen its Secretariat, reform its human rights structure, condemn international terrorism, and strengthen its capacity to respond to conflict. A new realism about the state of the world is taking hold, along with a search for a better balance among the various instruments of international relations (defense, diplomacy, development). The enormous cost of recent military interventions has highlighted the rewards of conflict prevention, peacebuilding, regional security arrangements, and long-term development cooperation. The once shunned concept of state building has been restored as a priority aid objective.[43] With inspired leadership, fragmented energies and resources could yet be mobilized to promote a more equitable and sustainable economic and social order.

Looking ahead, in order to avoid chaotic conditions in poor countries that may end up affecting depressed regions or even the entire world, rich countries may be induced to provide security as well as aid. Over time, the judicious promotion of democracy may provide an effective bulwark against extremism. Specifically, an incremental approach that stresses domestic ownership, judicial reform, transparent management of public spending, and the emergence of a civil society may be more effective than pressing for regime change or electoral breakthroughs through coercion. Thus, rich countries should provide poor countries with significant latitude in their poverty reduction and policy reform efforts. They should give priority to creating a more propitious policy climate for development and concentrate on strengthening the delivery of their own humanitarian and development activities.

A constructive approach to developing countries that treats them as partners remains central to success. Only then will the tensions between the priorities of poverty reduction and the legitimate demands of international stability be resolved constructively. Poor countries do have a stake in anti-terrorism efforts and their cooperation is critical. But their security needs differ from those of rich countries and policy coherence demands that a judicious balance be struck between "their" priorities and "ours." Nor should the human security label undermine the protection of human rights in a zealous effort to combat terrorism, since the suppression of civil liberties and the interdiction of legitimate dissent would only fuel future instability.[44]

What if the Climate for International Cooperation Turns Sour?

Two sets of risks should be considered. First, the United States may retreat into isolationism or militarism. This could occur if its economy suffers a hard landing or if another major terrorist attack takes place on the U.S. homeland. In such a circumstance, like-minded EU members would need to compensate for the withdrawal and team up to sustain an outward orientation for the European Union that would reach out not only to close European neighbors (such as Turkey, Ukraine, Serbia, and Montenegro) in Africa and the Middle East but also to Asia and even to Latin America and the Caribbean.

Second, Europe may lapse into a prolonged period of introspection. Under such a scenario, individual EU states would need to rely less on the EU partnership and more on activities where their individual foreign policies can achieve results on their own or in concert with non-European partners, including the United States. Here too, adjustments in the scope and direction of development cooperation policy would need to be considered.

Both scenarios would be politically and administratively demanding and both would require adjustments to the aid selectivity criteria currently promoted by the DAC, which are based on developing countries' performance. This said, the fundamental security and development policy emphases sketched in this book are unlikely to change and a policy of proactive engagement within Europe, the United States, and developing countries would continue to be appropriate for both the management of risks and the exercise of policy influence by individual European countries.

Appendix to Chapter 1: Survey of Policy Coherence Practices

Twenty-one policy researchers and practitioners in aid donor countries responded to a questionnaire about policy coherence for development in fragile states (Picciotto and others, 2004). Most of the respondents ranked humanitarian considerations and progress towards the Millennium Development Goals ahead of global security concerns and access to natural resources as rationales for donor countries' engagement in fragile states. By an overwhelming margin, they pointed to good governance as the first priority of engagement. Next, they stressed the importance of social services, safety nets, and youth employment and investments in skills and policy reform.

By a substantial margin, respondents perceived the "war on terrorism" as the greatest threat to policy coherence for development, well ahead of commercial interests and inadequate aid flows. They ranked poor coordination among donors as another major obstacle to policy coherence, slightly ahead of conflicting objectives between donors and the partner country and of inconsistencies between the goals and the means of aid policy. Thus, joined up government was viewed as the least important link in the policy coherence chain. Nonetheless, respondents still considered this approach as the most important thing that an individual donor country can do to improve policy coherence in difficult environments. For these environments, they ranked consistency between aid and non-aid policies ahead of improved policy research and analysis, an informed public opinion, or a more assertive legislature.

Neither giving the aid minister a seat at the cabinet nor efforts to align non-state actors with government policies were considered of high significance by a majority of survey respondents. Diplomacy, development, and defense (ranked in this order) were identified as the key policies that need "joining up," ahead of trade and migration.

Strikingly, about 85 percent of respondents considered that current aid allocation policies should be less restrictive towards fragile states. Further, 60 percent of respondents expressed doubt about the use of macroeconomic conditionality in difficult environments and 70 percent held the view that the comprehensive approach embodied by the MDGs remains valid in fragile states.

Almost half of the respondents were not prepared to abandon the prevailing country-led approach to aid even in the difficult circumstances of fragile states. On the other hand, about two thirds did not advocate using the central government as the main aid channel in these circumstances. Public-private partnerships ranked as the most preferred channel for assistance. Almost three times as many respondents opted for channeling aid through NGOs, sub-national levels of government, or social funds as opted for channeling aid through central government. Sectorwide programs, technical cooperation activities, and investment projects were perceived as more likely to deliver results in fragile states than were policy-based operations or lines of credit.

Only in Sweden, Switzerland, and the United Kingdom did respondents detect that a strong "whole of government" culture was taking root. Most respondents judged that non-aid ministries had only weak capacity to respond to the results of analysis of policy coherence for development (PCD). Thus, factors other than coordination—for example basic conflicts in objectives—were perceived as more limiting. While most respondents reported that development ministries are adequately represented in inter-ministerial working groups and committees, actual policy coordination was not rated highly in Italy, France, or Belgium.

The survey confirmed that in Belgium, Sweden, and the UK, security and military issues are fully integrated within the policy coherence agenda. Canadian, Swedish, UK, and U.S. survey participants reported that senior policymakers are adequately informed of policy coherence for development issues, depending on the political profile of the case. In Canada, Italy, Sweden, Switzerland, the UK, and the US, the quality of policy analysis was reported to be good or excellent while in Belgium, France, and Japan it was considered marginal or poor.

Nowhere except Canada and Switzerland were good public information programs reported to be in place. Views about the links of policy coherence to the private sector, universities, and NGOs were mixed and a majority of respondents did not consider that the media and NGOs exert positive pressure on PCD decisions. In Canada and the UK, the development ministers have Cabinet status. Elsewhere the development portfolio is lodged within the Ministry for Foreign Affairs although a development minister within the Foreign Affairs Ministry may have a seat at the cabinet table (as in the Netherlands and Sweden).

Respondents in Sweden and U.K. did not perceive the quantity of their aid as a constraint whereas respondents from France, Italy, Japan, and Switzerland did. All respondents except those from Sweden and Switzerland considered administrative budget allocations to be constraining. The frequent lack of reporting was noted: nowhere apart from Sweden and Switzerland are tracking systems in place and only in Canada and Switzerland has a specific group within government been tasked to monitor policy coherence.

Revealingly, a majority of survey participants expect defense and security agencies to gain increased clout over the level and allocation of aid as a result of intensified interdepartmental coordination, while none, except in the U.K. and U.S., expect the aid ministry to acquire more influence as a result of PCD efforts. Defense and geo-strategic considerations seem to prevail over development concerns more often in France, Italy, and the U.S., while commercial considerations and historical ties are considered especially influential in the U.K. and France.

Notes

1. World Bank, World Development Indicators Database, 2002.
2. Intra-national inequality is also increasing: out of forty-eight developing countries and transition economies, only 14 experienced a decreased Gini coefficient between the 1980s and the 1990s. Kanbur and Lustig (2000).
3. <http://www1.worldbank.org/prem/poverty/voices>
4. The 2002 survey results were released in June 2003. They are available on the World Bank website under <External/http://web.worldbank.org/WBSITE/EXTERNAL/

NEWS/0,,contentMDK:20114414>
5. The survey was carried out for the World Economic Forum. See <http://www.weforum.org>
6. American exceptionalism is the idea that the United States has a special place in the world that derives from its unique history, values, and constitutional norms focused on personal and economic freedom. The term connotes an ideal that may not always be upheld by the people and government of the nation.
7. The global war on terror shares the spotlight with regional hot spots (for example Taiwan, Iran, and North Korea) where the traditional competition for regional dominance continues to shape U.S. policy.
8. Cooper (2004) distinguishes "modern" states, which have achieved legitimacy and a monopoly of legitimate violence within their borders, from "pre-modern" states, which have not, and "post-modern" states (such as EU members), which accept a degree of mutual interference in each other's domestic affairs. "Post-modern" states reject the use of force for resolving disputes in favor of transparency, interdependence, and mutual vulnerability.
9. The inability to secure a united front among Security Council members explains why the Sudan government and the *janjaweed* militias have been allowed to conduct an ethnic cleansing campaign that has caused 200,000 civilian deaths and untold suffering in the Darfur region.
10. Beyond generalized assertions about the link between state weakness and security challenges, the strategy fails to relate identified shortfalls in state capacity, resilience, or political will to specific risks of instability.
11. The threat of genetically engineered bio-terror agents has induced the United States Defense Department to fund a USD 1.5 billion initiative to develop broad-spectrum medical countermeasures.
12. Innovative interventions combining civilian and military forces in combination with humanitarian and development assistance have begun to be used in Afghanistan to combat warlords and deprive combatants of the safety and comfort provided by local populations. Over the long run, "hearts and minds" strategies are likely to trump "search and destroy" tactics.
13. Deterrence is static, indefinite in its timing, and unambiguous in terms of the retaliation triggered by clearly specified adversary actions. By contrast, "compellence" seeks to reverse actions already underway (e.g., discouraging a spate of suicide bombings) or overturning a status quo (e.g. inducing an adversary to abjure the use of nuclear weapons). "Compellence" is designed to induce timely responses from adversaries through graduated incentives applied selectively and in a dynamic context (Schelling, 1966). The word is not yet in the dictionary but it is in widespread use in war studies.
14. They have not swayed world opinion: according to a May 2003 Pew attitudes survey of 16,000 people in twenty countries around the world, a vast majority of people broadly but guardedly approve of the growth in foreign trade and global communications and of the spread of international popular culture and are more inclined to credit globalization for conditions they see as improving. On the other hand, majorities in thirty-four of forty-four countries surveyed perceive job availability, health care, and the ability to save for one's old age as having deteriorated, and majorities in forty-two of those countries believe that their traditional way of life is getting lost and should be protected from foreign influence.
15. The debate about globalization goes awry when economic and social trends that result from technological change or from the governance characteristics of an individual state are attributed to increased market integration.

16. For example, more than half the people surveyed outside the United States by the Pew Research Center in December 2001 perceived the United States' policies to be contributing to the growing gap between rich and poor nations.
17. The main sticking points have been in agriculture, services, and special treatment for developing countries. However, prior trade rounds also incurred delays and skirted repeated failures before agreements were finally reached. The most likely outcome is a modest package of reforms with limited benefits for developing countries.
18. In 1998, the former Managing Director of the International Monetary Fund estimated the global flow of dirty money at 2-5 percent of the global economy.
19. The European Union announced on May 24, 2004 that its richest states will reach the historic target of 0.7 percent of national income by 2015 and that European aid to Africa and the rest of the developing world will double by 2010 when the richest 15 countries pass the 0.51 percent mark. This could mark a turning point if it induces other rich countries, including the United States and Japan, to follow suit. While the United States has increased its aid by USD 8 billion since the year 2000, its aid is only 0.16 percent of U.S. national income.
20. Joseph Stiglitz estimates that the Iraq war may end up costing USD 2 trillion if account is taken of lost productivity and the long-term impact of disability payments and general economic disruption.
21. Americans and non-Americans do not see eye to eye on global issues (Stokes, 2005). A poll taken by the British Broadcasting Corporation in 2004 found that 70 percent of U.S. respondents viewed their country as having a positive influence in the world whereas pluralities in all the other 21 countries surveyed saw U.S. influence as mostly negative.
22. Mexico (1994), East Asia (1997), Russia (1998), Brazil (1999), Argentina (2002).
23. The economic output of China is roughly that of California and India's economy is 20 percent smaller than that of Texas. China would have to grow by 21 percent and India by 56 percent to match the value of annual U.S. increases in production.
24. According to a *Washington Post*-ABC News poll, nearly six in ten Americans now believe that the Iraq war was not worth fighting and more than half assert that the war has not contributed to the security of the American public (*Wall Street Journal*, June 9, 2005).
25. The levels of protection of Norway and Switzerland are higher, at 19 percent and 12 percent, respectively.
26. Norway does even better (0.87 percent). Development Assistance Committee countries commit an average of 0.25 percent of GDP.
27. A short-list of principles for good international engagement with fragile states was formulated following a Senior-level Forum on Fragile States attended by officials of the OECD/DAC, the European Union, the UNDP, and the World Bank in London in January 2005. But these principles do not tackle issues beyond those under the control of aid ministries and therefore have limited value, since policies *other* than aid tend to be more important in such environments. The principles will be piloted in two to five countries before the end of 2005, and their implementation will be evaluated in 2007.
28. The U.K. Department for International Development has suggested the creation of a Multilateral Balancing Fund, while Mark McGillivray (2005) has proposed that the Development Assistance Committee (DAC) of the OECD, in conjunction with major multilateral agencies, should organize annual events to coordinate inter-recipient aid allocation.

29. UNESCO has established a Forum on Human Security <http://www.unesco.org/securipax>. The Development Studies Association has a set up a Conflict and Human Security study group. The International Peace Academy in New York and the universities of British Columbia, King's College (London), Harvard, Tufts, and Michigan run programs dedicated to the interface between conflict, security, and development (human security).
30. <http://humansecurity.gc.ca/menu-en.asp>
31. Human security promotes respect for the Hippocratic Oath, "first, do no harm." It respects the traditional notion that confines security to the imperative of survival of individuals, societies, and international systems. This was the meaning of security emphasized during the Cold War when security concepts were state-centered and focused on the military sector. But the emerging human security concept is broader in scope, and recognizes the individual as the privileged unit of account for policy impact.
32. The Human Security Gateway <http://www.humansecuritygateway.info> sponsored by the Ministry for Foreign Affairs of Canada, the Trust Fund for Human Security of the Ministry for Foreign Affairs of Japan <http://www.mofa.go.jp/policy/human_secu> and the Global Partnership for the Prevention of Armed Conflict <www.gppac.net> lists useful support sources for human security activities. See also <www.humansecuritynetwork.org> for information on an initiative that involves the governments of Austria, Canada, Chile, Costa Rica, Greece, Ireland, Jordan, Mali, the Netherlands, Norway, Switzerland, Slovenia, and Thailand, with that of South Africa as an observer.
33. For Mark Duffield (2006), the development enterprise has always sought to reconcile the disruptive effects of economic progress with the need for social order so that the current focus on human security is explained by a desire to sustain a dynamic equilibrium in fragile, "non-insured" societies through external intervention.
34. In finance, securitization is a technique that pools assets together and turns them into tradable securities. In political science, it refers to the labeling of an issue or activity so that it receives privileged treatment. Specifically, it means the politicization of an issue in ways that allow the short-circuiting of regular decision making rules, consultation procedures, etc. Development practitioners are ambivalent about "securitization." On the one hand it enhances the priority of their work. On the other hand, it could be a pretext for subverting the poverty reduction goals of aid, ignoring democratic safeguards, and undermining participation in decision making.
35. About half of the peace agreements intended to stop intra-state wars are breached.
36. Other policies matter too and they can help or hurt the cause of global poverty reduction. For example, fishing subsidies by OECD countries absorb USD 15-20 billion a year, benefit large companies more than poor fishing communities, and deplete the fish populations on which poor countries' coastal fisheries depend.
37. See Netherlands Minister for Foreign Affairs (2004). Denmark, Norway, and the United Kingdom also report on their contributions to MDG 8.
38. < http://aidharmonization.com/>
39. The perpetrators of 9/11 could be apprehended based on a variety of legal instruments, including the Hague Convention on the Suppression of Unlawful Seizure of Aircraft of 1970.
40. See for example, the *Journal of Conflict, Security & Development*, vol. 4, no. 3, December 2004, which is devoted to a discussion of issues at the intersection of security and development and the challenges of achieving closer links between the two disciplines.

41. Barring high level intervention by United States and European leaders, a "low ambition" outcome with limited development content (combining slight improvements in agriculture and mixed progress on industry and services) seems to be the most likely outcome as of March 2006: in exchange for proposed cuts in agricultural subsidy ceilings (which would not reduce actual spending or end dumping) developing countries would have to reduce their tariffs on industrial goods without offers of comparable concessions by industrial countries.
42. The United States, Israel, the Marshall Islands, and Palau voted against the measure since they favored approval of Council membership by a two thirds majority of the General Assembly (rather than an absolute majority of its members) so as to guarantee that human rights abusers would not join the Council. However, the United States ambassador (John Bolton) confirmed that his country was prepared to "work cooperatively with other member states to make the Council as strong and effective as it can be."
43. On February 16, 2005, the Administrator of USAID, Andrew Natsios, said that the United States is threatened more by "failed, failing, and recovering states" than by "conquering states" and that ignoring failed and failing states "can pose great risks, including the likelihood of terrorism taking root."
44. In some countries, the global war on terrorism has also helped to justify repression against dissidents of all stripes.

2

Towards a More Secure Global Development Agenda

> *"The central issue of contention is not globalization itself, nor is it the use of the market as an institution, but the inequity in the overall balance of institutional arrangements—which produces very unequal sharing of the benefits of globalization"*—Amartya Sen

This chapter focuses on the policies that OECD countries should adopt to help developing countries secure freedom from want as well as freedom from fear. These twin goals are anchored in the Millennium Declaration that was endorsed by all United Nations heads of state at the turn of the century. But are they mutually consistent? What policy instruments should be used to achieve them? What changes are needed in global policy directions and goals?

Section A highlights the need to break through the firewall that separates security and development: it presents the rationale for paying special attention to the coherence of policies towards fragile states. Section B describes the major policy coherence challenges of globalization—challenges that go well beyond increases in the quality and quantity of aid. Section C examines the other major policy vectors that need reorientation: trade, private financial flows, foreign direct investment, migration, the environment, and the arms trade. Section D proposes a new initiative that would enrich the Millennium Development Goals with complementary goals and indicators geared to the full human security agenda outlined in chapter 1. Section E concludes.

A. Policy Coherence and Security

Throughout the 1990s, the development agenda centered on facilitating globalization. Liberated from the strictures of the Cold War, the development cooperation business succeeded in building a distinctive professional identity focused on common principles and the vision of a world free of poverty. These are major achievements. In September 2005, despite initial reservations by the United States, world leaders at the UN Summit reiterated their support for the Millennium Development Goals.

Because the nations of the world have become more interconnected and interdependent than ever before, the penalties associated with inconsistent policies have risen. This applies to security as well as to development. It has become clear that neither development strategies nor peacebuilding policies can be fully effective unless they are formulated in concert. This means that the "rules of the game" that govern the relationships between OECD countries and developing countries should be adapted to the emerging global economic order but also that policy coherence should embrace security as well as development.

Fragile states are the weak links in the global system. Control of terrorism, health pandemics, or illegal drugs constitutes a global public good of the "weakest link" type. Control requires the participation of every state, since the smallest provision level determines the amount of the public good that generates benefit for all (Sandler, 2004). For example, adequate security screening of passengers in only one country is not enough to contain air travel risks for the citizens of that country. Beyond a certain level, upgrading national security in one country runs into diminishing returns if that country is surrounded by unstable, fragile, "weakest-link" states.

These are the states where violent conflict is concentrated, where global development meets its most challenging test, and where the proactive and coherent engagement of donor countries is needed the most. And yet, these are the very states that have been neglected by the international community and where the principles of development cooperation, patiently constructed to fit the circumstances of countries that perform well, are largely inapplicable.

Until recently, the aid business bypassed the issues faced in countries that are unable or unwilling to adopt market-oriented policies and poverty reduction programs. Ownership of the right policies was considered a prerequisite of donor engagement. Little if any attention was devoted to the needs of conflict prevention or reform of security systems. Conversely, national security strategies took no explicit account of the potential security benefits of aid. Finally, the Millennium Development

Goals focused on making poverty history without addressing a fundamental obstacle to poverty reduction: violent conflict.

Path dependence weighs heavily on government institutions, so the strategic upheaval of 9/11 has yet to be translated into major changes in the modalities of aid. People pay lip service to the convergence of security and development but actual changes in aid allocations, instruments, and practices have been slow and uneven. It is only in countries where a strong civil society has nurtured a political constituency for development assistance that the notion of joined up government has become a priority goal of public policy.

These are the same countries that have acknowledged the true dimensions of the challenge of policy convergence between security and development. Countries that have made the most progress along this road—the Netherlands, the UK, and Nordic countries—have included security within the agendas of all their major ministries.[1] But even these countries are still at the steep end of the learning curve.

Given the scope and complexity of operational issues at the intersection of security and development, more is required to achieve policy coherence than fine-tuning policy processes or executing small and symbolic projects that combine security and development objectives. Such initiatives are useful in testing new approaches and building local capacities. But what needs to emerge is a paradigm shift towards a comprehensive concept of human security that combines security system planning and embraces conflict prevention and peacemaking, together with broadly based development that aims to leave no country behind.

Development Aid as an Investment in Security

Aid is equivalent to only seven percent of the resources absorbed by the military worldwide. On average, rich countries devote 0.25 percent of their national incomes to development assistance, compared with 2.3 percent to the military. After the decline that followed the end of the Cold War, the resources allocated to aid have begun to rise again in absolute terms. The Development Assistance Committee estimates that aid disbursement by its members will rise from USD 78.6 billion in 2004 to USD 128 billion in 2010, an increment of nearly USD 50 billion (OECD/DAC, 2006). Other donors, such as China, Korea, and India, are also increasing their aid contributions. But defense expenditures are also trending up so that the imbalance may not be rectified any time soon.

Over the past ten years, world military expenditures have risen annually by 2.4 percent in real terms. The budgetary burden of military expenditures is especially heavy within developing countries. These countries currently absorb two thirds of arms exports by rich countries (Grimmet, 2001).[2] According to the Stockholm International Peace Research Institute, between 1993 and 2002 military expenditures grew much faster in developing regions than in the world as a whole: by 38 percent in the Middle East, 30 percent in Africa, and 23 percent in Asia. After 2002, the growth of world military expenditures accelerated sharply, driven by that of the United States, to reach USD 1,035 billion in 2004. The 2004 level is equivalent to 2.6 percent of world GDP[3] and USD 162 per capita. At current growth rates, world military spending will soon reach the level of 1988, when it was close to its Cold War peak.

Increases by the United States, with expenditures that account for 47 percent of the total, and by other powers trying to keep pace, will continue to fuel growth until the security situation of the world improves and/or the ballooning U.S. budget deficit induces a policy shift. For fiscal year 2005 alone, the U.S. military budget was USD 522 billion[4], compared to an average of USD 343 billion during the Cold War.[5] In 2005 U.S. fiscal year spending on the military was seven times larger than China's (the second largest spender), more than the combined spending of the next 14 nations, and 29 times as large as the combined spending of Cuba, Iran, Libya, North Korea, Sudan, and Syria.[6] In addition, intelligence operations absorbed about USD 41 billion annually.

By way of comparison, to meet the development objectives agreed at the Millennium Summit in 2000, the Millennium Project estimates that total aid would need to be USD 135 billion in 2006, rising to USD 195 billion in 2015; that is, 0.4 and 0.5 percent of donor GNP, or 17-25 percent of what is currently spent on the military. If the amounts required to reach the Millennium Development Goals have not been forthcoming while the military machine has continued to expand, it is because national security considerations continue to dominate public opinion.[7]

Whether current expenditure patterns reflect actual threats is debatable. Huge resources remain locked into military uses that reflect Cold War priorities.[8] Logically, arms transfers and military assistance should be subjected to impact assessments instead of responding to imaginary threats or narrow domestic policy considerations such as providing jobs in military bases that have dubious security value. Ideally, the value of additional military assets for security should be compared with the security gains that would flow from collective security arrangements and development assistance.

An integrated analytical approach would pay rich dividends. For example, it might show that the supply by OECD countries of reliable security guarantees (for example in support of collective regional security arrangements), would have very high security returns at modest cost, especially in zones where regional tensions are contributing to an arms race.

We know that poverty does not necessarily lead to violence and that security alone does not guarantee development. But we also know that development and peace are positively correlated (Collier and others, 2003). Developing countries that have achieved or are on track to achieve middle-income status face a risk of civil war just four times as high as that incurred by high-income countries of the OECD. By contrast, low-income countries that have been unable to adopt and sustain sound development policies face risks fifteen times as high.

The need for more and better aid geared to security as well as development is illustrated by the demographic situation of the Middle East, Africa, and Asia where a vast reservoir of unemployed youth constitutes a development challenge as well as a security risk. The Cold War ended when the military containment of the Soviet Union was combined with visible proof that open societies work better than authoritarian ones. Similarly, if the contest with fundamentalist ideologies (such as Maoism or *jihadism*) is to be won, it will be more through the promise of political participation and the provision of economic opportunity than through the use of military force.

In particular, extremist organizations will only be defeated when decision makers in regions currently plagued by unrepresentative governments and stagnant economies opt for economic and social reform and decide to restrain the extremists in their midst, or persuade them to abandon their radical ideologies through increased participation in the decisions that affect their lives.[9]

In Fragile States, Policy Coherence is the Key to Aid Effectiveness

In the United States and Southern Europe, public support for aid is shallow and short-run security concerns dominate. In other OECD countries, aid agencies seek early results and focus on countries that are willing and able to adopt market-friendly policies and manage poverty reduction programs. In most cases, a policy of benign neglect towards fragile states has been the preferred option. Yet, an integrated approach to security and development would emphasize long-term engagement with fragile, conflict-prone states. The results of a survey of donors' approaches to fragile states are outlined in the appendix to chapter 1.

The shift in approach that is needed should embrace the entire development community, since fair and predictable sharing of risks demands collaboration and consistency of goals and policies among donor countries. This is critical in difficult operating environments where administrative structures are weak and where effective donor coordination, reduced transaction costs, and harmonized procurement and disbursement procedures are crucial to aid efficiency. High-level coordination mechanisms are also needed to ensure that goals are congruent, but the most serious development effectiveness constraints are in the field.

Even if development initiatives are well coordinated within individual donor governments, they can impose excessive burdens on administrations in fragile states unless donors harmonize their practices with those of partner countries under strong, proactive, and sympathetic leadership, not only at headquarters but also "on the ground." Ultimately, greater reliance on multilateral channels would deliver policy coherence at low cost. But the injection of security issues into development has tended to "bilateralize" aid, so that harmonization and coordination among large numbers of donor agencies on a case-by-case basis remains the only practical option.

The problem of inadequate coordination was recognized by the UN Secretary-General's *In Larger Freedom* report (UN Secretary-General, 2005), which argued the need for a coherent approach by all parties concerned with conflict management. To achieve this approach will require stronger capacities within the UN, the World Bank, the EU, and the OECD. In parallel with reforms in the global governance system, the OECD would have to strengthen its ongoing efforts to harmonize the approaches of bilateral and multilateral agencies to policy coherence for development.

A significant achievement of the September 2005 Summit at the United Nations was the agreement to set up a Peacebuilding Commission, backed by a Support Office attached to the Secretary-General and focused on improved support processes for post-conflict interventions and monitoring. Obviously, the success of the Commission will hinge on what actual support is forthcoming from member states. The travails of the successive draft proposals reflected divergent views about the Commission's proper mandate, size, structure, and responsibilities.

On 20 December 2005, it was agreed that the Commission should focus on providing a coordinated, coherent, and integrated approach to post-conflict peacebuilding and to facilitating dialogue among key actors.[10] The mobilization of adequate resources, the sustained political attention of the Security Council, the provision of planning capacities, and the efficacy of coordination arrangements—without which progress will remain elusive—will hinge on getting individual member states to accept ownership of the outcome of peace operations.

Managing the interface between military, humanitarian, and developmental objectives will be especially critical. To ensure a smooth interaction, adjustments will be needed in the government-led model of aid. Fragile states, let alone failed states, cannot be expected to subscribe instantly to the liberal economic policies and social development goals that OECD countries hold dear. "Ownership" of specific poverty reduction goals by domestic authorities cannot be taken as given—nor should it be viewed as a prerequisite of donor country involvement.

On the other hand, broadly based engagement with non-state actors can lay the groundwork for a gradual evolution towards a transparent and responsive governance structure. Proactive engagement with domestic constituencies to achieve commonality of purposes—Type (iv) coherence, as defined in chapter 1—takes time and is worth nurturing since it is the most critical aspect of aid effectiveness in fragile states.

Given the distorted policies and the weak fiduciary standards that prevail in most fragile states, large-scale aid in the form of budget, sector, and balance of payments support may not be warranted. Other forms of assistance can be used but the commitment and participation of reform-minded actors requires careful and systematic support. Equally, aid practices need to be harmonized in order to avoid fragmentation of efforts and high transaction costs. This makes it all the more important to delegate appropriate authority to donor countries' country representatives and to set up a "unity of command" structure for external interventions in fragile states.

In other words, to achieve development effectiveness in fragile states, all four aspects of policy coherence should be tackled simultaneously. Security is "developmentalized" where defense professionals recognize that investments in development are investments in security. Equally, "securitization" has its place if it complies with basic development tenets capable of addressing the treacherous combination of human insecurity and social instability that plagues fragile countries. While the security agenda can and should be mainstreamed within development activities, its policy focus should not be distorted in the process or else the basic thrust of policy coherence *for* development would be lost.

Policy Coherence for Development Has Yet to Embrace Security

While all relevant aspects of security were included in the Millennium Declaration of 2000, the current policy coherence research initiative of the OECD does not extend much beyond issues geared to making the international marketplace fairer and more efficient and aid more conflict-sensitive. This selective approach is consistent with the focus of the initiative on the Eighth Millennium Development Goal. But recent shifts in the authorizing environment would justify broadening the agenda for policy coherence for development to embrace the full range of human security concerns—including the cost effectiveness of military spending, the consequences of weapons proliferation, and the economic consequences of international crime and terrorism, along with such topics as conflict prevention, security sector reform, and related issues such as disarmament, demobilization, and reintegration activities that have been tackled at the policy level but do not yet feature in the research agenda of OECD departments or the OECD Development Center.[11]

Both at the international and at the national level, security officials still tend to focus on protecting the state against direct internal and external threats instead of emphasizing conflict prevention and peacemaking. Peacemaking measures, by contrast, address the political, economic, and social consequences of war and aim to tackle the structural causes of conflict. Hence, a realignment of security strategies to take account of the relative weight of needed military and civil interventions is overdue. In particular, aid donors should consider giving greater weight to social protection and to the priority that poor people ascribe to individual security. This would mean adopting rights-based approaches, enhancing democratic governance, and promoting the participation and empowerment of the poor in decision making. Conflict prevention, conflict resolution, and post-conflict rehabilitation activities would have to be adequately resourced.

Many poor countries have no access to collective security arrangements. Hence, they reach out to OECD nations for loans and guarantees to facilitate their weapons purchases, some of which have been used for internal warfare (Nepal) or military incursions into neighboring countries (Uganda). Oxfam has shown that out of seventeen countries it surveyed that are parties to the European Union Code of Conduct and/or the principles of the Organization for Security and Cooperation in Europe, only ten would admit concerns about governance or conflict prevention as grounds for denying an export license for arms; only four have ever denied an arms export license on these grounds; and only two (U.K. and the Netherlands) have a policy of consulting their development departments before issuing such a license.[12]

In order to protect 250 jobs at home, the United Kingdom authorized the export to Tanzania of a USD 40 million air traffic control system, which was purchased on questionable defense grounds and over the objections of the U.K. Department for International Development and the World Bank. Countries such as Uzbekistan have used police equipment—imported to improve domestic security—to further internal coercion and human rights abuses. A huge quantity of small arms manufactured by OECD countries, China, Israel, Russia, and South Africa flows through a vast and unregulated network of independent arms dealers, brokers, middlemen, and criminal networks.[13] Too many of these arms end up in the hands of rebels in war-torn countries and make local wars bloodier and harder to control.

Regrettably, the war on terrorism has been used to justify increased military aid and arms sales to authoritarian regimes, and has provided a cover for human rights violations, ranging from lack of due legal process for suspected terrorists to unfair targeting of minorities and repression of political oppositions. A legal framework for better control of the arms trade has become urgently necessary for restraining violence in poor countries.

Hybrid Pilot Projects Have Begun to Combine Security and Development on the Ground

Military power is one way to exercise influence. Economic inducements are another. The two sets of incentives can be combined. Soft power—the "ability to entice and attract"—reduces the need for both (Keohane and Nye, 2000), but it does not substitute for either. Exclusive reliance on coercion can be counterproductive, since it may generate resentment and promote countervailing alliances. Conversely, a foreign policy geared to commercial considerations alone can reduce security, for example by facilitating access to sensitive military technologies.

Similarly, exclusive reliance on inclusion and attraction ignores the real risks that are posed by rogue states and non-state actors driven to violence by greed or ideology. A hybrid and flexible approach to diplomacy, combining military deterrence with development cooperation, is more effective than one that relies on either sticks or carrots. But ultimately, only a collective multilateral security system that ties all states together through mutually advantageous economic, political, and security links holds the promise of sustainable peace and global prosperity.

Meanwhile, the Afghanistan and Iraq wars (and before them the Balkan conflicts) used joined up approaches to security and development planning on the ground. "Mission-defined coalitions" have displaced multilateral initiatives. More private contractors are being used along with voluntary organizations in the delivery of social services. Along with smarter weapons that are designed to minimize collateral damage, humanitarian work is being called upon to mitigate the effects of military intervention and demonstrate to international public opinion the ethical values of open societies. In parallel, there is a clear trend towards greater government oversight of voluntary agencies that operate in insecure environments.

Thus, humanitarian agencies and international organizations are being invited to participate in conflict management and peacekeeping tasks in support of contested and politicized security agendas. If they refuse to participate, they forgo the opportunity to relieve the human costs of war to civilians and they risk losing their institutional relevance. If they join the effort, they risk abrogating the principles of impartiality and neutrality on which their credibility depends.

At stake is the fundamental question of whether the integration of security and development serves one goal at the expense of the other. New protocols, new operating practices, and new institutional arrangements will need to be forged to resolve the tension and ensure that, at a minimum, policy coherence does no harm. Already, at the operational level, like-minded partners have begun to pioneer more effective approaches to conflict management for use by the European Union[14] and NATO. The lessons of experience will have to be taken on board when designing policies at the intersection of security and development.

B. Managing Globalization

How should the rules of the game of the global market evolve to meet emerging threats to human security? First and foremost, all policy tools—not just aid—should be used in concert, since flows of trade, investment, knowledge, and people contribute more than aid to human welfare. Second, globalization should be managed better, rather than slowed down, since greater economic interconnectedness generates benefits that can be used to improve the well being of people everywhere. Third, since the insecurities associated with globalization are rooted in the weakest elements of the global system, development efforts should continue to concentrate on poverty reduction and give their due to fragile states: to the extent practicable, state building should be carried out upstream of full market integration. Fourth, the delivery of global public goods should be emphasized, since the network effects of globalization have negative as well as positive consequences and require public intervention.[15] Fifth, policies that protect the environment should be favored, since current patterns of development are not ecologically sustainable. In all five dimensions, briefly reviewed in what follows, the burdens of the adjustment process should be shared equitably by the public sector, the private sector, and the voluntary sector.

Aid is One Tool among Many

Aid is a very useful policy tool for making globalization work for all. In 2005, it assumed a high profile at the Gleneagles summit of the G8 in July and at the United Nations General Assembly Summit session of September. Commitments were made to raise official development assistance by more than 60 percent from 2004 to 2010. For countries that are performing well, agreement was reached to wipe out the debt owed to international financial institutions. A major debt reduction was agreed for Nigeria. These initiatives, as well as the "make poverty history" campaign spearheaded by international rock stars and civil society organizations, made 2005 "the year of development."

There is little doubt that aid matters hugely to development but to be fully effective, it should enhance the development impact of other policies, especially those that govern the international marketplace. These are the policies that increasingly affect the development prospects of poor countries, as shown by the experience of Bangladesh.

In the early 1990s, Bangladesh received USD 1.6 billion from foreign aid, USD 2 billion from exports, and USD 0.8 billion from remittances. By 2001, its aid receipts had shrunk to USD 1.4 billion, but its exports had risen by more than three times (to USD 6.5 billion)—and this despite an erosion of its terms of trade (by 10 percent over the past two decades).

Bangladesh's receipts of remittances have more than doubled, to USD 1.9 billion, and its inflows of foreign direct investment, at USD 222 million, are seven times what they were ten years ago. Bangladesh pays the United States more in import duties than France does, even though the value of French exports to the United States is thirteen times as high. This reflects the open trade regimes that tie rich economies together in contrast to the trade barriers that separate rich and poor countries (Rahman, 2004).

Even if recent aid commitments are met in full, aid volumes will lag behind the volume and value of transactions associated with other globalization links. Already, private capital flows to developing countries overall are four times larger than aid flows. However, the distribution of foreign direct investment (FDI) is skewed. Least developed countries collectively receive only 0.5 percent of global FDI flows, in reflection of their poverty and poor investment climates. Of this amount, 86 percent goes to ten countries, and more than half goes to four oil-producing countries.

The whole of Sub-Saharan Africa receives less than 2 percent of global FDI; even these receipts go only to a handful of countries and are mainly for natural resource extraction. In general, the policies that influence the volume and direction of private capital, knowledge, and technology transfers have been designed with the interests of OECD countries in mind without adequate consideration of the needs and potentials of poor countries.

The protection of intellectual property rights has been strengthened under World Trade Organization rules, in disregard of basic human needs in developing countries. Trade-related intellectual property regimes have restricted access to essential drugs and other knowledge-intensive products and services. Developing countries face growing pressure to strengthen intellectual property protection based on the current practices of developed countries. But in developing countries that are large net importers of technology, standards that may be suitable for developed countries produce more costs than benefits. As a result, USD 60 billion will flow from the South to the North to pay for patent protection, compared to USD 10 billion now. This projected reverse flow is nearly as large as all the aid that flows from the North to the South.

Migration regimes matter too: in 2002, while aid contributed about USD 49 billion in net official financing, migrants sent nearly twice that amount; their official gross remittances to developing countries were estimated at USD 93 billion.[16] Most OECD countries have rapidly aging populations, with all that that implies for the supply of labor. The very restrictions that are imposed on immigration on security grounds have created incentives for criminal rackets to smuggle human beings. Freer flows of people across borders, like freer flows of goods and services, would enhance global welfare,[17] but only if combined with measures to facilitate the integration of migrants in society and to protect homeland security. Tough but fair policy tradeoffs must be struck. To reach the right balance, the voices of developing countries in the corridors of Western power should be amplified to resist the extreme pressures applied by domestic vested interests.

Globalization Should be Managed Better, Rather than Slowed Down

The rapid expansion of cross-border flows made economic by the new information, transport, and communications technologies has made the protection of national markets harder to justify. Continuous technological advance should sustain the incentives for freer and more open cross-border exchanges. Further market integration has a strong economic justification, provided the risks attendant on globalization are managed judiciously. Currently, we seem to be experiencing a pause, and protectionist pressures are rising both in Europe and the United States,[18] but globalization has yet to run its course.

Despite the interregional variations shaped by colonial regimes and the exigencies of distance, markets for labor and capital were far more integrated at the start of the twentieth century than they are today. In the last twenty-five years only 2 percent of the world's people have changed their permanent residence, compared to 10 percent in the twenty-five years before World War I. While world trade grew twice as fast as world output in the second half of the twentieth century and foreign direct investment grew three times as fast, the ratio of trade to output has not increased much in Europe, and has declined in Japan, compared to what it was before World War I. The ratio of U.S. international trade to output would need to grow six-fold to achieve equivalence between internal and cross-border trade.

As the history of the first half of the twentieth century shows, a breakdown in the economic globalization process is not inconceivable. Such a development would be a major setback for people everywhere since the benefits that can flow from equitable and sustainable forms of economic integration are enormous. A reversal could be triggered by a major economic depression, a major environmental crisis triggered by energy shortages, or a combination of shocks resulting from dissension among major powers, policy mistakes, or sustained incoherence in policy responses. To withstand such challenges as these, states need market institutions, economic management skills, and the legitimacy required to mediate among competing claims.

There is no necessary trade-off between the growth of trade and the growth of government. This is because social spending is needed alongside the economic expansion associated with international trade. Historically, the industrial democracies have combined open trade with the welfare state.[19] Successful "globalizers" among developing countries have done the same. This is because open trade increases economic insecurity for workers as a direct result of the competition and innovation that drive productivity gains, and this in turn calls for policy responses that involve greater spending on social safety nets.

Hence, for globalization to proceed unimpeded over the medium and long run, governments must combine a market-friendly stance with people-friendly measures, including compensation, training, and social insurance, as well as environmental regulations designed to protect consumers and future generations. In the short run, differences in regulatory frameworks may arise as poor countries seek to attract foreign direct investment through a "race to the bottom." Over time, however, labor, environmental, and other standards are likely to converge and create a virtuous circle that helps to balance growth and equity concerns.

Fragile States Need Assistance for Capacity Building and Market Integration

There is considerable room for further integration of national economies, and well-managed globalization has the potential to unlock major benefits for all. But state fragility is an obstacle to equitable globalization and it also creates security risks. This is why state building through development cooperation should acquire new salience in policymaking.

Policy coherence is critical to the security as well as the prosperity of fragile states. Under the rules of globalization, these states are marginal players. Shunned by private investors, many of them rely economically on natural resource extraction activities that do not generate the gains in employment and productivity associated with diversified economies.

Without fiduciary controls and transparency, the public revenues secured from taxes and royalties are diverted to private ends by corrupt elites.

Fragile states will remain poorly equipped to connect to the global marketplace as long as they lack the institutions needed to protect property rights, to observe the rule of law, and to offer good infrastructure and the comfort of sound economic policies to private investors. To achieve these institution-building objectives, they need external support and "policy space" to reform their institutions and acquire the skills needed to function as full-fledged development partners. But they also need "security space" to create auspicious business conditions and make poverty reduction programs easier to implement. Thus, the economic and social prospects of fragile states must improve, not only to avoid international instability but also to ensure that globalization is not stopped in its tracks. Avoiding this outcome through humane globalization policies is a matter of self-interest for rich and poor countries alike.

The Network Effects of Globalization Can Only Be Tackled through Cooperation

Globalization has increased the flow of ideas, goods, services, capital, and people by expanding the scope and the intensity of relationships over long distances and across borders. This has increased the thickness of global networks and the speed of communications through them, and therefore the spread and extent of positive as well as negative spillovers. The resulting network effects can generate chain reactions, amplify relatively small fluctuations, and result in volatile or chaotic outcomes. Good ideas and productive innovations often spread like wildfire. But so can noxious ideologies and dangerous substances, with potentially catastrophic consequences.[20]

Some of the risks associated with economic growth (climate change, for example) are inherently non-territorial, and can only be managed through global agreements designed to change national behaviors in a coherent fashion. Others (for example land erosion in a watershed fully within a country's borders) are purely territorial and have no discernible impact on other states. Still other risks (infectious diseases, itinerant terrorists) can be isolated through border controls (quarantine).

Such controls create inconvenience and unintended costs (such as a reduction in travel for business and tourism), but if they are not exercised—for example if an infected passenger or a terrorist originates in or passes through a state that does not exercise effective border controls—an event such as a global pandemic or a terrorist act can ensue, with consequences that spill over national borders. The probability of such an outcome depends on the fragility of the weakest links in the chain of states involved in the transaction, while the instability that results depends on the scope and density of the network in question.

The management of globalization is contested. The dominant influence has been driven by neo-liberal thinking: *corporate globalization* has been instrumental in shaping trade, investment, and financial flows. But limits on the process have been set by a *civic globalization* movement that contests the market-driven model, embraces human rights, and operates on a global scale using the same information and communications technologies as the multinational firms.

Last but not least, *governments* have played a moderating role by screening the negative network effects of globalization and seeking to protect citizens from insecurity. As a result, the management of network effects has required formal or informal agreements between the public, private, and voluntary sectors. This has meant agreeing on operating standards and constructing dedicated partnerships. Diverse governance structures have resulted. These have one thing in common: they operate within interlinked and disaggregated networks that bring together governments, the business sector, and the global civil society.

In this fluid and interconnected context, where the weakest link in the system can create problems for all network participants, neglecting fragile states poses a strategic risk. This explains why state fragility has become a pivotal issue for sustainable and equitable development. Programs to provide global public goods and standards are critically needed to compensate for the inevitable failures of the global market. In designing them it is important to discriminate between risks of globalization that are genuinely trans-national in character and risks that a state can handle without consequences for other states. To avoid the transaction costs of cumbersome global bureaucracies, risk management is best left to the lowest level at which it can be handled, whether individuals, corporations, local communities, or individual states, based on agreed standards.

This still leaves a wide range of risks that can only be managed multilaterally. In response, collaborative programs that generate norms and standards or deliver regional or global public goods have proliferated. Some of these programs have been voluntary and based in the private sector. Others have been embedded within international organizations.

Still others have been handled by coalitions of states under the aegis of specialized United Nations agencies. Typically, donor countries have financed programs for global and regional public goods not as core activities of international agencies but through trust funds that they themselves control. Rich countries' reluctance to relinquish control helps to explain the ad hoc nature of these programs. All too often, the end result has been weak results orientation, high transaction costs, and a lack of voice of developing countries in their management (World Bank Operations Evaluation Department, 2004a).

Greater use of multilateral agencies to promote global public goods would be rational, but these agencies are perceived to suffer from a democratic deficit, and they are fiercely criticized from both the extreme right and left, while the silent majority ignores them or takes them for granted. Their public image is unlikely to improve until the expectations set for them become more realistic and until broadly based advocacy strengthens public support for them. [21]

Currently, rich and powerful states have the larger say in setting global standards and initiating global collaborative alliances. Looking ahead, they will need to reach out to developing countries, not only the rising economic powers of Brazil, China, India, and Russia, but also marginalized states. They should also give regional organizations and global multilateral bodies more authority than in the past. Only then will ownership and control of global security and development initiatives be perceived as legitimate and equitable.

Current Development Patterns Damage the Environment

Current production and consumption patterns in rich countries, emulated by poor countries, are producing unprecedented pressures on the physical environment. The same characteristics of dense networks that are associated with the integrated global economy have facilitated an extraordinary increase in production and productivity, accompanied by rising environmental stress. During the second half of the twentieth century, the human population increased 2.4 times—from 2.5 billion to 6.2 billion. In the same period, wheat, steel, and wood pulp production increased by 4.1 times, 4.3 times, and 14.2 times respectively. Numbers of registered motor vehicles, electricity generating capacity, and oil consumption rose 10.3 times, 21 times, and 7.2 times respectively.

By mid-century, the world's population will approach 9 billion. Virtually all of the growth will be in developing countries, where the population will rise from 5.1 billion to 7.7 billion. According to an assessment commissioned by the United Nations Secretary-General, "human activity is putting such strain on the natural functions of Earth that the ability of the planet's ecosystems to sustain future generations can no longer be taken for granted" (Board of the Millennium Ecosystem Assessment, 2005). A worldwide health check of twenty-four ecosystems, carried out by 1,360 experts, found that only four were increasing their ability to benefit human populations and that fifteen were in decline.

Industrialized countries dominate global environmental management through the heavy ecological footprint of their production and consumption patterns, and indirectly through their influence over the global regimes that govern the global commons. These countries' lack of environmental leadership, combined with the rapid growth of the Asian giants, presages no early relief from further environmental degradation. Red lights are flashing for climate change, air quality, wild fish, freshwater sources, wetlands, and tropical forests.

The World Resources Institute warns that China and India are currently on a growth path consistent with a per capita environmental footprint equivalent to that of today's Japan by 2030.[22] Based on current technologies, their needs would absorb the entire resources of planet earth. Some environmentalists believe that natural resources are being drawn down and pollutants are being produced at such a rate that the world is already in an "overshoot" mode.[23] Others believe that investments in cleaner technologies, proactive conservation policies, public education, and empowerment of local communities could reverse the ongoing degradation of ecosystems.

Canada's environment minister has called climate change a bigger threat than terrorism. While the threat has attracted considerable scientific interest and public attention, fully tested technological solutions have yet to be found and a global consensus about policy actions has remained elusive. Rich countries, home to 20 percent of the world's population, account for 63 percent of the carbon dioxide that has accumulated in the atmosphere since 1900. The United States, with a population of 288 million, is responsible for more greenhouse gas emissions than 151 developing countries with a population of 2.6 billion people.

According to the Intergovernmental Panel on Climate Change, there is enough evidence to conclude that carbon dioxide, surface temperature, rain, and ocean levels will increase significantly during the twenty-first century unless government policies change decisively. Scientific models estimate increases in temperature of about 0.3 degree per decade. While only indicative, the projections are worrisome: global warming could add 1.4 – 5.8 degrees to land surface temperatures and ocean levels may rise by up to 80-90 centimeters during the century.

A doubling of carbon dioxide emissions may cause economic losses of 1.6 - 2.7 percent of GDP for developing countries. There could be more heat waves, floods, droughts, fires, cyclones, and pest outbreaks. Small island economies are especially vulnerable. Africa's food security is likely to be set back. Severe flooding would threaten many parts of Asia. Agricultural productivity would drop in tropical and subtropical regions. Water availability may decrease in water-scarce regions, especially in the subtropics.

Mortality may rise, as the result of insect-borne and water-borne diseases. Bangladesh would lose 15-35 percent of its land surface. Tens of millions of people would be displaced. Coral reefs, glaciers, and alpine systems may be damaged. Plant scientists from Asia project reductions in crop yields of 30 percent over the next fifty years due to rising temperatures. The fight to achieve food security will have to be fought not only on the energy and transport front, in order to reduce greenhouse gas emissions, but also on the science and technology front, to come up with economically viable solutions.

Fisheries are being depleted due to rich countries' subsidies, fishing fleet overcapacity, and poor resource management practices. Three out of every four major fisheries are being harvested beyond their biological limit. New fish detection technologies and dragnets lead to unsustainable patterns of exploitation. Aquaculture, which now accounts for a third of fish production, involves chemical pollution and biological risks. Sustainable approaches to resource management exist but they require exploitation ceilings and fishing bans that have proven politically hard to enforce.

Forests in developing countries are shrinking at about one percent a year. A fifth of tropical and subtropical forests have disappeared over the past forty years. Unwise road investments, subsidized livestock production, slash-and-burn agriculture, and commercial logging are degrading forest areas. Forest fires are becoming more destructive and more frequent. With reduced forest cover in water catchments, effective watershed management is hindered. Sustainable forestry management and plantation development solutions exist but have not been promoted aggressively enough. There is no legally binding international instrument regulating all aspects of sustainable forest use.

Biodiversity losses are increasing at an alarming rate. Sixty percent of coral reefs that provide habitats for fish are threatened. Half of the world's coastal mangroves have already disappeared. Twenty percent of mammal species and twelve percent of bird species are at risk. Collective action is needed to preserve the resilience of ecosystems and the diversity needed for crop breeding and pharmaceutical research, through area ecosystem management, protection of environmental hot spots, trade regulation, and sustainability certification.

Ecosystems in China are severely stressed by extraordinary economic growth and large-scale displacement of people. In Rwanda, while causal links cannot be precisely established, heavy demographic pressures, rapid declines in farm size, and burgeoning income inequalities intensified the long-standing political confrontation and the social tensions that eventually led to the genocide (Piron and McKayu, 2004).

C. The Transmission Belts of Globalization Need Adjustment

Managing globalization means adjusting the policies that govern the international flows of goods, services, and factors of production. As noted in chapter 1, the rules of the global economic system have widened the inequality among nations and exacerbated social tensions and security risks. But conversely, the closer interconnectedness made possible by globalization has increased the rewards of international cooperation. The untapped potential for global welfare gains through policy coherence and further integration of the global market economy is enormous.

Unfair Global Trade Rules Should be Changed

Rich countries impose trade obstacles on poor countries that are much more serious than those they impose on each other. Average tariffs on agricultural commodities are twice as high as those on manufactures. Tariff peaks are imposed on labor-intensive products that poor countries can produce competitively, such as textiles, clothing, and processed foods. The end result is to undermine the economic security of poor people in poor countries. The protection implied by rich countries' agricultural subsidies, at USD 311 billion in 2001, means that resource transfers to OECD farmers were six times the volume of aid accorded to poor countries (USD 52 billion in that year).

United States subsidies to cotton producers are three to four times larger than U.S. aid to Africa. These subsidies benefit very few, relatively prosperous, farmers, and agro-industrial firms. Rich countries' subsidies encourage intensive agriculture with negative consequences for the environment. They support uneconomic production of meat, dairy products, sugar, rice, cotton, and other crops that developing countries can produce at a fraction of the cost. One-sided fishing agreements, onerous rules of origin, and massive subsidies to OECD fishing boats operating in poor countries' waters undermine local fishing industries.

The cost of trade policy distortions is borne not only by consumers and taxpayers in OECD countries but also by poor farmers in the developing world. Similarly, the highest tariffs on industrial goods imposed by OECD countries affect products—such as steel, textiles, clothing, leather—that are critical to economic prospects in developing countries and consumed by relatively poor consumers. According to research models, the welfare benefits for developing countries of trade liberalization for agriculture and manufactures range anywhere from USD 108 billion to USD 760 billion.[24] Including the liberalization of trade in services raises the estimated benefits by a factor of four to five (World Bank, 2002).

Non-tariff barriers almost double the protection afforded to rich countries' producers. They take different forms (including shipment inspections, rules of origin, quotas, cumbersome food safety requirements, administrative procedures, and customs fees). Anti-dumping measures with no economic justification are especially damaging. Preferential trading arrangements discriminate against excluded countries and distort trade flows. While World Bank models are known to exaggerate the benefits of trade liberalization in agriculture, industry, and services, they generate striking numbers: a notional USD 1,400 billion addition to developing countries' incomes, equivalent to 22 percent of their aggregate GDP.

Beyond the economic benefits, the social benefits of trade liberalization would be considerable, since unskilled and rural populations would benefit the most. On the other hand, substantial adjustment problems would need to be managed. In particular, food importing countries and poor countries now benefiting from preferential trade regimes would need to receive substantial assistance in the transition period.

Finally, steep declines in commodity prices have caused severe economic harm to developing countries. More than fifty developing countries depend on three or fewer commodities for more than half their export earnings. From 1980 to 2000, prices of tropical beverages were 60 percent below their 1980 levels. Those of agricultural raw materials, ores, and metals were down by about 30 percent. The collapse of coffee prices between 1995 and 2001 cost Uganda USD 323 million in export earnings. Stabilization of prices through supply management would require cooperation among developing countries as well as support from rich countries.

In the European Union, which is the largest protector of agriculture in the world, a drastic reform of the Common Agricultural Policy is needed.

International trade reform should concentrate on:

(i) removing tariffs, quotas, rules of origin, and other barriers to access to the markets of developed countries, under the Doha round of trade negotiations, with special emphasis on immediate elimination of trade-distorting support for cotton, sugar, and fish;
(ii) pressing for firm agreements by developed countries to end all export subsidies and trade-distorting support for agriculture by 2010 and to bring all tariffs to zero by 2015 while reducing non-tariff obstacles;
(iii) promoting removal of developing countries' own trade barriers while providing these countries with enough policy space for judicious sequencing and adjustment;
(iv) providing transitional aid to poor countries to adapt to the freer trading environment;
(v) gearing aid to the reduction of commodity dependency by poor countries through economic diversification, encouragement of private sector investment in primary product processing, and exploration of new approaches to stabilizing the international prices of primary commodities; and
(vi) enhancing poor countries' capacity to trade by providing assistance for customs reform, removal of restraints on transport and trade, improved governance, and regional integration.

The Global Financial Architecture Needs to be Strengthened

The mobility of capital limits the capacity of countries to tax it. Competition among countries to keep their business taxes low restrains excessive government spending but it can be inefficient and inequitable, given the tax avoidance that offshore havens make possible. Equally, the international financial system is highly prone to volatility because of highly leveraged banking operations, the contagion effects associated with panic withdrawal of funds, and the lack of global regulation.

Financial crises are particularly severe in countries with shallow, narrow, and poorly regulated capital markets and they are especially cruel to poor people in poor countries that lack social safety nets. The East Asian crisis caused 4-5 million Indonesian workers to lose their jobs and threw 40 million people into poverty. In Argentina following the peso crisis, unemployment shot up to more than 25 percent and more than half the population was impoverished. Worldwide, the economic downturn following 9/11 destroyed 11 million jobs in the travel and tourism industry alone.

The volatility of short-term capital flows is a major problem for economic management in developing countries. It is linked in part to the large debt overhang of some developing countries. Capital surges affect real exchange rates and domestic demand, with consequent disruptions in the real economy. The existing international financial architecture relies on international financial institutions that provide liquidity and impose conditionality to restore solvency. This is appropriate when lack of fiscal discipline is the culprit, but not when a crisis is related to private sector deflation and lack of liquidity. No procedure exists to declare bankruptcy, write off unserviceable debt, and replace management. Ultimately, such a crisis is resolved by transferring part of the private debt to the international financial institutions.

The design of a new financial architecture is beset with dilemmas. National sovereignty is not compatible simultaneously with market regulation and capital market integration, but politicians are loath to choose only two of these three objectives. Efforts to limit volatility by providing more information can have only a limited impact, since different analysts may interpret the same indicator as strength or weakness. Uncertainty, grounded in the reflexivity of markets, cannot be hedged.[25] Financial regimes are freer than ever before, as the result of investment and double taxation treaties, but no multilateral investment or taxation agreement exists, nor are there bright prospects for reaching agreement on international commercial legislation.

This is ultimately why capital mobility has limits. Conferring more regulatory authority on the international financial institutions to make the system more equitable is not in the cards, because the move would be opposed by the financial industry and would go against the imperative of national sovereignty. The creation of a global central bank would require existing central banks to cede their authority. The creation of a single global currency is another unlikely prospect. Global regulation by a board of overseers that would develop standards and evaluate institutions under its purview begs the question of which political authority it could be made accountable to. The same applies to proposals for international bankruptcy courts that would sit in judgment over sovereign governments.

In sum, structural reform has limits, and imperfect information creates dilemmas, but there are nonetheless several ways to make current financial arrangements more resilient to financial crises:

(i) increase the participation of developing countries in global financial governance and the definition of international norms as overseen by, for example, the international financial institutions, the Bank for International Settlements, and Basle Committees;
(ii) improve transparency, disclosure, and dissemination of financial information on developing countries and on international capital and banking markets;
(iii) assist developing countries in sound economic management, prudential regulation of capital inflows, commercial banking oversight, and crisis prevention through judicious regulatory restraints (especially in boom years); and
(iv) encourage stronger supervision and regulation of the international financial system (for example to prevent excessive leverage by hedge funds);
(v) improve communication among financial authorities (for example through an expanded and strengthened Financial Stability Forum) and strengthen information disclosure requirements for offshore centers.

Enhancing the Benefits of Foreign Direct Investment

The Millennium Development Goals emphasize socioeconomic outcomes but their achievement rests substantially on the mobilization of private capital and skills. Profitable, socially responsible businesses (whether large multinationals, small and medium-sized enterprises, or individual entrepreneurs) hold the key to wealth creation, technical innovation, and quality of life for developing countries. Conversely, unsound and corrupt business practices increase social tensions and contribute to environmental stress.

The removal of rich countries' restrictions on capital flows and the increased convertibility of currencies and trade liberalization have created a propitious environment for increased foreign direct investment in poor countries. The overwhelming evidence is that FDI benefits developing countries by creating employment, enhancing competition, connecting their emerging economies to world markets, transferring technology, and disseminating modern management practices. FDI can promote a more competitive business environment and generate domestic and enterprise development. But it may yield only limited benefits to host countries if it is associated with capital-intensive development, corrupt use of royalties, limited links to the local economy, negative environmental impacts, or deleterious social consequences for local communities. Thus, policy coherence for development requires the encouragement of appropriate corporate behavior through government regulation and civil society suasion.

Up to now, FDI has been concentrated in relatively few developing countries, as detailed above. But in contrast to fickle flows of debt and private portfolio investment, FDI has been a relatively secure source of long-term finance for those developing countries able to attract it. According to the United Nations Conference on Trade and Development, foreign direct investment made up three quarters of the net capital flows to developing countries in 2002, compared to 25 percent in 1990 and 6 percent in 1980. In 1992, FDI into developing countries was roughly equal to official capital inflows, but by ten years later it had become about three times as large.

The Uruguay Round Agreement on Trade-related Investment Measures (TRIMS) forbids World Trade Organization members to maintain local content requirements and preferences, import-export balancing requirements, foreign exchange balancing requirements, and export requirements. However, TRIMS does not address the protection of foreign investment from expropriation, restrictions on remittances, technology transfer requirements, domestic sales requirements, government-mandated offset programs, or limitations on equity or majority ownership. Thus, there remains scope for further liberalizing FDI rules. But developing country policymakers and nongovernmental organizations fear that further liberalization of foreign investment rules under WTO would reduce unduly the industrial policy space that developing countries need to promote domestic infant industries.

Except for national security restrictions, rich countries impose no restraint on outward FDI. Balance of payments concerns in these countries no longer constrain FDI. Differences in tax treatments among different destinations have become less pronounced as bilateral investment treaties inspired by OECD guidelines have spread. On the supply side, stronger global competition is driving private firms offshore to the developing world in search of cost savings, new markets, and access to natural resources. On the demand side, poor countries (prodded by the international financial institutions) are improving their investment climates.

Multinational companies contribute a third of world output. They compete through economies of size and scale and increasingly through branding, knowledge, and innovation. Numbering some 60,000, with some 800,000 affiliates in 190 countries, they constitute a bewildering variety of firms. Some are small and networked, while others are large and diversified; some are specialized and still others use franchises and licensing to expand their production and their markets. Given their global reach, they have contributed to the spread of international standards, especially in manufacturing and finance. Most multinational companies espouse more rigorous social and environmental standards than domestic firms and their operations are more closely scrutinized by nongovernmental organizations.

Information and communications companies appear especially suited for priming the FDI pump in risky environments.[26] Here as in other industrial and service activities that promise quick paybacks, diaspora entrepreneurs tend to lead the way in post-conflict environments.

Generally, FDI has been constrained by lack of infrastructure and skills, over-regulation, corruption, weak judicial systems, poor economic management, and political instability. OECD tariffs have discouraged investment in the processing of primary commodities within producing countries (their tariffs are typically 3-7 percent on imports of processed copper, aluminum, zinc, and oil, for example).

From a human security perspective, the key to enhancing the flow and the benefits of FDI is to promote helpful policy environments in poor countries. The triumph of market-based economic policies improved the efficiency of resource allocation in most countries, but serious policy mistakes have raised doubts about blueprint approaches to freeing and privatizing markets (World Economic Forum, 2005). Where social safety nets are absent, governments are plagued by graft, and where market distortions are rampant, premature privatization damages the society. To sustain the private provision of basic social services (water supply, transport, education, and health services), operators need to provide equitable access and affordable pricing. In military and security services, public oversight over private suppliers is needed to ensure that human rights are protected.

Only within a framework of good governance can the private sector contribute fully to socially and environmentally sustainable development. The critical priority is to ensure that the public revenues generated by FDI are invested for poverty reduction and that they benefit local communities. To start with, governments and companies must ensure that FDI does no harm. Voluntary and regulatory efforts must prevent corrupt use of revenues, poor labor practices, complicity in human rights violations, and environmentally damaging project designs. But in addition, source countries should encourage companies that promote domestic employment, spread innovation, and champion corporate social responsibility.

Rules for FDI are multifaceted, multilayered, and constantly evolving both at the national and international levels (UNCTAD, 2004). Service regimes in particular are changing fast. Complexities and inconsistencies in coverage and obligations abound. The challenge is to find a judicious balance between forging international investment agreements that attract FDI and protecting the policy space needed to pursue national poverty reduction strategies. Many industries are deeply embedded in the political and social fabric of poor countries that lack the regulatory framework needed for nurturing a freer and more competitive environment. The pace and sequence of liberalization should be governed by the speed at which adequate infrastructure and sound regulatory capacities can be established.

From a human security perspective, the following policy directions should be emphasized in order to enhance the benefits of FDI:

(i) Encourage FDI in developing countries and especially in the least developed countries that are now marginalized, by ensuring that international investment agreements are flexible enough to provide developing countries with the policy space they need to adopt judicious sequences of liberalization and privatization.
(ii) Support harmonization initiatives that are geared to simplification and to removing inconsistencies between national regulatory frameworks and bilateral, regional, and international agreements; and support developing countries' involvement in such processes (for example the OECD Initiative on Investment for Development[27]).
(iii) Enhance the role of aid in developing market institutions, improving the investment climate, creating appropriate regulatory frameworks for private investment, and enhancing the transparency and effectiveness of public expenditure management in poor countries.
(iv) Encourage multinational companies to adopt voluntary codes of conduct that reflect sound norms of corporate social responsibility and transparency and help developing countries and international financial institutions to harmonize domestic regulatory frameworks with current social and environmental safeguard policies.

(v) Ensure that support for FDI by official sources and financial intermediaries is contingent on the strict application of social and environmental safeguard policies (such as the Equator Principles[28]).
(vi) Explore with banks and investment guarantee organizations the provision of incentives to multinational companies that comply with sound social and environmental safeguard policies.

New Migration Policies Should be Forged to Balance the Needs of Rich and Poor Countries

When economic opportunity is lacking, people seek to migrate in search of a better life. Migration has historically acted as a major means to reduce differences in living standards, and today greater labor mobility would generate a much wider dispersion of the gains from international economic exchange (Pedroni, 2004). But in rich countries, immigration is severely restricted. Wage differentials between rich and poor countries are large, leading rich countries' electorates to strongly resist increases in immigration. Yet, with the aging of their populations, the rich countries will have fewer workers to meet a growing demand for services, especially in health care and domestic services.[29]

Immigration can help but on its own it cannot deal with the demographic imbalance, given the social difficulties of large-scale absorption of immigrants and also because migrants themselves grow old. The share of migrants in the world's population is modest (about 3 percent) but political opposition to increased immigration is strong in part because the numbers are rising rapidly—from 70 million in 1970 to 200 million in 2005.[30] Populist exploitation of the "immigration issue" is frequent because policies to integrate migrants into the receiving country are often weak and also because the costs and benefits of immigration are unequally distributed.

The impact of migration on wages is quite small on average, but in certain occupations it may be significant. As a result, aggregate economic benefits to the society are perceived as costs from the perspective of vocal interest groups. Country nationals often fear immigration. They feel that they "own" the infrastructure, institutions, and cultural traits that contribute to the economic productivity of the nation and do not wish to see their equity share diluted. They do not recognize that immigrants often work harder and pay more taxes than native citizens, relative to the welfare benefits they receive, and that immigrants often work in occupations that most native citizens are unwilling to perform. Thus, given the political sensitivity of immigration, rich countries have been more willing to consider increased mobility of temporary labor and to allow selective immigration that allows the import of scarce skills.

On the supply side, migration is often part of livelihood strategies aimed at enhancing the security of the household. Remittances act as a safety net for poor families. Family reunification provides additional comfort to family members. It has become the largest cause of migration from poor to rich countries (60 percent in Europe and 75-80 percent in the United States). Community and ethnic ties, too, play a large role in determining the direction of migration flows. Illegal migration may account for 10-20 percent of the total number of migrants. Smugglers and criminal syndicates assist or forcibly move about half of illegal migrants. Migrant women play a growing role as family providers and development agents in Africa and Asia. But they also constitute the majority of illegal trafficking victims.

The United Nations Convention Relating to the Status of Refugees regulates humanitarian migration. Given the restrictions placed on migration for employment in Europe, the Convention has become a major channel of migration: refugees account for about one third of all entries into Europe, compared to 8 percent in the United States. Globally, 9 percent of international migrants are refugees (16 million out of 175 million migrants in 2000). In addition, in 2002 more than 25 million people were internally displaced as the result of armed conflict and human rights violations.

Educated people leave for the West when their home countries provide a discouraging environment for private enterprise and professional advancement. Where sending countries are severely short of skills, the emigration of the educated has a high opportunity cost, and often a substantial fiscal cost. On the other hand, globalization has expanded the ways in which migrants can remain actively involved in the economic and social development of the sending countries. Enhanced exports of food, cultural, and other products consumed by emigrants abroad give an economic boost to migrants' countries of origin. Equally, remittances, business partnerships, Internet communications, hometown associations, and holiday travel provide links to the motherland that can be strengthened by policies in both sending and receiving countries. Finally, temporary migration also leads to brain gains and to inflows of savings by returning migrants. Migration is critical for drawing developing countries into the global economy through the intermediation of migrant communities (International Organization for Migration, 2005).

Heightened security concerns in rich countries have had a chilling effect on migration, as have stigmas arising from perceptions of poor migrant health. Targeted policies and development aid that can address migration health issues have been neglected. More stringent visa restrictions, profiling, detention without due process, and forcible repatriation have become frequent. Efforts have been made to justify increased development assistance on the grounds that it will reduce the supply of migrants. But poverty reduction efforts may in fact have the opposite effect by providing potential migrants with the resources they need to undertake the journey. From a development perspective, the considerable economic benefits of remittances must be weighed against the loss of skilled people.

Labor immigration policy must strike a balance between collective welfare and individual rights; and among the interests of citizens of receiving countries, the migrant workers, and their countries of origin. Policy coherence for development does not mean that citizens should waive their rights to preferential access to the national labor market. But it does mean that the basic rights of migrant workers should be protected and that the import of skills should be managed in development-friendly ways. In particular, given the critical importance of migration for development, coherent policies regarding labor mobility, family reunification, brain drain, brain gain, and remittances are needed to ensure a fair balance between the needs of rich and poor countries. Human security also requires coordinated action towards expanded resettlement and reintegration opportunities for refugees and internally displaced peoples, ensuring the safety of migrants, fair burden sharing for asylum needs, and control of illegal human trafficking.

New policies should be forged to tap the considerable human security benefits of migration while minimizing their costs. A comprehensive set of principles for action by the international community is laid out in the Report of the Global Commission on International Migration (2005) set up by the United Nations. A selective list follows:

(i) Promote public understanding of the positive role that a managed liberalization of migration could play in stabilizing the labor force and social security systems of rich countries, in order to increase mutually beneficial migration from poor countries and, in conjunction with improved border controls, to reduce the incentives for illegal migration.

(ii) Press for progress on liberalizing services in the Doha round of trade talks in order to encourage temporary (Mode 4) migration.
(iii) Facilitate a dialogue between rich and poor countries about the design and management of temporary foreign workers' programs, including measures to achieve a judicious balance between brain drain and brawn drain and to ensure a fairer distribution of costs and benefits between sending and receiving countries.
(iv) Focus public policy in sending and receiving countries on migration health issues to address the special health issues faced by migrant workers, to promote human resource development in the health professions, and to minimize the disruptive impact of large-scale exports of nurses and doctors on poor countries' health systems.
(v) Assist developing countries to design tailor-made policies that focus on the three Rs—recruitment, remittances, and return—in order to minimize the impact of skills exports through human resource development, reduce the transaction costs of remittances, and encourage brain gain and enterprise development by returning migrants.
(vi) Promote a global consensus on the governance of international migration issues, drawing on current initiatives (International Labor Conference, International Dialogue on Migration, Berne Initiative, and Global Commission on International Migration) so that the United Nations General Assembly High-level Dialogue on Migration and Development in 2006 will yield concrete results.

More International Cooperation is Needed to Achieve Environmentally Sustainable Development

Environmentally sustainable development is an essential feature of human security. Demographic trends combined with heedless consumption have caused unprecedented stress on the natural environment. From the last decade of the nineteenth century to the last decade of the twentieth century, world output rose fourteen times, energy use thirteen times and the fish catch thirty five times (Ginsborg, 2005).

Despite growing fuel efficiency, carbon emissions have quadrupled over the past half century. More evidence of global warming emerged in 2004 (UNEP, 2005). Atmospheric carbon dioxide levels surged and weather events were severe, including four severe hurricanes. The European Environment Agency detected impacts of climate change on glaciers, marine systems, and biodiversity.

Rich countries are better placed to adopt sustainable solutions and are less likely than poor countries to suffer from the results of environmental mismanagement. Thus, they bear a special responsibility to act as responsible stewards of the global commons. But the rapid growth of large middle-income countries that have adopted the same consumption and production patterns as high-income countries will impose further burdens on an already fragile environment, and within regulatory frameworks that are far less effective.

There are ways to address the global warming problem. They involve decreeing emission ceilings, eliminating fossil fuel subsidies, increasing energy taxes, increasing forest areas, relaxing current restraints on nuclear power plant construction, and implementing measures to promote clean energy development. Political support for the full range of measures needed is scarce, given the inevitable costs to economic growth that the measures would entail in the short and medium run.

With its ratification by fifty-five countries, the Kyoto Protocol entered into force in 2005, but the United States has rejected it[31] and even its modest targets may not actually be implemented. On the other hand, many countries are promoting renewable energy sources and setting specific targets for increasing their share in total energy use. Over and above mitigation measures, addressing the adaptation needs of vulnerable countries deserves priority.

In 2004, international agreements were reached with respect to chemicals management, biodiversity on land and in marine ecosystems, and bio-safety. An international treaty to conserve plant genetic resources has come into force and in 2005 the United Nations completed ten-year reviews of key environmental agreements on disaster reduction and vulnerable small-island states.

Key policy priorities include:

(i) Strengthened monitoring and verification of existing international environmental undertakings and agreements, with special emphasis on small island states.
(ii) International cooperation and dialogue on global warming to help ensure that Kyoto Protocol targets are reached, with emphasis on market-based solutions and intensified research.
(iii) Substantive progress towards improved governance of global forests and better management of international fisheries.
(iv) Intensified support for environmental management capacity development in poor countries and for country based strategies of adaptation to global warming.

Regulating Trade in Arms and Weapons

To maintain their defense production facilities, all major military powers have sought to promote their exports of conventional weapons systems, with the result that competitive pressures have made advanced weapons technologies more readily available. Demand has been sustained by concerns over the growing military clout of China and the general turmoil in the Middle East. New methods of financing have been devised, prices have declined, and proliferation risks have grown. Large defense companies have also sought to compete by subcontracting part of their supply chains to advanced developing countries, and the liberalization and globalization of the arms trade has increased the competitive pressures.

Weapons are perhaps the largest manufacturing sector worldwide. In real terms, total military spending, fuelled by the U.S. military build-up, grew by 6.5 percent in 2002 and 11 percent in 2003. It is now about a trillion dollars. The United States dominates the export market with about half of the total sales and 40 percent of the sales to developing countries. Private companies are now integrated in the global market, so that an increasing share of technology sales for advanced weapons systems is out of military control and in private hands, raising questions about the ultimate destination of arms and weapons supplies. Commercial competition among arms suppliers for a share of developing country markets has increased, and the diffusion of military hardware has become especially pronounced at the small arms end of the spectrum.

Technology has made many small arms cheap, light, portable, and easy to use even by a child. Assault rifles, grenades, rocket launchers, landmines, and explosives do not require logistical support or elaborate maintenance. They are omnipresent and represent a much greater risk to human welfare than the formal arms trade geared to inter-state wars. Small arms are responsible for most of the casualties in intra-state conflicts.

In weak states, economic necessity—more perhaps than greed or grievance—combined with the ready availability of cheap arms, explains the culture of violence; many young people caught in the conflict trap of intra-state wars have few choices other than violence to make ends meet. In the face of severe deprivation, the resort to small arms has become a rational tactic of survival for criminals, warlords, and their recruits. They routinely engage in systematic looting of natural resources and keep forced labor in line through intimidation and violence.

The downsizing of official arms stocks and the collapse of the Warsaw Pact at the end of the Cold War increased the supply of second-hand weapons disposed of at cut-rate prices. This has been a major factor in triggering and sustaining chronic violence and intra-state conflicts. Plentiful supplies of small arms in constant circulation among fragile states have created pervasive insecurity. The easy access to small arms has encouraged arms races among local factions and contributed to large-scale refugee movements induced by pillage, rape, and ethnic cleansing. There is evidence that despite international decisions to stop the flow of arms to the Sudan, brokers continue to export arms to that country.

As recommended by the Commission for Africa (2005), a key priority for the international community is to reduce the proliferation of small arms and light weapons by filling gaps in current control agreements, and to independently verify the implementation of existing and future agreements:

(i) Negotiations for an international arms trade treaty should be launched without delay.
(ii) More effective and legally binding agreements on arms brokering and common standards for monitoring and enforcement should be integrated into the international trade treaty.
(iii) To curtail trafficking in illicit weapons, the oversight of transport should be tightened through better policing, registration of transport agents, and new insurance rules.
(iv) National and regional capacities to monitor compliance should be strengthened.

D. Missing Goals?

Security and development policies need to converge for a simple reason: the emerging threats to international stability and prosperity demand it. First, intra-state warfare at the periphery has supplanted the ideological confrontation between East and West as the major threat to international stability. Second, the growing interconnectedness of nations and societies has led to the globalization of violence. Third, a proliferation of frail and failed states is causing international instability.

Global security requires collective action by capable states. The new security challenges cannot be met with policy instruments conceived for the Cold War era. Nor can global prosperity be secured by focusing aid on states that perform well while neglecting the special needs of those that are fragile. The increased role of non-state actors, the emergence of asymmetric warfare,[32] and the strategic risks posed by state fragility mean that development has become an instrument of security. Conversely, development priorities must now extend beyond global economic integration, if only because the spread of intra-state violence associated with state failure hinders the achievement of the Millennium Development Goals.

The Millennium Development Goals themselves are a very valuable asset for the international community. However, they do not respond adequately to the legitimate security aspirations that are expressed by people worldwide—even though the Millennium Declaration in which they are embedded addressed peace, security, and disarmament. (Specifically, the Declaration advocated action against international terrorism, organized crime, and traffic in small arms and light weapons.)

Such a broad conception of the historic compact between rich and poor countries ought to be translated into agreed security goals for the international community. The report of the High-level Panel on Threats, Challenges, and Change (UN, 2004) opens up an opportunity to bridge the divide between security and development concerns. Is it time to broaden the policy coherence for development initiative to include Millennium Security Goals?

Some would argue that the Millennium Development Goals should be achieved first before taking on more global commitments. But given the heavy weight of conflict-prone states among least developed countries, and considering the vast waste of resources currently taking place in the security arena, it seems illogical not to seek agreement on Millennium Security Goals. They should be grounded in people's—and especially poor people's—own interpretation of their vulnerabilities; a human security orientation would provide a useful test of relevance for state-centered approaches to collective security.

A useful first step towards a human security consensus would be to prioritize the 101 recommendations of the UN High-level Panel on Threats, Challenges, and Change (UN, 2004) and translate them into action. These far-reaching recommendations are consistent with the Millennium Declaration and they complement the Millennium Development Goals. If agreed by member country governments, the recommendations would add up to a comprehensive system of collective security, with capable and responsible states as its lynchpin. The eight major security goals embedded in the High-level Panel report are:

(i) Reduce the number, length, and intensity of conflicts between and within states.
(ii) Reduce the number and severity of terrorist attacks.
(iii) Reduce the number of refugees and displaced persons.
(iv) Regulate the arms trade.

(v) Reduce the extent and severity of core human rights violations.
(vi) Protect civilians and reduce women's and children's participation and victimization in war.
(vii) Reverse weapons proliferation and achieve progress towards nuclear, radiological, chemical, and biological disarmament.
(viii) Combat trans-national crime and illegal trafficking.

Endorsement of these goals and of related progress indicators should be backed by agreements to enforce effective sanctions to protect human security; prevent genocide; authorize the use of force based on explicit criteria; strengthen peace enforcement, peacekeeping, and peacebuilding; protect civilians; reform the United Nations; and strengthen regional organizations to meet the challenges of human security.

E. Conclusions

Working to achieve policy coherence for development in an age of interdependence and insecurity is essential but it is also fraught with problems, especially at the global level. Agreements must be reached through intergovernmental processes in consultation with the private sector and the civil society. Since it is not politically feasible to override the national interest of a rich country in order to assist a poor country, it is best to focus on policy options that improve aggregate welfare in both.

Fortunately, the scope for policy reform within this domain is vast. To reconcile policy objectives, a commonly agreed set of security and development goals should be constructed. Each donor government should adopt a "whole of government" approach. Equally, policy coordination among countries should be improved. This raises very tough issues of international relations at the multilateral level. To facilitate progress in the adjustment of aid, trade (including trade in arms), international migration, foreign direct investment, intellectual property, and environmental policies, the United Nations should sponsor a participatory process to review progress towards the Eighth Millennium Development Goal, leading to specific indicators of progress that would be tracked as rigorously and independently as those for the other development goals.

Achieving harmony among the policy goals of individual donor countries in support of global security and development is very demanding, especially within conflict-ridden countries. The relationship between humanitarian, peacekeeping, and development interventions raises conceptual issues. There is a clear trend towards greater military oversight of nongovernmental organizations that operate in insecure environments. The extent of outsourcing to private security contractors is growing. Proposals for mixed military-civilian intervention forces are under consideration. A priority task for the Peacebuilding Commission would be the design of generally accepted norms for the participation of humanitarian agencies and international organizations in conflict management and peacekeeping.

Notes

1. In the United Kingdom, the first explicit policy connection between conflict and poverty was made in the 2000 White Paper (*Eliminating World Poverty: Making Globalization Work for the Poor*). This highlighted the links between security and development, related violence to governance issues, identified personal safety as a prerequisite of sustainable livelihood, argued for integrated security and development approaches, and stressed that partnership is essential for conflict prevention and management. Policy work continued with a focus on small arms, security sector reform, conflict assessment, and fragile states.

    Public service agreements (PSAs) have provided a ready-made incentives framework to help promote joined up approaches to strategy formulation by the Ministry of Defense, the Foreign and Commonwealth Office, and DFID. The Global Conflict Prevention Pool (GBP 74 million a year) and the Africa Conflict Prevention Pool (GBP 60 million a year) gave further impetus to interdepartmental cooperation.

    A common committee structure allocates funds and oversees the implementation of projects. Joint Public Service Agreement targets monitored by the Treasury, and expanded budget envelopes for departmental initiatives, have induced interaction and sharing of policy analysis both across departments and in the field. The new integrated Post-conflict Reconstruction Unit (350 trained civil and military personnel) confirms a readiness to change and adapt processes and practices to evolving security and development challenges. Recently, DFID began to explore ways and means of rapidly assessing the impact of its aid and non-aid policies on some pilot developing countries.
2. Developing countries used USD 43 billion for arms imports in 1999, according to the United States Department of State.
3. Many developing countries allocate a far larger share of their national income to the military; they include Angola (4.7 percent), Burundi (5.9 percent), Eritrea (19.4 percent), Iran (3.8 percent), Morocco (4.2 percent), and Turkey (4.9 percent).
4. Including expenditures on Afghanistan and Iraq.
5. The U.S. military budget request for fiscal year 2007 is USD 463 billion. This includes the Defense Department budget, funding for the Department of Energy (which includes funding for nuclear weapons), and "other" related expenditures. It does not include money for the Afghan and Iraq wars—USD 50 billion for fiscal year 2007 and an extra USD 70 billion for FY 2006, on top of the USD 50 billion approved by Congress.
6. According to the *Washington Post* of May 1, 2005, the aggregate of United States budget expenditures for the Iraq war and for reconstruction for fiscal years 2003, 2004, and 2005 rivals the total aid provided by OECD countries to all developing countries in the same period.
7. Liberal critics of the Bush administration detect a dangerous trend away from the nation's democratic ideals towards the militarization of the popular culture (Rieff, 2005; Bacevitch, 2005).

8. The *2006 Quadrennial Defense Review* does not propose cutting back on hugely expensive and controversial equipment such as the F22 and F35 fighter planes and the U.S. Navy's DD(X) destroyer.
9. A key reason why religious totalitarians have the upper hand in many parts of the world is that they have secured the loyalty of the common people through religious charities that provide efficient social services that the state has been unwilling or unable to provide.
10. The Commission will comprise an intergovernmental Organizational Committee to address country-specific situations, a Peacebuilding Support Office within the Secretariat, and a multi-year standing Peacebuilding Fund to support initiatives on post-conflict stabilization and capacity building.
11. The Development Center plans to hold an expert workshop about the human security dimensions of development cooperation in 2006 or 2007.
12. See <http://www.id21.org/insights50/insights-iss50-art04.html>
13. The legal trade in small arms and light weapons is worth USD 4-6 billion. Another USD 1 billion worth flows through semi-legal and illegal channels (Burrows, 2002).
14. The European Union is preparing 7,500-man crisis groups for peacekeeping and a 60,000-man rapid reaction force.
15. Unless the weakest links of a network are reinforced or replaced, the benefits of interconnectedness cannot be tapped. This is why all network beneficiaries should contribute to the central delivery of goods and services that are not generated locally because of weaknesses in network links.
16. This estimate excludes reverse flows (migrants' transfers of funds to rich countries or among developing countries) that may be as high as USD 40 billion. On the other hand, unofficial remittances to developing countries may be as high as USD 30-35 billion, and official aid numbers should also be discounted (International Organization for Migration, 2005).
17. Letting poor workers into rich countries in modest numbers (equivalent to 3 percent of the labor force) for a limited period would yield benefits to the developing world worth USD 200 billion a year, according to Rodrik (2002).
18. In Europe, nationalistic impulses led the governments of Spain and France to act to prevent national energy companies being taken over by foreign firms. In the United States, the security concerns of congressmen on both sides of the aisle blocked the sale of facilities at six U.S. ports to a Dubai firm.
19. Recently, the expansion of the European Union has made it less cohesive so that the Union has had more difficulty sheltering its social and welfare systems from the rest of the world. Its new boundaries are more porous and its industries are increasingly vulnerable to competition from the fast-growing, low-cost economies of China and India.
20. Free trade enthusiasts do not recognize the unintended risks associated with the transmission of "problems without passports" through thick networks. Conversely, misplaced attribution of "weak link" effects to increased market integration underlies the anti-globalization opposition to open trade. The remedy for these negative network effects is appropriate sequencing of trade reform in relation to institutional strengthening.
21. "It has become commonplace to say that our global institutions are not up to the challenge of our unprecedented global interdependence. But the reason for this mismatch lies partly in our schizophrenia. Sometimes we pour scorn on …international bodies, and starve them of resources. Sometimes we talk as though they must have superhuman strength, and we lumber them with impossible objectives." (Mallaby, 2005.)

22. The "footprint" concept comes from ecology. It measures the productive land area it takes to sustain a human population.
23. Economic growth is not sustainable if it is achieved simply by running down the stock of natural capital, without making compensatory increases in agricultural capital, industrial assets, knowledge, skills, and/or institutional capacities. Ecological devastation caused the collapse of the Easter Islanders, Anasazi, Mayans, and Norse (Greenland) civilizations due to their inability to replace increasingly scarce natural capital with other forms of productive capital (intellectual, physical, human, institutional, etc.). "Green" national accounts that track the value of all forms of wealth would be needed to rank the sustainable development performance of nations. According to Dasgupta (2005), such accounts would show that "development in the poor world (barring China) has been unsustainable."
24. The high end of the range is drawn from Dessus and others (1999) and is based on a dynamic model with productivity growth. The low end of the range is from Anderson and others (2000) and is based on a steady-state model.
25. In psychology, reflexivity is the interaction between the passive "cognitive function" and the active "participating function." It constitutes a two-way feedback mechanism in which reality helps shape the participants' thinking and the participants' thinking helps shape reality—an unending process. The inherent divergence between participants' views and reality introduces an element of indeterminacy into social events that is absent in the natural sciences.
26. In Afghanistan in the two years following the fall of the Taliban, private investment in telecommunications reached USD 130 million. In post-Saddam Iraq, 200 private consortia submitted bids for phone licenses.
27. See <http://www.oecd.org/about/0,2337,en_2649_34893_1_1_1_1_1,00.html>
28. In 2003, ten major banks from seven countries agreed to a series of guidelines known as the Equator Principles on social and environmental issues in loans to developing countries. The Equator Principles are based on policies and guidelines of the World Bank and the International Finance Corporation. The banks apply the principles globally and in all industry sectors, including mining, oil and gas, and forestry.
29. In particular, by 2050, the median age of Europe's population will have risen to forty-eight years from thirty-eight years at the turn of the century. In 2004 there were more deaths than births in 43 percent of the 211 regions that make up the European Union.
30. In the year 2000 the share of immigrants in the total population was 19 percent in Australia, 13 percent in North America, 8 percent in Europe, 2 percent in Africa, and 1 percent in Asia and Latin America. The three most important host countries were the United States (35 million), Russia (13 million), and Germany (7 million). The three most important origin countries were China (35 million), India (20 million), and the Philippines (7 million).
31. The United States participates in the Carbon Sequestration Leadership Forum and the Methane to Markets partnership. Eight U.S. states and New York City have a lawsuit against five power companies pressing for a reduction in their emissions.
32. Asymmetric warfare is a military term to describe conflicts in which the two belligerents are mismatched in their capabilities or accustomed methods of engagement, such that the militarily disadvantaged power presses its special advantages and effectively exploits its enemy's weaknesses in order to prevail.

3

The New Security Landscape

> *"War is an act of force, and there is no logical limit to the application of that force. Each side, therefore, compels its opponent to follow suit; a reciprocal action is started which must lead, in theory, to extremes."*—Carl von Clausewitz[1]

This chapter lays out the key variables of the new security equation that must be mastered before the international community can achieve a consensus on a set of Millennium Security Goals. Section A presents alternative conceptions of conflict and analyzes historical trends. Section B reviews the state of knowledge regarding intra-state wars. Section C examines the nature of the international terrorist threat and the policy options available to counter it. Section D outlines the proliferation dilemma. Section E draws the security policy implications of these threats and their interconnections with the development issues covered in chapter 2. Section F concludes.

A. The Antecedents and Trends of Violent Conflict

The peaceful resolution of social conflict is part and parcel of the democratic experience. According to Albert O. Hirschman (1995a), conflict is essential for socialization. Indeed, democracy can be defined as the capacity to negotiate conflicting claims without resort to force. Conversely, through a social learning process, the peaceful resolution of conflict is an eminently efficient producer of integration and cohesion. This "democratic miracle" is akin to Adam Smith's "invisible hand" that shapes a positive overall outcome even though the intent of participants is to pursue their own selfish gains.

But just as markets function well only where property rights are protected, social antagonisms get resolved without violence (and leave behind a beneficial residue of social capital) only where the enabling environment is propitious. Where such conditions do not obtain, direct violence results from the combined effect of structural violence (that is, social and political structures that repress and harm people) and cultural violence (that is, the beliefs and customs that legitimize direct and structural violence). In such environments, conflict acts as a solvent rather than as a glue.

Typically, structural violence occurs when huge income disparities and retrograde political structures are sustained by security institutions that protect the rich and oppress the poor and operate without democratic safeguards. Such security establishments tend to be large and to drain resources away from social programs, while the political structures in place severely limit citizens' ability to realize their human potential. With excessive militarization and wide income disparities, structural violence takes place at the local, national, and global levels.

Inequitable resource allocations, corrupt legal systems, lopsided political power relations, and biases in the provision of social services provide fertile ground for social grievances, while brutality subdues people who would otherwise have protested against social injustice. The resulting violence may be chronic, latent, and covert. It is embedded in path-dependent institutions rooted in past conquests or colonial history. Ideologies that condone violence towards persons who are seen as different or inferior (in terms of class, gender, ethnicity, or religion) are often so deeply rooted in society that they go unnoticed. Occasionally, a glimpse of their destructive potential is offered to the world when flagrant human rights violations that routinely take place are made visible by civic action, a free press, or the mass media.

Obviously, structural and cultural violence are problematic in and of themselves but they can also erupt in widespread direct violence, with major economic and political consequences. The number of deaths caused by unequal distribution of wealth and power within a society (or across societies) may be viewed as a measure of structural violence. On this basis, structural violence is sixty times greater than the annual average number of battle-related deaths or 1.5 times as great as the annual average number of civilian and battlefield deaths during World War II. Every four days, it is the equivalent of Hiroshima.

This radical analysis (Galtung, 1969) is consistent with the view that the community spirit that democratic market societies need to function smoothly does not arise spontaneously. It requires a subtle combination of shared values, political leadership, and social entrepreneurship embedded in cultural norms and legitimate institutions. This means that it is hard to distinguish whether or not a society is just prone to conflict or already in conflict.

Cooperative outcomes may emerge through principled debate even where the debaters' interests diverge. This is where specialized nongovernmental organizations that operate in the zones of turmoil of the developing world are making important contributions to conflict management, mediation, and resolution. These NGOs are adept proponents of techniques for dialogue facilitation and negotiation that originated in the management of domestic and industrial disputes. Their activities help to de-legitimize the belief prevalent in fragile societies that violence is an acceptable way to resolve disputes.

Peace, if achieved, is unlikely to be sustained unless it is buttressed by appropriate domestic institutions. This calls for the development of legitimate, well functioning, and socially accepted institutional arrangements capable of resolving conflict before violence erupts.

Conflict sensitivity is not conflict avoidance. Thus, helping individuals and groups to negotiate conflicting claims without resort to violence is a social learning process. This is why aid operations should work "in" and "on" conflict rather than simply "around" conflict. Governments should be equipped to deploy their coercive means against improper uses of violence. Therefore, building the core capacities of the state to nurture individual safety, protect human rights, and enforce the rule of law should be a central priority of development cooperation.

Aberrant social behavior may be the consequence of private or public grievances that cannot be resolved constructively, given a lack of institutional capacity to mediate conflict or an absence of accepted norms. Where individuals are involved, criminality becomes rampant. Where large identity groups feel singled out for discriminatory treatment, large-scale violence may be ignited. Thus, within a state, criminality and war constitute a continuum. Equally, dispute resolution is not always a linear and unidirectional process—stable results cannot be ensured.

Most conflicts are settled through a mixture of confrontation and cooperation. If the balance tips excessively towards confrontation, this may reignite large-scale violence, sometimes for trivial reasons. This is why the comforting conflict cycle metaphor whereby all conflicts are resolved once and for all does not fit the reality. It is also why a mix of policing and military forces is needed to prevent, resolve, or manage intra-state conflicts: most of the underlying crises require hybrid solutions that combine mediation skills, law enforcement capacities, and combat readiness. This is the rationale of the human security response force proposed by the Barcelona Report to the European Union (Study Group on Europe's Security Capabilities, 2004; Glasius and Kaldor, eds., 2005).

Three major explanations of poor countries' proneness to violent conflict compete for policymakers' attention. The first connects poverty and conflict through political antecedents. It holds that democracy and activism hold the key to peace and prosperity: democracies do not fight one another and they are more prosperous than autocracies (Siegle and others, 2004). The evidence regarding this doctrine is mixed. First, not all authoritarian governments adopt radical policies or threaten global stability (Gerard Alexander, 2004). Second, the path towards democracy tends to be perilous. Indeed, statistical evidence shows that rapid transitions to democracy are associated with violence, especially where civil society is weak (Mansfield and Snyder, 2004). When social mobilization runs ahead of economic and institutional development, ethnic violence tends to erupt (Rwanda), secession may occur (former Yugoslavia), or the state is captured (Taliban in Afghanistan) (Burnell, 2004).

An alternative explanation links both poverty and conflict to gaps in state capacity. It postulates that where the state cannot raise taxes, deliver public goods, or make productive investments in development, poverty grows as well as discontent, social strife, and eventually violence. But capacity shortfalls are not enough to explain why violence erupts or states fail; out of 32 insecure countries, 12 are in the top three capacity quintiles of state strength, according to the Center for Global Development (2004).

The third explanation of the poverty-conflict association points to competition for resources, demographic characteristics, group inequalities, and social grievances as the major antecedents of violent conflict in poor societies. Here too, examples can be found to counter the hypothesis. They suggest that it is the absence of reliable mediation mechanisms among competing identity groups that causes social tensions to escalate and provide the space for political entrepreneurs to break the monopoly of violence and capture the levers of state power.

In short, each of the three explanations has value as well as limitations. The mechanisms that link poverty and conflict are complex and diverse. Conflict and state disintegration are the combined result of fragility, exposure, and shocks. Fragility is structural. It is linked to capacity constraints (as in Liberia or Sierra Leone) as well as to lack of legitimacy (as in Poland under communism, or Ukraine until the Orange Revolution). By contrast, exposure is a function of location and geopolitical status: shifting alliances, abrupt political transitions, and bad neighborhood influences, all of which can generate mortal threats. Finally, economic fluctuations and natural disasters can produce brutal shocks, whose effect depends on the country's economic and social resilience.

Consequently, predicting conflict is a highly speculative venture. But all conflict prevention options are linked by a common thread: an effective role for the state. Thus, effective external engagement with the state is the key to achieving results. Hence, development cooperation programs should be tailor-made, based on conflict assessments. The upshot should be nimble, adaptive, flexible donor engagement strategies that combine defense, diplomacy, and development in a coherent package.

Security in Historical Perspective

The stability of the state-centric world order that originated in Europe with the treaties of Westphalia in 1648 depended on maintaining a balance of power among sovereign states that were nominally equal under international law but varied in size, wealth, and power. The tension between states' territorial sovereignty and political equality, on the one hand, and the disparities in military and economic power, on the other, gave rise to shifting coalitions. The needed adjustments in international relations were achieved either through diplomacy or through violent conflict.

The changing fortunes of individual states and the dynamics of international competition led to imperial wars in the nineteenth century, inter-state European wars in the first half of the twentieth century, and civil wars with international ramifications in developing and transition countries after 1945. By then, the two superpowers were vying for world domination, and the availability of new weapons of awesome destructive power made all states vulnerable to catastrophic attack. A balance of terror prevailed.

Since the end of the Cold War, when there were thirty major conflicts in twenty-five locations, the worldwide number of conflicts has declined.[2] 2004 witnessed nineteen conflicts in seventeen locations, the lowest on record. It was also the first year when the Stockholm International Peace Research Institute reported no inter-state war (Dwan and Holmqvist 2005).

Major conflicts have become shorter on average—from twelve years pre-1990 to four years post-1990—and less costly—from eleven to six months of pre-conflict economic activity (Staines, 2004). Asia and Africa are now the theaters for six conflicts each—more than in the other regions. But they are also the regions that have seen the largest net drop in the number of conflicts. For Asia, the peak year was 1990 (twelve conflicts) and for Africa it was 1998 (eleven conflicts). In relative terms, on the other hand, a similar decline occurred in the Middle East (from six during 1993-96 to three in 2004) while the steepest drop was in Europe (from a peak of four in 1994 to one in 2004) and the smallest drop was in the Americas (from a peak of five in 1990 to three in 2004).

The number of battle-related deaths, which peaked during the two staggeringly brutal world wars, has also been trending downwards. Data on non-battle-related deaths in war are scarce, especially for inter-state wars. Yet, both inter-state wars and intra-state wars cause massive deaths of civilians not only from violence but also from disease and starvation. The two world wars involved 23 million deaths in the military and 40 million civilian deaths. The Korean War caused about 1 million military deaths and 5-6 million civilian deaths. The second half of the 1960s and the first half of the 1970s witnessed intensifying conflicts in Vietnam, Cambodia, and Laos, which generated new though lower peaks in battle deaths. Following the end of the Cold War, battle deaths rose again for a time due to conflicts in the Balkans, the former Soviet republics, and the Gulf War. Still another (again lower) spike of military fatalities emerged with the Soviet invasion of Afghanistan and the Iran-Iraq war. The war in the South of Sudan involved 100,000 combat deaths and about 1.2 million civilian deaths until 1997. But since 1997 the general trend has again turned down.

Battle death statistics convey key messages about conflict trends. First, though the international community has become somewhat more adept at resolving and managing conflict, international war has not been banished, and violent intra-state conflicts have continued to erupt, many of them with international ramifications. This means that conventional military preparedness will continue to feature in national security strategies.

Second, intra-state wars of various kinds have come to dominate the security environment.[3] Intra-state wars resist classification and require tailor-made treatment. The pattern of casualties has changed radically:

civilians rather than combatants have become the major victims of warfare. This raises humanitarian and human rights concerns and creates an ethical justification for external intervention. Finally, the endgame of most wars is no longer characterized by a formal military cease-fire, still less an explicit surrender. Instead, a political agreement by external actors is imposed well before a clear victor emerges. Hence hostilities tend to be bottled up rather than resolved. In about half of the cases they resume with tragic consequences (as in Liberia and Rwanda). Of course, violent conflict is costly. Major international wars in the quarter century since 1980 have involved direct costs estimated at USD 550 billion (equivalent to about half the annual total military expenditure around the globe).[4]

In a disordered and fragmented world system, centripetal economic forces interact with centrifugal political forces. Civil strife weakens states and they become prone to social fragmentation. Chaotic conditions left unattended can lead to war. In sum, post-modern conflicts are both a cause and a symptom of a systemic disorder that arises because of the network effects described in chapter 2. They reflect the dispersion of political power in the world and the reluctance or inability of the sole remaining superpower and its allies to devote enough resources to contain turmoil at the periphery (Cooper, 2004).

Whereas conflict in the nineteenth and twentieth centuries was driven largely by competition among strong states, in the twenty-first century, conflict originates mostly through implosion, rebellion, and/or external interference within weak states. War casualties are lopsided towards civilians, especially women and children. In Africa alone the number of internally displaced people is 13 million and the number of refugees is 3.5 million. Localized violence due to communal fighting, lack of effective and honest civilian policing, and weak legal systems also claims victims.

Thus far, the response of the international community has been hesitant and weak, except in conflicts that obviously endangered international security or access to natural resources. The humanitarian and development rationales for intervention have been accepted in principle but applied in an inconsistent and uncertain manner. Yet experience demonstrates that the human costs of war can be drastically reduced through conflict prevention or external intervention.

Medical aid, food, and shelter for displaced persons, economic reintegration of refugees and former combatants, and security sector reform have begun to account for a significant part of aid programs. As noted in chapter 2, further expansion of aid under fire would require new ways of providing security so that humanitarian workers are assured of safe access to victims and threatened populations. Post-conflict rehabilitation, reconstruction, and development will need to be pursued in parallel with peacekeeping activities, in order to tap synergies and avoid discontinuities in the transition to peace.

State fragility is correctly perceived as a strategic risk, but strictly military solutions to the new global security equation do not exist. Initially, the global war on terrorism received wide support. Good will towards the United States was sustained through the robust military response in Afghanistan. But the costly military intervention in Iraq and the protracted and costly "war after the war" that it spawned have harmed rather than helped the war on terrorism.[5] By now, the military hegemony of the United States has generated worldwide unease (out of concern about "imperial globalization"[6]), and as a result, goodwill towards the United States has dissipated. This is contributing to an anxious and uncertain mood that is not conducive to international cooperation.[7]

Inter-State Wars Remain Part of the Equation

Most contemporary conflicts have been classified as intra-state wars, but traditional wars between two or more states have not been banished and their destructiveness is exceptionally high, especially when rich and middle-income countries are involved. They illustrate the fundamental asymmetry between the slow and painstaking process of development and the staggeringly rapid devastation of war. In the last twenty-five years the most destructive example of traditional war has been the armed conflict that pitted Iraq against Iran (1980-88). It accounted for at least 800,000 of the one million or so battle deaths ascribed to traditional wars during the quarter century. It unleashed once again the specter of human wave attacks, chemical weapons, and indiscriminate use of missiles against civilians. It also threatened to interfere with Gulf shipping routes.

The most internationally significant wars have been the two Gulf interventions of 1991 and 2003. They pitted a wide, and then a narrow, coalition against Saddam Hussein's Iraq. Victory in the first war, in liberating Kuwait, proved to have a number of unintended consequences both for Iraq and for the allied coalition that was assembled to fight it. Saddam's defeat led to further repression inside Iraq, international monitoring of the country's infrastructure, and an air war between some of the allies and Iraq. The Iraq war that began in 2003 involved more ambiguous allied motives. Its effects on the Greater Middle East and the insurgency that followed are still being assessed. However they eventually play out, the effects on international politics will be fundamental. No other traditional war during the last quarter century has had anything like the human or political consequences of this conflict.

Thus, it is critical to integrate inter-state war perspectives into the search for new security paradigms. The ongoing threat of instability arising from inter-state war must be taken seriously for the foreseeable future. Each decade seems to produce at least one significant inter-state conflict. Competition for resources, disputes over the jurisdiction of territory or peoples, demographic and environmental pressures, autocratic aggrandizement, or sheer miscalculation must still be expected to occur between states, as well as within the more vaguely defined societies of the present chaotic system. Some of these tensions may result in traditional war.

If the twenty-first century is destined to be the "Asian Century"—given current population and productivity trends—international wars that are fought for the motives mentioned above could have massive human and political consequences. Western powers may have technical superiority in their military forces but some Asian powers maintain massive armies.[8] In 2001, after five Kashmiri separatists attacked the Indian Parliament, killing nine people, the resulting crisis between India and Pakistan led these powers to mobilize more than a million troops on their joint border. Both countries possessed usable nuclear weapons, and there was little the outside world could do to contain the crisis. In the end, it was defused by the protagonists themselves.

Any war arising from a Chinese attempt at military seizure of Taiwan, even without U.S. involvement, would involve no less than a million troops in total. Any war in the Korean peninsula between the Democratic People's Republic of Korea and the Republic of Korea (again leaving aside potential U.S. or Chinese involvement), would involve more than a million troops and threaten widespread urban destruction, given the weight of artillery and conventional airpower that could be brought to bear.[9] In short, if the international system cannot contain the tensions behind these plausible war scenarios, or if the deterrence of the major powers fails to prevent their outbreak, any of them could turn into hugely destructive conflicts with crucial international implications. In the present environment these prospective wars may be regarded as low-risk but high consequence possibilities that must be factored into any security strategy

The potential for the unintended consequences of war to become internationally destabilizing is heightened by the fluid state of current world politics and the tendency for war to exacerbate or even cause the failure of states. Many international wars have a tendency to become open-ended and to drift into civil conflict. The clear-cut defeat of Iraqi forces in 1991 sparked a Western-inspired revolt in both northern and southern Iraq that, in the north at least, continued for a decade. Similarly, the victory of U.S.-led forces in 2003 may have laid the foundations for a civil war in Iraq. The insurgency it provoked has undermined the wider political objectives of the U.S. coalition.

A traditional military response to 9/11 took place in Afghanistan, where the U.S. invoked the principles of national self-defense to attack a state that had harbored its terrorist attackers. This was not a straightforward response, even though the world generally accepted its legitimacy and the right of the U.S. to respond. The resulting small war was conducted in a proxy fashion and resulted in the routing of the Afghani government and the occupation of the country by foreign forces, pending the installation of a new government. Here too, a traditional battlefield victory has turned into an insurgency, and the entire international community confronts the need for a nation-building exercise in the midst of continued insecurity and unrest.

B. Intra-State Wars Resist Classification

All ongoing intra-state wars are taking place within national borders and they all share the distinction of involving one or more non-state groups. But it is otherwise hard to generalize about them. Some are highly localized but eventually acquire international and sometimes trans-national characteristics in their dynamics and consequences. Others remain bottled up and hidden from international scrutiny, and without external engagement they generate hardship, suffering, and death over decades. Some countries (Afghanistan and Iraq) endure occupation by foreign troops. Others (Sudan's neighbors) face large-scale refugee inflows. Still others provoke the incursion of combatants from neighboring territories (Cote d'Ivoire, Democratic Republic of Congo). Diasporas often contribute money and arms (as in Sri Lanka). In truth, the classification between intra-state and inter-state warfare has become blurred.[10]

The management of contemporary intra-state armed conflict cannot rely on general precepts, given the wide range of situations, the multiplicity of causal factors, and their complex interplay (Dwan and Holmqvist, 2005).[11] Typically, many rebel groups are involved (as in Burundi, Colombia, Indonesia, Sudan), whose agendas tend to differ and may not conform to the grievances that the rebels articulate. War tactics are diverse. They tend to cause more casualties among civilians than among combatants (including indirectly, through disease and hunger) and there is often no difference in the kinds of outrages committed by rebel groups and government special forces.

The extent of cross-border impact varies. It has been high in the successor states of former Yugoslavia, in the African Great Lakes Region, and in West Africa but relatively confined elsewhere (Algeria, Colombia, Myanmar, Sudan, and Turkey). Even though their direct impact on regional and global security may be limited, most intra-state wars have destabilizing international dimensions in the form of smuggling, infiltration, refugee flows, environmental stress, and the general lawlessness that results from warfare.

The new strategic focus on intra-state wars has major implications for Western military policy. Expeditionary operations are gradually becoming a significant part of the role of the North Atlantic Treaty Organization. The transformation has been incremental, given the opposition of some members to a major shift away from NATO's traditional territorial defensive posture. But NATO intervened in Kosovo, its high-readiness response force is now operational, and it has assumed command of a significant share of security assistance operations in Afghanistan. The division of labor between nationally led troops, NATO, and the European Union remains unclear. For a long time to come, it is likely that the arrangements for coordination between NATO and the EU (and hence between defense forces, counter-terrorism units, and humanitarian action) will need to be designed on a case-by-case basis.

Poverty and Conflict Go Together

Recent policy research about poverty and conflict suggests that security and development are two sides of the same coin. There is a strong association between low levels of GDP per capita, low growth rates, and prevalence of conflict. Conversely, war and civil strife are associated with economic stagnation and poverty. Thus, while development has always been viewed as dependent on adequate security conditions, there is evidence of a two-way association (Stewart, 2004): once a country experiences conflict it can get trapped in a vicious cycle of poverty that undermines the prospects for peace.

First, security facilitates development: insecurity reduces a country's growth, exports, consumption, calorie consumption, government revenue (although not always), and the propensity to invest. Second, development helps to achieve security, certainly in the long run. However, in the short run, economic growth may generate local disruption or expectations that cannot be satisfied quickly enough, thus creating instability. Hence, rapid economic growth from a low baseline has to be handled carefully to avoid an insecurity backlash.

For any individual country the best predictors of internal conflict are low average incomes, low growth, and high dependence on primary products. When a country's income per person doubles, the risk of civil war is halved. Economies in conflict grow 1-2 percent more slowly than economies at peace. For each additional percentage point of growth, the risk of conflict falls by a point.

In other words, common variables animate the security and development equations. Civil strife and conflict are associated with decline/stagnation in per capita incomes, low life expectancy, horizontal inequality (income inequality among regions and groups), vertical inequality (inequality within the same identity group), poverty, reduced government revenue, cuts in social spending, lack of political participation, weak oversight over natural resources, and tolerance of illegal activities. The numerous feedback loops create vicious (though sometimes virtuous) cycles. The links are complex and hard to disentangle at both the micro and macro levels. They exist at both ends of the results chain—goals as well as means. Development and security are inputs as well as outputs.

At the aggregate level, there is a strong and robust statistical correlation between violent conflict and poverty, as well as between violent conflict and poor growth performance. Research shows that the per capita income of a conflict-affected country is only one-third that of a peaceful country. A country with an income of USD 4,000 per capita is three times less likely to be affected by a new conflict than is a country with USD 1,000 per capita. A country whose economy is shrinking by 6 percent a year is twice as prone to conflict as a country whose economy is growing by 6 percent. From this perspective, traditional growth-oriented prescriptions are antidotes to conflict. Out of twenty countries with the lowest human development index values in 2002, sixteen were in conflict or just emerging from conflict.

We do not know for sure why these relationships hold or how noneconomic factors intervene to explain the poverty-conflict linkage. But the evidence that conflict prevention should have top priority is strong. On average the cost of a civil war is two and a half times the value of the country's GDP at the time the conflict starts. Just as wars create poverty, negative income shocks matter to security: it has been estimated that a 5 percent negative income shock raises a country's risk of civil war by 50 percent. Yet another reason why poverty and conflict are linked is that poor states tend to be weak states that are more vulnerable to takeover, and hence more likely to be attacked by neighbors and/or captured by insurgents.

As discussed more fully in chapter 4, these relationships mean that aid can deliver security benefits when it is focused on fragile states and on the building of state capacity. Sound and equitable economic management is equally important since failed economic strategies can lead to conflict. In turn, conflict may weaken the resolve of the state to adopt the demanding measures required to rekindle growth.

Broadly based development, focusing on reducing group and regional inequities, should be the goal, since rapid increases in horizontal inequality and exclusion of cultural identity groups are more likely to induce conflict than are inequalities within the same identity group. Provision of health services is also critical since infectious disease may affect a society's most productive elements and increase its vulnerability to conflict. In turn, conflict may spread disease and increase poverty.

Breaking the Iron Triangle of Poverty, State Failure, and Conflict

In brief, there is no single explanation for the poverty-conflict linkage. Common sense suggests that diverse causality chains link poverty and conflict. Demography certainly plays a role. Wars are fought mostly by the young and it is therefore not surprising that youth bulges should be associated with civil strife and unrest, especially in societies that do not empower the young and create jobs. Beyond demography, variable combinations of poor economic management, weak government capacity, environmental stress, natural resource dependence, and neighborhood effects link poverty and conflict.

In stagnant economies the opportunity cost of taking up arms is low. It stands to reason that weak states are less able to protect themselves. Equally, competition for access to depleted natural resources is bound to exacerbate social tensions. Greed considerations aside, it is rational for excluded groups with no prospect of sustainable livelihood to take up arms. Without economic diversification, heavy unemployment tends to prevail with dire social consequences.

Intrastate wars are not easy to contain. Civil conflict that explodes as a result of entirely local tensions frequently spreads and escalates with unintended consequences. This is because weak governments do not, or more precisely cannot, respond appropriately to local instabilities. As a result, violence often overwhelms weak societies simply because there is nothing to stop it (Fukuda-Parr, forthcoming).). Such violence may also institutionalize itself within a society as aspiring leaders bid for a constituency—whether a regional, ethnic, religious, or socioeconomic group—by heightening local grievances to the point that they become political fissures in the social fabric.

The process of disintegration in Lebanon or in the former Yugoslavia, as Woodward (1995) demonstrates, followed this latter logic to create a dynamic of violence that could not be halted by any of the forces within society (and was not addressed early or powerfully enough by the international forces outside). In a different context, and even in the midst of an international occupation, a similar dynamic of disintegration may be taking hold in Iraq, where a severe economic dislocation has occurred and where a protracted political vacuum is increasingly filled by local politicians bidding for constituencies while violent local flare-ups take on a momentum of their own.

Past development interventions have not been sufficiently attuned to such context-specific risks. A deliberate reorientation of the development enterprise towards security would reflect hard-won lessons of experience. Tailor-made, conflict-sensitive country strategies are needed to address the most relevant structural obstacles to security and development. Without such strategies, reoriented security and development policies will not deliver results. From this perspective, it is unfortunate that world leaders did not include early warning and conflict prevention in the remit of the Peacebuilding Commission.

No single model can explain the dynamics that create conflict but it is clear that state weakness, poor leadership, underdevelopment, and inequality predispose a society to conflict. This means that development cooperation deployed judiciously is a conflict prevention mechanism. Conversely, military supremacy does not automatically translate into a capacity to impose order, especially when force is exercised unilaterally. Unfortunately, the sheer size of the U.S. military establishment has encouraged the use of force—even in contexts where coercive power is not the appropriate instrument.

In many developing country contexts where intra-state wars are concentrated, diplomacy and aid may be more effective means to peace than the use of brute military force. Exercised unilaterally, force is illegitimate. Conversely, well managed development assistance boosts the image of donor countries, as demonstrated by the shifts in public perceptions of the United States in Indonesia following the *tsunami*. Of course, within the development sphere, aid does not always yield peace dividends. Here too, there can unintended consequences, such as when aid is captured by warlords or by one side of a public policy contest.

But, as elaborated in chapter 4, aid can be used to reduce poverty, create youth employment, diversify the economy, improve natural resource management, and encourage conflict resolution and peace making. The security benefits from a balanced approach combining diplomacy and development vastly outweigh those from a heavy reliance on military interventions. In the new wars of the twenty-first century, human security strategies are more effective in cost benefit terms than purely military interventions.

Military tactics that kill and maim civilians generate deep public resentment and swell support for terrorists and insurgents. Thus, the heavy collateral damage of aerial bombing in Iraq, though unintended, has deprived the U.S. of moral legitimacy. In the public mind, democratic ends do not justify the degrading treatment of prisoners, the lack of due process for detainees, or their extraordinary rendition. Nor does a coercive regime change followed by elections automatically lead to a peaceful democracy.

Even in situations where violent conflict is absent, development cooperation requires attention to human security. At the level of individual projects funded by aid, pressure from advocacy groups has led the development community to adopt social and environmental safeguards to mitigate the social and environmental costs of development interventions. But broader support for domestic policy reform and capacity building geared to the protection of local communities and weaker elements of society has lagged.

In particular, progress in mainstreaming gender considerations within development strategies has been slow and the rights of indigenous peoples and minorities have been given short shrift. Finally, economic policy has tended to be neglected during and soon after a conflict, with significant consequences for growth (Staines, 2004): policy performance starts to deteriorate soon after a conflict starts and this worsens the negative impact of conflict itself on the economy. After a violent conflict, good policy performance can yield very rich dividends.

Violence is often sustained by vested interests that capture scarce national resources at the expense of the common people, thus feeding grievances among deprived groups and perpetuating violence. Hence, in peace settlements, power-sharing arrangements that favor narrow interests ought to be discouraged, and during the reconstruction phase broadly based economic strategies should be put in place (Addison, 2003).

Identifying the Links between State Weakness and Global Security

The general notion that weak and poor states in the developing world constitute a risk to international stability has become widespread in security circles. But policy research has only begun to uncover which state characteristics are associated with different global insecurities. Equally, the transmission mechanisms that link local turmoil with global security have yet to be identified with precision.

State weaknesses come in different packages and the links between state failure, violent conflict, and international stability are diverse and complex. Among the factors relevant to instability risks are the size of the country, its location, the extent of its poverty, the political will and orientation of its leadership, the nature of its capacity shortfalls, and the vulnerability of its governance arrangements. Weak states do not all contribute to international security risks in the same way or to the same degree (Patrick, 2006).

First, the spread of violence across borders is not the only spillover challenge to global or regional security: infectious diseases and environmental stress also pose existential threats. More than terrorism or international crime, the rapid spread of disease is a major security risk associated with governance weaknesses: fragile states are the weak link of the health supply chain. Equally, adaptation to global warming risks and natural resource preparedness are serious issues for poor, isolated, low lying, or mountainous areas.

Second, the weakest states are not necessarily the poorest. Nor are poverty and capacity shortfalls the defining characteristics of countries that pose the most serious risks to international peace. While Iran, North Korea, and Saudi Arabia are of strategic regional importance and critical to the security of OECD countries, they do not feature on the lists of "low-income countries under stress" that development assistance agencies have used to design and implement their policies towards fragile states.

Third, transnational terrorism does not always originate in developing countries. It is often incubated within the alienated suburbs of OECD countries or in countries aligned with the West that do not have the political will to crack down on *jihadists*. Nor is terrorism a significant security problem in the least developed countries. When it takes place (as it has in Colombia, Kashmir, Nepal, or Sri Lanka, for example), it is largely focused on domestic political objectives and does not necessarily create a clear and present danger for OECD countries Nor is a failed state necessarily a good platform for training terrorists or staging terrorist attacks: paradoxically, it is the Iraq invasion that turned a middle-income, secular authoritarian country into a recruitment magnet and a symbol of anti-Western resistance for international terrorists.

Fourth, while illegal drug production and human trafficking are associated with state poverty and weakness, other transnational criminal activities (such as financial fraud, cyber-crime, money laundering, the counterfeit trade) often take root in states where judicial institutions are weak but other state capacity problems are not very serious and private sector economic activity is buoyant.

Fifth, lack of resilience in political institutions (as distinct from state incapacity) is often a feature of countries vastly endowed with oil or other resources for extractive industries, or situated along energy supply routes. The extraordinary dependence of the global economy on secure sources of energy and minerals means that developing countries that export oil and minerals can exert considerable leverage over OECD countries. This constrains the implementation of coherent security and development policies.

In sum, better analysis of the connections between the diverse dimensions of state weakness and individual security threats is critical to the design of effective engagement strategies for donor countries in fragile states. Attention should be directed not only to low-income countries but also to middle-income countries, since the latter group command substantial influence in security affairs and their fragility poses especially tricky challenges. Hence, development cooperation with middle-income countries under stress merits attention in conjunction with other policy instruments.

In general, diverse governance gaps (political, economic, social) translate into highly differentiated transnational security risks (terrorism, proliferation of weapons of mass destruction, international crime, pandemics, energy insecurity) so that the risks of state fragility should be assessed in terms of their specific implications for regional and global stability.

C. Terrorism Can be Tackled through Democratic Means

Terrorism has diverse and complex causes and a long history. Given problems of data and definitions, no resilient trend can be ascertained with respect to international terrorist incidents, but a recent report by the U.S. National Counterterrorism Center (2005) confirms that terrorism is diverse and that most international terrorist incidents are small and take place in developing countries.[12]

In the first half of 2004, for example, India accounted for 47 percent and Iraq for 31 percent of 283 incidents; by contrast, OECD countries accounted for five, or fewer than two percent. Out of 651 significant incidents in the whole of 2004 (involving 9,321 victims), only sixty-four involved a U.S. citizen and/or a U.S. facility (103 U.S. victims). South Asia and the Near East together accounted for 597 attacks and 5,194 victims.[13]

Pape (2005) has compiled a database of every suicide bombing and attack around the globe from 1980 to 2003 (315 in all) and finds that the connection with religious fundamentalism is less pronounced than commonly believed. Most of the suicide bombings (96 percent) took place as part of organized political or military campaigns. Democracies (France, India, Israel, Russia, Sri Lanka, Turkey, the United States) were the main targets. The attacks were invariably directed at a strategic objective and geared at establishing political self-determination, and they usually involved resistance to a military presence.

Of course, religion is used to recruit and motivate terrorist bombers. Except for radical leftist or Maoist groups active in Colombia, Nepal, and Turkey, most terrorist groups that have claimed responsibility for attacks listed by the U.S. National Counterterrorism Center are Islamic militants (for example, the Taliban in Afghanistan, Al Qaeda in Saudi

Arabia and Spain, Al Aqsa and Hamas in Israel, and a variety of *jihadist* groups in Kashmir).

The *jihadists* use tactics that make military deterrence impractical. They rely on a network of private donors. Their suicide bombings and kidnappings are modest in cost; even the 9/11 attacks are estimated to have cost no more than USD 500,000 in total, and the Madrid bombing to have cost less than a tenth of that. Their shadowy, diffuse, and decentralized organizational structure is resilient. Their movement—in reality a shifting network of networks—can survive the death or the capture of individual cadres given the vast pool of idle, discontented, motivated, and educated youths ready to serve the *jihadist* cause.

Terrorism is as old as warfare itself. Some terrorism has had significant impacts on domestic societies in provoking governmental responses that have served to change the course of national politics, for both good and bad. But no terrorist campaign until now can be said to have significantly affected the international system as such. The present terrorist phenomenon does have this potential impact, however, partly because it has shown itself able to tap into a growing wellspring of anti-Western sentiment around the world, and also because it has provoked the sole superpower—a major pillar of the international system—into a war mentality.[14]

Current terrorism must also be seen in a different light because the ambitions of *jihadist* terrorism unite an aspiration to global revolution with the prospects of political chaos generated by failing states and the possibility of access to technologies of mass destruction. The current chances of terrorists getting hold of a functioning nuclear device or a highly destructive chemical or biological weapon are unknown but they are bound to rise over time, and the outcome of such an attack would be catastrophic.[15] Judicious preemptive action is justified because there is strong evidence that terrorists are striving to secure nuclear and biological weapons and their constituent elements.[16]

Jihadist terrorists constantly search for novel ways, both high-tech and low-tech, of wreaking destruction and causing panic. If they can use the inherent openness, and the day-to-day routines and technologies, of Western societies to perpetrate panic, then so much the better for their cause. And though the statistical incidence of successful terrorist attacks of this sort against Western society is much lower than that of terrorist attacks within warring societies such as the territories of the Arab-Israeli dispute, Algeria, Chechnya, Iraq, or Turkey, they have nevertheless created a specter of potentially destabilizing terror that deserves to be regarded as new and different from previous strands of terrorist behavior.

Economic and political grievances matter in the fight against terrorism. If terrorism is to be successfully contained and its political salience reduced to traditional levels where it is not regarded as a threat to international stability, then intelligence and policing must be combined with a positive policy towards developing countries: a "hearts and minds" campaign carried out globally as well as locally through development cooperation and the judicious promotion of democracy.

Towards a Balanced Anti-Terrorism Strategy

At the country level, draining the swamp of insurgency requires military pressure in combination with a special effort to protect civilian non-combatants. Avoiding collateral damage, cordoning off areas where the insurgency lies and providing safety to those who opt not to provide insurgents with support and cover are critical elements of a winning "hearts and minds" strategy. But in the last analysis, insurgencies can only be expected to fade away once a political settlement is reached.

The Iraq military intervention has its own separate origins and may not presage future actions along similar lines. It is likely to fuel more terrorist attacks as veterans of the ongoing insurgency export their techniques to soft targets outside Iraq. A long twilight struggle lies in store as long as the industrial democracies maintain troops and military installations in fragile states run by governments that lack popular support and in territories that terrorists consider their homeland (Tertrais, 2005).

Though the impact of modernity on the rigid societies and stagnant economies of the Middle East has been destabilizing (Zakaria, 2002)[17], the current root cause of Islamic terrorism is more political than cultural or economic. More than half the population of the Middle East is less than 25 years old. Thousands of young people lack jobs and find no productive outlets for their energies. They are frustrated by the lack of political participation and the vast disparities in wealth and power in their societies. They are disoriented by the alien and hedonistic lifestyles of the West displayed by the mass media. They feel humiliated by the economic and military dominance of Israel and express outrage at the plight of the Palestinians. No wonder then that some of them seek solace in extreme forms of religious fundamentalism and (following systematic indoctrination) are willing to sacrifice their lives for their faith and the lofty dream of Islamic resurgence.[18,19]

Terror spreads where domestic political grievances are left unattended. Struggles for national identity or regional autonomy have always used terror. They are doing so in Afghanistan, Chechnya, Iraq, Kashmir, Pakistan, Saudi Arabia, Sudan, and the West Bank. To be sure, the strong military responses triggered by 9/11, the brutal treatment of prisoners, and the discriminatory treatment of West Asian immigrants and Muslims in Western Europe and North America have encouraged the spread of radical Islam. Al Qaeda leaders have made it clear that their goal is to expel foreign forces from all Muslim lands, take power in Arab states now aligned with the West, and ultimately spread their brand of the Islamic faith throughout the world.[20] Such ambitions constitute a goal of world revolution, not for a twentieth-century ideological revival (for which Western nations have been psychologically well prepared) but for a twenty-first-century religious revival (for which they have not).

Leaders in the West as well as the Middle East describe the Al Qaeda movement as a fanatical strain of religious extremism. Yet, radical Islamists justify suicide bombing as the only effective way to resist.[21] Whereas the West should be exploiting the fault lines among disparate terrorist movements around the world and seeking alliances with moderate leaders in Islamic communities, the rhetoric of the long global war on terrorism has conflated all terrorist threats into a single adversary, thus playing into the hands of those who seek to promote a global struggle against the West (Barkawi, 2004). The United States is unlikely to mount another military intervention as a counter-terrorism measure but Iraq is already serving as a training ground and an indoctrination center for *jihadists* around the world.

The International Legal Issues Raised by Terrorism Should be Settled

Whatever the root causes of terrorism (and a strong case can be made that a fair solution to the Israeli-Palestinian conflict, the gradual democratization of the Middle East, and the accession of Turkey to the European Union would do much to reduce the appeal of radical Islam), the development of a cogent anti-terrorism policy in OECD countries has emerged as a prerequisite of peacemaking in our times.

To be sure, the perception of international terrorism as a clear and present danger to the security of industrial countries will gradually fade if these countries are spared periodic attacks. But this seems increasingly unlikely, so that the voting public is likely to insist on further security and retaliatory measures that could lead to an endless spiral of violence—unless strong and enlightened leadership that respects the very democratic norms that are challenged by the terrorists comes into play.

After decades of wrangling among international lawyers and diplomats about the meaning of terrorism, the United Nations Secretary-General delivered an authoritative definition in his *In Larger Freedom* report (UN Secretary-General, 2005): "Any action…intended to cause death or serious bodily harm to civilians or non-combatants with the purpose of intimidating a population or compelling a government or an international organization to do or abstain from doing any act."[22] Based on the UN Secretary-General's proposals, attacks on civilians should henceforth be viewed as illegitimate by the international community always, everywhere, and by anyone, even in support of a just cause.

Thus, the targeting of civilians (for example through suicide bombing) would not be considered legally justified even if done by stateless people with legitimate grievances or by national minorities seeking secession from an oppressive regime. Already, the resort to and use of force by states is regulated under international conventions under which states cannot legitimately target civilians. But the lack of agreement on a definition of terrorism at the September 2005 UN summit reflects widespread anger at the numerous civilian casualties that state power is actually inflicting within occupied lands. It also demonstrates that the United States and its allies are no longer credible as standard bearers on human rights given their post-9/11 policies that tolerate inhuman and degrading treatment of detainees. Respect of the Geneva Convention should be an integral part of the "long war" on terror.

Democratic Countries Can Fight Terrorism and Remain Democratic

If militant groups are prevented from launching major attacks using biological, chemical, radiological, or even nuclear weapons, the threat of terrorism may gradually cease to dominate international security policy. But success will require patience and a change in tactics towards those that were recommended by the Club of Madrid in March 2005.[23]

First, the Club of Madrid meeting endorsed the same definition of terrorism proposed by the United Nations High-level Panel and espoused by the UN Secretary-General. It urged zero tolerance for terrorism and the ratification and implementation of all anti-terrorism-related conventions by all states, as well as the speedy completion of a comprehensive convention on international terrorism. It concluded that coercive or repressive counter-terrorism actions, even if successful in the short run, may alienate the population and create a backlash that increases the risks of terrorist attacks over the medium term.

Second, the Madrid agenda proposed the protection of human rights as the acid test of legitimacy for anti-terrorism activities and posited that democratic principles and values should be observed in all circumstances. Wherever possible, terrorism should be treated as a criminal act to be handled with full respect for the rule of law. Accordingly, human rights laws should be incorporated in all anti-terrorism programs and policies of national governments and international bodies. A special rapporteur would be appointed who would report to the United Nations Commission on Human Rights on the compatibility of counter-terrorism measures with human rights law.

Third, the Madrid conference highlighted the need for solidarity and cooperation among democracies. The transatlantic rift that had resulted from the American-led campaign in Iraq was a victory for the terrorist networks. The rift was the result of different perceptions regarding the justification for military action against a threat that, while not imminent, could have turned calamitous with little or no warning. Hence a practical doctrine that empowers the UN Security Council to deal with such threats in a legal manner that is timely, proportionate, and effective would reduce the risk of unilateral action and allow forcible action against terrorists in conformity with United Nations values and principles.

Fourth, terrorists tend to target democracies, and the transition to democracy may destabilize a country and make it vulnerable to terrorism. The Madrid conference concluded that to minimize the risks, democracy assistance programs should respect local values and cultures and reach beyond support for free and fair elections to emphasize the rights of minorities, the enhancement of capacities in fragile states, the need to strengthen the economic foundations of democracy in poor countries, and the active participation of the civil society, especially women's groups. The establishment of a global citizens' network, that would provide early warning of terrorist threats and help to defuse local conflict, was also proposed.

Fifth, the Madrid conference warned against explaining terrorism simply in terms of background conditions. As participants recognized, poverty as such is not a cause of terrorism. Nor can globalization be considered responsible for poverty. But both can provide pools of potential support from which determined terrorist groups can draw and in which terrorist acts can be regarded as morally acceptable. Economic and social policy should therefore mitigate social exclusion and the impact of disruptive economic change. Hence, the Madrid conference endorsed the implementation of the Millennium Development Goals and the adoption of long-term trade, aid, and investment policies that promote participation and empower marginal groups.

Finally, the Madrid agenda stressed the global nature of the terrorist threat and recommended the establishment of international mechanisms to strengthen and coordinate bilateral, regional, and global law enforcement, intelligence activities, and databases, as well as the systematic interdiction of funding for terrorist networks.[24] It recommended the provision of assistance to states that need to build their financial resources and capacity if they are to implement their anti-terrorism obligations. It also called for new mediation and peacekeeping initiatives in conflict-prone societies, a focus on accountability mechanisms for addressing political grievances, and measures to protect against the proliferation of weapons of mass destruction.

In sum, the Madrid meeting confirmed that international terrorism ought to be regarded as a unique and frightening phenomenon that requires special approaches to policing, intelligence, and homeland security. But countering terrorism also requires the same commitment to international cooperation, broadly based development, and state building as does peacemaking. Only far-flung networks of cooperation involving governments, the private sector, and civil society can undermine the effectiveness of terrorist networks and divorce them from their potential bases of public support. Only development can drain the swamp of insecurity and despair within which terrorism flourishes.

D. Weapons Proliferation Should be Reversed

During the Cold War, the balance of terror between the two competing spheres of influence restrained the spread of nuclear weapons. Since then, the demand for these weapons has grown. A black market in nuclear technologies and materials has developed. The disdain of the most powerful states for a rules-based approach to international relations is evident in their attitudes towards the 1970 Nuclear Non-Proliferation Treaty (NPT). This stands in the way of the further agreements that are urgently needed to remedy the treaty's weaknesses. In particular, the 2006 landmark nuclear deal between India and the United States (once it is approved by the U.S. Congress) will increase the risks of proliferation just at a time when the international community is seeking to persuade Iran to curb its nuclear activities.

This is unfortunate, as the NPT has been more successful than most other arms control regimes, and certainly more successful than most analysts expected in the late 1960s. The NPT combines an undertaking by non-nuclear ratifying countries not to develop nuclear weapons with an agreement by the five "declared" states that possess nuclear weapons (US, UK, France, the Soviet Union, and China) to provide non-nuclear states with access to nuclear technologies for peaceful purposes and to pursue negotiations in good faith on general and complete disarmament. The NPT has induced many states to abandon (or not take up) nuclear weapons programs. But it has now run into difficulty not only as a treaty but also in respect to the regime-centered approach to arms control that it embodies (Byers, 2005).

The countries that have acquired nuclear weapons since the NPT came into force (India, Pakistan, almost certainly Israel, and probably North Korea) currently stand outside of the treaty and are therefore not subject to international safeguards and inspection. They are not even defined as "nuclear powers"—a term reserved for countries that exploded a nuclear device before 1967. The NPT signatories are allowed to build the capacity to enrich uranium and reprocess plutonium that can be used both to generate nuclear power and to manufacture nuclear bombs. No incentives or penalties have been agreed to encourage restraint. Therefore, Iran is exploiting the loophole and Egypt, South Korea, and Taiwan could follow suit.

Nuclear disarmament and non-proliferation must go together. The goal of general disarmament by the nuclear states has proven elusive. More than 30,000 nuclear weapons remain in their arsenals. A New Agenda Coalition has brought together Brazil, Egypt, Ireland, Mexico, New Zealand, Slovenia, South Africa, and Sweden. This aims to encourage nuclear weapon states to proceed towards disarmament. Yet the United States has not ratified the 1996 Comprehensive Test Ban treaty. It has turned its back on the 1972 Anti-Ballistic Missile Treaty and it has announced its intention to develop ballistic missile defense and new tactical nuclear weapons. Its executive branch is seeking congressional approval for the development and testing of a new generation of "cleaner" and smaller nuclear weapons.

This stance creates incentives for other states to join the nuclear club and develop other unconventional weapons of mass destruction. On the positive side of the ledger, Libya abandoned its clandestine program in 2004 and the United States has sought to strengthen the enforcement of measures designed to prevent non-nuclear states from developing nuclear weapons. These measures include export controls and vessel interdiction on the high seas; a Proliferation Security Initiative led by the United States and comprising fifteen "core" countries and sixty collaborating countries has engaged in search and seizure of vessels carrying nuclear materials, missiles, and related technologies.

The fundamental weakness of the Nuclear Non-Proliferation Treaty is that it addresses arms control from the state-centric perspective of the 1960s, whereas current concerns regarding nuclear proliferation pertain to non-state actors as well. Unfortunately the recent five-year review of the NPT has failed to produce a consensus about the road ahead. The United Nations Secretary-General, Kofi Annan, has called the failure at the 2005 September summit to agree on a strategy to prevent the spread of nuclear weapons "a real disgrace."

Fortunately, the number of warheads in the world has dropped from 65,000 to 20,000 and the United States and Russia have agreed to reduce their arsenals to between 1,700 and 2,200 warheads apiece by 2012. However, Russia's massive nuclear stockpiles remain uncertainly secured, and its decommissioning programs are lagging. And no nuclear state has announced an unequivocal commitment to dismantle its nuclear arsenal.

There is no universal agreement among nuclear states to abjure first use against non-nuclear states, although various declarations point in a positive direction. The comprehensive test ban treaty is no longer honored. The costly development of a missile shield by the United States has not been shelved and may induce other nations to follow suit. A perception of double standards is palpable given that nuclear states are not honoring their commitment to total nuclear disarmament—which they made in exchange for non-nuclear states' agreement to forsake the development of nuclear weapons.

It is generally believed that some twenty regional powers have now secured or are actively seeking access to chemical weapons, eleven to biological weapons, and 6 to nuclear weapons. All these powers have the potential industrial infrastructure to pursue credible programs for weapons of mass destruction and produce or operate workable delivery systems. North Korea quit the Nuclear Non-Proliferation Treaty two years ago and has announced that it is reprocessing more plutonium for its nuclear weapons program. Iran intends to end its voluntary freeze on uranium enrichment activities and may exit the NPT if the ongoing negotiations fail. The lack of sanctions on some non-members of the NPT (India, Israel, and Pakistan) and the unwillingness of nuclear states to fulfill their own long-standing obligations to disarm adds to the temptation to withdraw from the NPT. Other nuclear-capable states may be induced to acquire a nuclear capability, especially following the United States' decision to assist India's nuclear program.

The treaty allows countries to enrich and reprocess nuclear fuel provided that they keep the International Atomic Energy Agency (IAEA) informed. Iran has failed to inform IAEA of such activities, which means that action to curb them cannot be taken under the multilateral treaty, leaving unilateral action (or action by a coalition, whether endorsed by the Security Council or not) as the only option. A tougher inspection regime is clearly required since substantial quantities of weapons-grade plutonium are known to have gone missing, especially in Russia but even in the United Kingdom and Japan.

Of course, national security considerations are likely to drive proliferation, so that the number of states embarking on a nuclear weapons program may well remain small. The greater risk lies in access by nonstate actors, which is not regulated or monitored by the NPT. This risk is hard to measure and may be small, but it is not impossible to visualize and its human and geopolitical consequences would be dramatic.

An ambiguity at the heart of the current treaty regime, explicitly built into the original bargain, is that it gives NPT signatories an inalienable right of access to nuclear technology for peaceful purposes (the founding principle of "atoms for peace" that underlies IAEA) and it also allows them to withdraw from the treaty after ninety days, without having to return equipment or fuel enriched under the provisions of NPT membership. Lack of progress on how to identify violations and penalize the violators compounds the risks of non-compliance. The worthwhile suggestion by the IAEA during the May 2005 non-proliferation treaty review, that *all* states should forgo new enrichment activities until a foolproof inspection regime is in place, was not endorsed.

The miniaturization and modernization of nuclear weapons as a way of countering other threats such as biochemical warfare may also weaken the taboo against their use and erode existing psychological barriers to proliferation. The High-level Panel Report on Threats, Challenges, and Change (UN, 2004) makes a number of detailed proposals to address these deficiencies in the current regime, but it is not yet clear whether the UN member states will be prepared to implement any or all of them, as they consider in a broad package the future of the UN. Thus, many obstacles stand in the way of nuclear non-proliferation thirty-five years after the international community agreed to promote it.

Proliferation of chemical and biological weapons, too, poses serious risks of large-scale casualties. With more than 6,000 chemical facilities worldwide, chemical agents are in abundant supply and relatively easy to obtain. The deadline for complete destruction of 70,000 tons of declared chemical weapons agents under the Chemical Weapons Convention has been postponed till 2012 and the extended deadline is unlikely to be met. Similarly, research facilities capable of producing biological weapons are numerous and cannot be readily identified. Evidence exists that terrorist cells have had ready access to ricin, a biological toxin, one gram of which could produce fatalities that would rival those of a nuclear explosion. Nor do obstacles exist to the use of new DNA technologies to design new diseases or revive eradicated diseases in forms that will resist treatment (Pearson and Dando, 2005).

The consensus of expert opinion is that a multi-layered web of assurance is needed to protect the public from the dire risks posed by chemical and biological weapons. Existing international and national regimes should be strengthened to totally prohibit production and use and provide verification. Control measures should be instituted nationally and internationally to address handling, use, storage, and transfer of dangerous pathogens and chemicals. Protective measures spanning civilian and public health defenses should be put in place to ensure preparedness, detection, diagnosis, and medical support. Finally, enforcement through diplomatic actions, sanctions, and interventions should be instituted under the aegis of the Security Council. [25]

E. Implications for Security Policy

Frail and Failed States

Frail and failed states are likely to move to the top of the international security agenda for at least four reasons. First, fragmenting or collapsing states provoke local insecurity and create pressures for external intervention whether for national gain, regional competition, or reasons of conscience. While not all such states have attracted international involvement, the overall pattern of the last fifteen years indicates increasingly powerful inducements for external intervention, albeit for diverse and sometimes confused (and confusing) reasons reflecting the need to combine diverse domestic constituencies (e.g., humanitarian activists and fundamentalist Christians in the case of Southern Sudan).

Second, though terrorists have often concealed their operations within relatively strong states (Afghanistan, Iran, Northern Sudan, Saudi Arabia as well as OECD countries), frail and failed states (such as Somalia) have been used as safe havens, transit facilities, and recruitment platforms for terrorist and criminal networks. Thus, engagement with weak states is a form of conflict prevention.

Third, frail and failed states offer fertile ground for promoting anti-Western resentment and extremist ideology. With their wellsprings of angry resentment, particularly among the young, they can be used as exemplars of failed Western economic and social policies. Ignoring them involves risks of regional instability.

Fourth, military interventions aimed at spreading democracy have been prone to unintended consequences and costly miscalculations. In societies that lack liberal traditions, civic institutions, and social cohesion, long-term development efforts are more likely to succeed than coercive interventions. More generally, in terms of relative effectiveness, the role of the military needs to be reconsidered so as to make room for diplomacy and development assistance (aid for peace).

Reconsidering Coercion

The military establishment and the security policies of the United States, while in flux, are still shaped by the experience of World War II and the Cold War, when the overarching objective was to defeat a powerful state animated by a hostile ideology. This meant deterring, pre-empting, or preventing other states from challenging western military primacy. With the collapse of the Soviet Union, the United States is now without rivals in military might given its mastery of modern technology and the awesome destructive capacity of its armed forces,

But, as stressed above, among the major new threats to international stability are the consequences of intra-national wars and the activities of non-state actors. The latter disdain the rules of traditional warfare (Byman and Waxman, 2002) and react in unpredictable, unconventional, and innovative ways to inflict maximum damage, sap morale, and spread fear. They do not respect neutrality protocols. They deny their adversaries visible military targets. They exploit the restrictive rules of engagement of states intent on minimizing civilian casualties. They evade capture by mingling with non-combatants, use women and children as human shields, and take refuge in churches, mosques, and cemeteries. They do not hesitate to use violence against reporters, diplomats, or aid workers. They are ready to die for their cause. Against them, the threat of brute force is not particularly effective.

It is the strategy of such non-state actors to sustain their violent opposition until public opinion in the industrial democracies tires of the financial and human costs of coercion. They are adept at eroding support for military intervention by denouncing foreign intervention, showing resilience in the face of adversity, and appealing to the peace-loving public. Since they have no incentive to protect civilians or to spare the national infrastructure, they deliberately blur the distinction between combatants and non-combatants and are keen to provoke counter-attacks that cause collateral damage. The resulting destruction and the associated civilian tragedies are then used to manipulate public opinion and undermine the legitimacy of military responses. These tactics are deliberately designed to reduce the value of military assets.[26]

Thus conventional military force is not very effective in asymmetrical warfare. It still has a role to play towards hostile states intent on challenging the United States and its allies on matters of vital interest. On the other hand, severe limits to military coercion would arise if a nuclear state falls prey to a radical ideology hostile to Western interests or if non-state actors prove able to add weapons of mass destruction to their terrorist arsenal. The sheer scale of the damage that nuclear weapons would inflict and the potential readiness of *jihadists* to act as suicide bombers (and of authoritarian regimes such as North Korea to suffer large-scale casualties) severely restrict the capacity of the United States to turn its massive capability advantage into actual influence. Here again, diplomacy and development emerge as valuable adjuncts to the military.

Emphasizing Conflict Resolution

New mechanisms for resolving human conflict emerged when the development of nuclear weapons threatened human survival and when multidisciplinary research groups discovered that the conflicts that arise among individuals, families, and communities share common elements with conflicts in industrial relations, national politics, and international relations. Mediation techniques made their mark in labor relations and community affairs, and have been extended to the diplomatic and security arenas after overcoming stiff resistance. By the 1980s, the new ideas were achieving some success in Northern Ireland and South Africa. The new specialist field came of age after the dissolution of the Soviet Union, when the historic ideological contest subsided and left room for intranational struggles aiming at state capture, secession, ethnic dominance, or looting of natural resources for personal gain.

Just as entrepreneurs of violence occupied themselves by dislocating weak states, voluntary organizations and foundations (such as the Carter Center, Nyerere Foundation, and International Alert) sprang up to apply a wide range of conflict mediation and resolution techniques to the divisions and social tensions associated with globalization. Since then, controversy has swirled around the impact of such initiatives. Does the involvement of voluntary organizations undermine diplomatic and military efforts? Does neutral intervention prolong conflict through moral hazard (for example by enhancing the legitimacy of warlords, drug kingpins, war criminals, and terrorists)? Does it promote moral relativism by failing to take sides in an unjust contest that victimizes the weak? Does it favor the strong and help perpetuate inequality and oppression? Are theories and techniques that were forged during the Cold War relevant to the post-Cold War era?

On the one hand, conflict resolution quickly runs into diminishing returns if it does not address root causes. On the other, it has become a vital instrument of peacemaking in governance environments where state sovereignty has broken down, social bonds have dissolved, and violence has become decentralized and privatized (Miall and others, 1999). In such contexts, conflict has many sources and responses are required at various levels. High-level negotiations with top leaders are now combined with problem-solving events at the middle level and training interactions at the grassroots. Force itself may have a role to play, for example as part of a peace support operation designed to stop ethnic cleansing or genocide or to counter the sabotaging of a peace settlement.

A multi-track approach is therefore required. It needs to involve the United Nations, aid agencies, and international financial institutions as well as international NGOs, church groups, and private businesses. The approach should use such tools and techniques as constituency building within the contending groups, involvement of indigenous champions of peaceful solutions (many of whom are women), and coalitions between external third parties and peacemaking parties embedded within the local culture. Simultaneous action is needed within and outside the country since diasporas are usually involved on one side or the other, outside governments may be covert or overt parties to the conflict, and local peacemakers are often connected to international advocacy or church groups.

Promoting Inclusion

European powers have used robust military force to hold on to their empires, but their own experience of horrific industrial warfare has made them averse to military solutions to international disagreements.[27] The European Union idea is grounded in shared values and the promise of inclusion in a community of nations that protects the safety of its citizens, combines pluralism with tolerance, renounces violence as a way of settling disputes, and delivers economic growth to its citizens. The broad popular appeal of this vision has acted as a powerful incentive for adjoining countries to adopt democratic reforms and market-based policies.

Of course, this foreign policy stance has been made possible by the security guarantees offered by the United States. Europe has yet to develop its own defense shield against the use of force by hostile powers. It has only begun to plan, deploy, and test shared European capacities for security and defense. The main focus of these shared capacities has been on peacekeeping missions, where 50,000 troops have been deployed in support of a common security strategy that aims at securing Europe in a better world. The transformation of military establishments into nimble instruments of warfare able to project European power over distant theaters of war is still at an early stage. Integrated crisis management capacities, including intelligence support and logistics, are still embryonic. So is the pooling of resources for research and development and the standardization of weapons and systems across European nations.

More advanced is Europe's "soft power" arsenal, built out of the extraordinary human suffering of two world wars. This emphasizes market-friendly and people-friendly economics, greater freedom of movement of people and goods, and a readiness to impose limits on national sovereignty to facilitate international cooperation. The translation of power into influence ("compellence") requires the combined use of "carrots and sticks." Despite its growing pains and the democracy gap implicit in its governance structure, the European Union has embodied a compelling post-modern vision of political governance.

Geographical, cultural, and political obstacles are hindering the further expansion of the European commonwealth, but might be overcome as electorates realize the enormous security value of a broader union. Such a union may eventually resort to thresholds of rights and obligations for different categories of members (as in the case of the single European currency, which some EU members have not adopted).

Leadership by example and a proven ability to carry out state building through advice, suasion, and the magnet of membership would help to maintain Europe's edge in foreign policy. Many of Europe's new Eastern neighbors have not fared well following the transition from the plan to the market. Their industries have collapsed. Their standards of living are low. Many are managed by oligarchies. They pose security risks to the EU, given porous borders and the prevalence of criminal networks. Further enlargement of the EU would be an effective way to promote institutional change within them and to protect EU security.

In any event, strong links with these countries should be nurtured across a variety of economic and cultural domains. In addition, the EU should define a mutually beneficial strategic partnership with Russia that facilitates constructive engagement with shared neighbors. Special emphasis should be given to conflict prevention and mediation (for example in Moldova), and to security sector reform, which has not been a focus of European Community cooperation thus far. Benign neglect is not a useful approach even for such difficult partners as Belarus; an imaginative approach needs to be designed that mixes positive and negative incentives. Intensified relationships with South Caucasus countries (for example with a Black Sea dimension) should be explored (Lynch, 2005).

Beyond the near-abroad, systematic use of trade, investment, and aid instruments would favor regional and sub-regional coalitions and reduce the risks of conflict. Proactive support for regional bodies, say in the Mediterranean region, would sow the seeds of collaboration in support of economic cooperation and collective security. Thus, like-minded developing nations would translate their yearning for peace and stability into concrete collaborative initiatives across borders, including encouragement of foreign direct investment, support for civil society organizations, research institutes, and environmental initiatives.

In this way, the European Union would help fragile states to build their capacities towards achieving a more democratic future, and to improve their economic prospects through economic reform. In support of such strategies, soft power instruments such as information sharing, cultural exchanges, people-to-people contacts, and involvement of diasporas would be brought to bear along with aid. But much remains to be done to translate such a European vision of peaceful inclusion into specific policies that tap synergies between security and development

In the final analysis, the highest security priority for Europe's neighbors may be Europe's readiness and capacity to provide security for countries victimized by intra-state conflicts. The crises previously faced in the Balkans, the tragedy of Darfur, and the travails of the United Nations in the Democratic Republic of Congo show that, at least in the short and medium term, global and regional security organizations are unlikely to shoulder the full burdens of peacekeeping unless Europe and the United States team up to provide military and financial support.

Dealing with the Terrorist Menace

The success of terrorism depends in large part on whether or not it succeeds in amplifying fear and causing changes in government behavior that can be used to spread anti-Western sentiment and to foster division among the industrial democracies. Evidence is growing that the structural impact of the 9/11 attacks on the international order may be smaller than originally feared. However, international terrorism does require a concerted and well-considered global response because it is a telling symptom of global disorder. Other consequences, such as far deadlier international crime than experienced so far, could materialize.

Addressing Proliferation

Fragile states are a problem in the proliferation picture. First, fragile statehood destabilizes regimes in regions that are subject to proliferation pressures, notably South Asia, Central Asia, and the Middle East. Second, state failure, if ignored by the world community, increases the incentives for regional powers to pursue major weapons programs, so as to compensate for the lack of the reliable security guarantees that the Cold War era had provided.

Third, in areas where nuclear technologies are available, state fragility increases the risk of nuclear devices falling into the hands of determined terrorists. As emphasized above, the destructive potential of this possibility is so large that the risk must be considered with the utmost seriousness.

Fourth, the success of the regime-centered approach under the Nuclear Non-proliferation Treaty needs to be buttressed by collective security measures that deal with non-state actors based in fragile states and working in cahoots with rogue regimes. So far, the problem of leakage of nuclear materials and of other elements of weapons of mass destruction has been dealt with largely through a series of bilateral or trilateral initiatives, such as those between the U.S. and Russia or Ukraine.

The European Dimension

The new global politics are shaped by a lone superpower, a few primary regional powers, several secondary regional powers, and a growing number of minor but largely autonomous local powers. In this evolving context, regional and sub-regional cooperation among states that share economic interests and cultural values offers major scope for improved collective security.

As the largest and most successful regional player, the European Union is well placed to share in the responsibility for global security. It favors multiple decision making structures and diverse networks of influence that can aid the resolution of specific regional security dilemmas. Thus, it adopts flexible and at times competitive relationships among global and regional organizations. It is committed to effective multilateralism and a rule-based international order and therefore, with various degrees of success, it has sought to constrain or channel the unilateral predilections of the United States.

The 2003 European Security Strategy (EU, 2003) recognizes that the security threats of the post-Cold War era cannot be tackled by purely military means. Dealing with proliferation calls for harmonized export controls along with political pressures and diplomacy; anti-terrorism requires a mixture of police, judicial, and military means; restoration of order in failed states involves a combination of humanitarian, development, and crisis management interventions; and regional conflicts call for political solutions backed up by military assets and civilian crisis management.

Inevitably, the European Union has concentrated its resources on threats and challenges lying close to its borders. There are political constraints on the further expansion of the European commonwealth, although these may be overcome if electorates are made to realize the security value of a broader union. In addition to continued efforts to sustain the peace in the Balkans, and taking a stronger interest in the Southern Caucasus, Europe's Security Strategy is giving priority to proactive engagement with Mediterranean partners and resolution of the Arab/Israeli conflict.

Improving Relations with European Muslim Communities

Europe's security strategy will be difficult to implement without a constructive engagement with Muslim societies, which today account for one in five of the world's people and in twenty years' time will account for about one in four. Over the past three decades, Europe's Muslim population has more than doubled, to about 23 million, and its rate of growth is accelerating. Already, Muslims constitute about 5 percent of Europe's population. With Turkey included, the figures are 90 million and 15 percent.

By 2015 these numbers are expected to double while the non-Muslim population is likely to fall by about 3.5 percent. Within Europe, birth rates are now more than three times higher among Muslims than among non-Muslims while, at the edge of Europe, the population of the Middle East and North Africa is likely to double over the next three decades. Given labor shortages in Europe, and chronic youth unemployment in the Middle East and North Africa, most of the future legal and illegal migrants into Europe are likely to be Muslims.

The Europe-Islam security and development nexus has several strands (economic, political, diplomatic, cultural, and theological). The challenge is external as well as internal. The enlargement of the European Union and the strategic opportunities offered by Turkey's potential EU accession imply a need for strong and positive links with Muslim-populated states that stretch from Casablanca to the Caucasus. Most of the Muslim states that border Europe face serious problems of unemployment and social stress. Many suffer from economic stagnation and lack of political participation.

European Muslims do not constitute a monolithic group, but especially the young among them increasingly identify with Islam rather than with the country where they reside or their country of origin. They are proud of their heritage and wish to maintain their Islamic identity. That is, they seek integration but resist assimilation. Unfortunately, the general public in European countries tends to perceive them as foreigners or immigrants rather than as full-fledged fellow citizens.

Discrimination in employment, low educational achievements, limited economic participation by Muslim women, and intense security surveillance characterize Europe's relations with its Muslim communities. The global war on terrorism, the forcible removal by Western powers of Muslim governments in Afghanistan and Iraq, restraints on domestic civil liberties in Western countries, and fissures in the Atlantic alliance have induced mistrust and misunderstanding among Muslim countries and communities. Especially in Europe, the extremism of a minority of fundamentalists has distorted perceptions of Islam.

European governments will need to make a combination of adjustments in domestic and foreign relations to achieve a coherent and constructive policy stance towards Muslim communities. A fresh discourse of tolerance combined with proactive engagement will be needed so that relations between Europe and Muslim communities improve.[28] Involving the diasporas of Middle Eastern countries can play a useful role in improving mutual understanding. Policy dialogue should be part of the strategy, since the domestic dimensions of Europe's relations with Islamic communities are critical and inextricably linked with the foreign policies that EU member countries pursue towards the Middle East, as well as with the conflict patterns within Muslim societies.

F. Conclusions

At a time of anxiety and division, the international community should seek to balance the demands of international stability, security, and justice. 2006 could mark a turning point. Recent progress in resolving and managing conflict should be strengthened. International war has not been banished and therefore, it is critical to integrate inter-state war perspectives into the search for new security paradigms. But the prevention of intra-state wars, as well as sustainable conflict resolution, should move to center stage in the design of security and development policies. Intra-state wars resist classification and require tailor-made treatment. Better protection of civilians is an imperative.

The policy research literature confirms that the security and development equations are interconnected. There is a strong and robust statistical correlation between violent conflict and poverty, as well as between violent conflict and poor growth performance. We do not know for sure why these relationships hold or how non-economic factors intervene to explain the poverty-conflict linkage. But we know enough to change the direction of development policy and to view equitable and sustainable growth as a conflict prevention mechanism. The policy of inclusion of the European Union has been an effective tool of security policy and the promise of gradual enlargement should be kept alive.

International terrorism requires a concerted global response consistent with democratic principles. Policy should aim at denying terrorists the leverage unwittingly provided by restraints on civil liberties, ill-considered military responses, or discord among the industrial democracies. State failure should not be ignored since it can lead to violent conflict that spills over borders and facilitates terrorist and criminal activity. The catastrophic risk of a nuclear device falling into the hands of non-state actors should be tackled with the utmost seriousness through international cooperation and this means addressing the problems of leakage of nuclear technology and materials.

The international community should continue to support conflict resolution and mediation initiatives by the United Nations, regional bodies, and the international voluntary sector. It should be prepared to offer its own good offices for conflict resolution when so requested. It should support compliance with a stronger Nuclear Non-proliferation Treaty and promote the anti-terrorism policies designed by the Club of Madrid. European Union members should adopt a proactive foreign policy towards Europe's neighbors, with special emphasis on preventing and mediating conflict and on security sector reform. In particular, they should help connect Europe and its neighbors through a continued focus on enlargement of the European Union and outreach, trade, information sharing, cultural exchanges, and people-to-people contacts. Finally, they should promote substantive dialogue with Muslim communities inside and outside Europe.

Notes

1. For Clausewitz, "absolute war" was a Platonic ideal whereas real war was "an act of policy" subject to inevitable resource limits which eventually constrained the intensity and duration of the conflict. Weapons of mass destruction at the hands of terrorists may have made this logic obsolete.
2. The Conflict Barometer of the Heidelberg Institute on International Conflict Research also records a decrease in the number of high intensity conflicts—from forty-seven in 1991 in the wake of the Soviet Union collapse to thirty-six in

2004—following a rapid rise from a level of only 7 following the end of World War II. <http://www.hiik.de/en/main.htm>
3. The growing dominance of intra-state vs. inter-state conflicts is confirmed by the statistics of the Conflict Barometer of the Heidelberg Institute on International Conflict Research. These report no inter-state high intensity conflicts, but thirty-six intra-state high intensity conflicts. However, other states were sometimes involved in the conflicts, as was the U.S. coalition in Iraq, or Pakistan in Kashmir.
4. This gross figure hides some significant variations that reflect the very different severity of such wars. The Iran-Iraq war is estimated to have cost both countries around USD 150 billion; the 1991 Gulf War is calculated at USD 102 billion; and the 2003 war at USD 150 billion, in constant 2003 dollars. By contrast, the Falklands War cost both sides around USD 5 billion; the Peru/Ecuador conflict USD 2 billion; and Ethiopia/Eritrea perhaps USD 1 billion. The Kashmir conflict is estimated to have cost India and Pakistan together around USD 35 billion. The source for these estimates is the International Institute for Strategic Studies.
5. The war on terrorism is favored by half or more of public opinion in the U.S. (81 percent); Russia (73 percent); Britain (63 percent); Germany (55 percent) and France (50 percent) but only by 37 percent in Turkey; 28 percent in Morocco; 16 percent in Pakistan, and 12 percent in Jordan according to a nine-country Pew opinion survey dated March 16, 2004. In eight countries surveyed by the Pew Attitudes Survey in the same month, a majority of respondents said that the Iraq war had done more harm than good in the global war on terrorism.
6. According to a nine-country survey by the Pew Research Center for the People and the Press dated March 16, 2004, unfavorable ratings of the United States reached 42 percent in the United Kingdom, 63 percent in France, 62 percent in Germany, 53 percent in Russia, 70 percent in Turkey, 79 percent in Pakistan, 95 percent in Jordan and 73 percent in Morocco. According to a June 23, 2005 Pew survey of sixteen nations, anti-Americanism shows modest signs of abating but the United States remains broadly disliked in most countries, especially in the Muslim world.
7. Public confidence in the United Nations was a major casualty of the Iraq conflict. According to a Pew survey of 16,000 people in 20 countries conducted in May 2003, more than half of the respondents in sixteen countries believe that the UN is less relevant than it used to be.
8. China is believed to field around 2.4 million active service personnel, India more than one million, and Pakistan some 600,000. Indonesia fields around 300,000, and Japan around 230,000. Taiwan keeps a very competent 370,000 active military personnel and the two Koreas between them maintain more than 1.6 million military personnel. For comparison, even the U.S. now only fields around 1.2 million active service personnel and Russia around 1 million. More typically, Sri Lanka, with an active list of about 110,000, fields an army of 95,000, only slightly smaller than the current British army of 100,000.
9. Both coalition wars in the Gulf in 1991 and 2003 involved major mobilizations from the Western powers that brought fewer than half a million troops to the battlefields, fighting against Iraqi forces who effectively numbered less than 100,000 on both occasions.
10. Casualties in ongoing armed conflicts have been the largest in Algeria, Colombia, Russia, Sri Lanka, and Sudan (total deaths in the 40,000-70,000 range) followed by India, Myanmar, Peru, the Philippines, and Turkey (20,000-40,000 deaths) and by Burundi, Iraq, Israel, Nepal, Rwanda, and Uganda (up to 20,000 deaths).
11. Though every complex human emergency is unique, common challenges and constraints recur. The specificities of context should not be an excuse for repeating

the same mistakes, nor should they stand in the way of using theory to illuminate practice.

12. According to the *Washington Post* (May 1, 2005), tighter border security and counter-terrorism efforts may be yielding results. While the U.S. homeland security system remains vulnerable (for example in sea ports, chemical plants, nuclear plants), intelligence officials report that credible terrorist threats against the United States, while still "elevated," are 25-50 percent fewer than they were over the previous two years.

13. Definitions of terrorist attacks are to some extent arbitrary. According to the *Financial Times* (July 6, 2005), the Bush administration has released new figures for global terrorism. Whereas in April, the U.S. State Department had reported 651 "international" terrorism incidents for 2004, using a broader definition—to include attacks that "deliberately hit civilians or non-combatants"—the National Counterterrorism Center has raised the number to 3,192 for the same year. The incidents resulted in deaths, injuries, or kidnappings of almost 28,500 people.

14. While Al Qaeda had targeted U.S. interests in Yemen (1992), New York (1993), Somalia (1995), and Saudi Arabia (1996), the United States did not declare "war on terror" until the spectacular terrorist hits on New York and Washington. Since then, there has been no significant terrorist incident on the U.S. mainland, so that the impact of 9/11 on the popular mood is waning. While a policy legacy remains, "search and destroy" tactics are beginning to be complemented by "transformational" diplomacy and increased support to fragile states.

15. Even if the destruction caused turned out to be less than is popularly imagined, attacks on urban centers involving a weapon of mass destruction would certainly have a powerful psychological effect on Western societies.

16. "If terrorists do get their hands on nuclear weapons, the most momentous result will not be the death of hundreds of thousands of innocent people. It will be the fact that all the democracies will have to place themselves on a war footing. The measures their governments will consider it necessary to impose are likely to bring about the end of many of the socio-political institutions that emerged in Europe and North America in the two centuries since the bourgeois revolutions. They may return the West to something like feudalism." Rorty (2004). Access to chemical weapons and dangerous precursor chemicals is far more prevalent and represents a significant threat in areas of instability and state fragility, but the destructive impact of chemical warfare would not be as great.

17. In 2003, according to the Annual Report on Conflict by the Institute for International Conflict Research at University of Heidelberg, seventeen of the world's thirty-six high-intensity conflicts involved member states of the Islamic Conference, of which seven are in the Arab League. Out of nineteen major conflicts listed by the Stockholm International Peace Research Institute (SIPRI), eight involve members of the Islamic Conference, of which four are in the Arab League.

18. Among Muslims from twelve countries who were surveyed by the Pew Research Center Global Attitudes Project for 2002, about a third responded positively to the question of whether suicide terrorism against civilians in defense of Islam can be justified. See Harris (2005).

19. The reduction of suicide bombings in Israel has required extraordinary measures that have taken a heavy toll on the welfare of a majority of Palestinians.

20. The Afghanistan and Iraq wars are in part the consequence of failed policies in the region. During the 1950s the United States helped to overthrow the nationalist Mossadegh government in Iran. In 1980, Arab states and Russia encouraged Iraq to invade Iran. Following the first Gulf war the victorious coalition imposed sanc-

tions that had serious humanitarian consequences. Next, the United States and its Arab allies provided funds and arms to radical Islamists to defeat the Soviet Union in Afghanistan. They also failed to stop meddling by neighbors after the Soviets withdrew and did not provide major economic assistance, thus laying the foundation for the Taliban takeover.
21. Suicide as a military strategy has long history. The current revulsion of Westerners towards suicide bombings in Iraq (60-70 a month) resembles the horrified reaction to the martyrdom of early Christians in pagan Rome. Japan and the Soviet Union used suicide missions to destroy enemy targets in World War II. The Tamil Tigers perfected the technique for political assassinations. There have been 1,000 suicides to bear witness to a cause since the immolation of a Buddhist monk in Vietnam in 1963. Bunting (2005).
22. He thereby endorsed the definition of terrorism proposed by the United Nations High-level Panel on Threats, Challenges, and Change in December 2004: "Any action, in addition to actions already specified by the existing conventions on aspects of terrorism, the Geneva Conventions and Security Council resolution 1566 (2004) that is intended to cause death or serious bodily harm to civilians and non-combatants, when the purpose of such an act, by its nature or context, is to intimidate a population, or to compel a government or an international organization to do or to abstain from doing any act."
23. On March 11, 2004, an international terrorist network caused ten bombs to explode in four trains during the Madrid rush hour. Almost 200 persons died and 2,000 were injured. On the first anniversary of this traumatic attack, a comprehensive plan of action to confront terrorism emerged from a conference in Madrid that brought together fifty-seven current and former heads of state, 250 leading experts, official delegations from 40 countries, and heads of inter-governmental and international organizations.
24. According to Cecilia Wikstrom (*International Herald Tribune*, June 6, 2005), European Union governments remain reluctant to share sensitive intelligence, to coordinate investigations into terrorist crimes, and to support Eurojust, the judicial cooperation agency, in the fight against terrorism.
25. United Nations Security Council Resolution 1540 was designed to create a mandatory international regime to keep weapons of mass destruction out of unauthorized hands. But it remains very preliminary and has been sufficiently controversial to prevent it being a major step, so far, towards a new international regime.
26. The Iraq war and its aftermath demonstrate the deadly impact of asymmetrical tactics as well as their disproportionate impact on local security forces and civilians. While the United States coalition has incurred about 1,800 military deaths, Iraqi security forces have lost 3,600 men and Iraqi civilian deaths are about 21,000-24,000. *Washington Post,* May 1, 2005.
27. According to Stokes (2005), from a 2004 German Marshall Plan Fund poll, one in three Americans believe that the West should threaten Teheran with military action to thwart its nuclear ambitions, whereas only one in eight French citizens and one in sixteen Germans support such an approach.
28. Deep feelings of fear, insecurity, and disempowerment underlie the violent demonstrations that took place in Islamic countries in reaction to the publication of Muhammad cartoons in 2006 by *Jyllands-Posten*, a Danish newspaper.

4

Rethinking Development Cooperation

> *"Although problems and catastrophes may be inevitable, solutions are not."* — Isaac Asimov

Geopolitical upheavals and disillusion with the asymmetries of globalization are propelling human security to the top of the development cooperation agenda. The downside risks of the current international order need better management. Towards this end, chapter 1 considered the conceptual and strategic issues involved in the convergence of security and development. Chapter 2 identified the policy adjustments that rich countries should consider to level and secure the playing field of the international economy while chapter 3 examined the security threats that need to be tackled to protect human security.

The present chapter shifts the spotlight to development cooperation at the country level. Looking at human security from the vantage point of an aid industry in transition, section A reviews how conceptions of development have evolved to fit changes in the international order. Section B traces the relevance of state fragility to conflict and poverty reduction. Section C takes a human security perspective and identifies new policy directions for development cooperation. Section D outlines the aid reform agenda. Section E concludes.

A. Changing Conceptions of Development Cooperation

The development enterprise has always reflected a mix of geopolitical concerns, economic interests, and democratic ideals. At the end of World War II, foreign assistance was dominated by the reconstruction challenge of war-torn Europe. Next, it focused on the overseas possessions that colonial powers yielded to national independence movements. The transition was marked by a rise in the number of violent intra-state conflicts. The complex human emergencies they created brought forth a vast increase in humanitarian relief operations. These absorbed a steadily growing share of aid flows, drew the international civil society into aid operations, and turned voluntary organizations and multilateral institutions into influential development actors.

Throughout the Cold War, aid to the developing world was used as an ideological weapon in the East-West contest. Accordingly, a significant share of aid was used to prop up unpopular, corrupt, and illegitimate governments that cared only for their hold on power and privilege, mismanaged their economies, and violated human rights. In these instances, aid fed corruption, contributed to internal coercion, and perpetuated economic mismanagement. As a result, the geopolitical approach to aid distorted priorities and yielded mixed development results. Conversely, it provided a "self-interest" justification for increased aid flows and it exposed rich countries' citizens to the realities of turmoil and deprivation in poor countries.

The ending of the Cold War raised hopes for rapid progress towards peace and democracy. But with the disintegration of the bipolar international order, civil strife spread and separatist conflicts broke out. These induced violent conflicts and large refugee flows that the United Nations and the voluntary sector were called upon to mitigate—often with inadequate military protection, as in Bosnia and Rwanda—demonstrating the reluctance of powerful governments to intervene with sufficient force except where they had pressing domestic policy imperatives to do so (Ogata, 2005). Outside the zones of turmoil and violence, aid was pressed into service to promote market-based policies and global economic integration.

By then, policy leverage had become a fixture of development cooperation. It was used to promote global market integration. But the political fallout proved disruptive so that the conditionality instrument (which was used with considerable success to pry open borders for trade and foreign investment) eventually fell into disrepute. In parallel, doctrinal tensions among human rights activists, humanitarian aid practitioners, and advocates of economic reform intensified. But while the radical and vocal wing of the anti-globalization movement captured the attention of the media, the mainstream of the various development constituencies sought pragmatic ways to work together. Eventually, they joined forces behind a debt reduction agenda and a poverty reduction focus that was adopted by all members of the United Nations at the turn of the century.

Thus, from the fall of the Berlin wall to the collapse of the Twin Towers, remarkable progress was made towards a common normative framework for development cooperation. The effort was shaped by a variety of concerns: the imperative of saving lives, human rights values, democratic governance ideals, and the drive to globalization. The Millennium Declaration of 2000 was consistent with a broadly based, comprehensive, and cosmopolitan vision supportive of a globalization process that was expected to benefit all. At its core was a consensus that was made explicit at the Monterrey Conference of 2002.

That historic compact, outlined in chapter 1 above, matched improved governance and implementation of poverty reduction strategies in poor countries with adjustment of policies in rich countries, including more and better aid, debt reduction, and more open markets. By 2002, however, terrorism had emerged as a looming transnational threat that was to revolutionize international relations. Even though terrorism inflicts far fewer casualties than intra-state wars or the scourge of poverty,[1] it has a unique capacity to instill fear—the most powerful of human emotions, according to Machiavelli. Terrorism also benefits from the unintended results of the coercive responses it generates. Thus, the military intervention in Iraq has caused unprecedented upheavals in international relations and induced a precipitous decline of international good will towards the United States. It has also undermined the international harmony that had made the universal adoption of the Millennium Declaration possible.

On the development front, the Millennium Development Goals now seem out of reach. The means deployed to achieve them have proved inadequate. Weaknesses in governance throughout the developing world (and the intra-state conflicts they have spawned) help to explain the disappointing outcomes. But in addition, the Monterrey compact has failed to elicit the necessary aid commitments or the political will required within rich countries to level the playing field of the global economy. The Monterrey consensus also sidestepped conflict and security issues that had in the meantime emerged as matters of urgent concern to people everywhere.

These gaps in coverage will need to be addressed by a new development cooperation agenda. Securing a consensus to this end is a tough challenge. But the stakes are such that progressive politicians, development activists, and people of goodwill everywhere should join forces to induce a sea change in global policies towards human security.

The Meaning of Risk has Evolved

The time is ripe for a new development consensus. The international environment is volatile, uncertain, and risky. Already, the concept of risk has acquired new prominence in public policy. In the halcyon days of development, risk was simply the probability of an event combined with the associated gain or loss. The term still carries this meaning in science, insurance, and gambling but not in public affairs, where it has come to refer only to potentially negative outcomes. This evolution in the meaning of risk reflects a gradual erosion of trust in public institutions. Transparency, oversight, and legal recourse are now perceived as prerequisites of development effectiveness.

Disillusion with aid performance, in relation to unrealistic expectations, has contributed to aid fatigue. In part this is because chronic optimism in program design and systematic underestimation of potential human hardships have been all too common. A growing awareness of the obstacles to development effectiveness in poor countries has undermined trust in the accuracy and relevance of cost-benefit calculations. Aid critics allege that downside risks have been deliberately downplayed so as to get dubious projects funded. Responding to these perceptions, aid agencies have shifted from rate of return "point estimates" to qualitative risk assessments that assert rights, claim privileges, and express aspirations, without producing professionally derived "best estimates" of collective gains and losses.

International conventions and safeguard policy norms are now expected to provide social and environmental guarantees to individuals and communities affected by development activities. Public officials and international bureaucrats have become accountable for results on the ground. "Pareto optimality," whereby no one is made worse off as a result of the intervention, has become a central test of development effectiveness. Anyone who suggests that no battery of safeguards can guard against all possible dangers is taken to shirk responsibility. The same climate of opinion has generated rights-based approaches in development agencies, corporate social responsibility initiatives in the business sector, and a bewildering proliferation of social audits and impact assessments in the voluntary sector.

Typically, risk assessments emerge out of consultative processes that are designed to empower individuals or groups who may be negatively affected by a public investment or a policy decision. These processes zero in on the potential damage that policies, programs, and projects may cause to poor people and future generations. As a result, the concept of risk has become a stick that the weak wield against authority: an instrument of accountability, a way to amplify the voices of the poor, and a forensic resource. Thus in development as in medicine, the Hippocratic Oath, "first, do no harm," has become a key performance benchmark.

At the same time, security strategists have come to recognize the limits of military might, and the disenchantment with the industrialization of war and its bloody consequences has led to the innovative use of new information and communications technologies in military combat. Its object is to achieve victory while reducing human casualties, minimizing collateral damage, and reducing the risk of battle (Coker, 2004). This post-industrial doctrine of warfare is grounded in the notion that success should be measured, not in "body count" or in the capacity to level cities and immobilize armies, but in the ability to use information to direct firepower towards critical nodes and to neutralize the opponent with minimum harm.

Thus, the new millennium has started with a "re-enchantment of war" within influential policymaking circles. Cinematic depictions of "high tech" warfare underlie current reforms of the United States military establishment. However, this post-modern vision of combat has proven to be a hallucination in the Iraq quagmire where the most sophisticated military systems have failed to overcome simple and flexible intermediate technologies wielded by highly motivated insurgents. Nevertheless, the concept of low-casualty conflict retains its hold on the imagination of influential security policymakers, who have also come to realize that diplomacy and development are prized strategic assets in the asymmetric confrontations favored by insurgents.

The Convergence between Security and Development is Raising Concerns

In this new security context, the aid industry is once again under pressure to advance the geopolitical and security interests of rich countries. Not surprisingly, these interests do not always coincide with (or match the priority demands of) poverty reduction. As a result, the risks of policy incoherence in development cooperation have risen. During the Cold War, Western development assistance was marshaled towards common political goals while the post-Cold War era produced a historic consensus behind a vision of equitable globalization. By contrast, the trends in aid since 9/11 signal a diffusion of development cooperation goals. This raises the risk of fragmentation and incoherence in development strategies.

In particular, since perceptions of security risks differ among donor countries, efforts to align aid with foreign policy objectives have induced a retreat from multilateralism. International financial institutions, restrained by constitutional charters that prevent them from taking account of political considerations in their operations, have begun to lose ground to bilateral agencies. Weakened support for the United Nations in the wake of the Iraq oil-for-food scandal has accelerated the trend. Aid activists and professionals now worry that security fears are diluting the focus on human rights and undermining the credibility and independence of aid. While they perceive "joined up" government as critical for aid effectiveness, they insist that policy coherence should remain firmly geared to poverty reduction rather than refocused to serve donor countries' short-term security interests. These concerns are not altogether misplaced.

Aid Resources Risk Being Diverted Away from Poverty Reduction

Based on Cold War experience, massive resources could be wasted if once again aid became subservient to narrow geopolitical imperatives. Short-changing the legitimate poverty reduction aspirations of developing countries in order to satisfy rich countries' security concerns would be an ironic outcome of the desired rapprochement between security and development. While the record to date does not suggest that major diversions have occurred, pressures to reward states that support the war on terrorism have been and remain high.

A close association between aid, foreign affairs, and defense bureaucracies is desirable if it serves the interests of the global poor. For example, post-conflict experience in Africa has confirmed the utility of combining conflict management and development activities for achieving results on the ground. But if the legitimate need to protect homeland security is allowed to dilute the focus on poverty reduction, this undercuts the credibility of aid givers. This is what happened when the United States coalition supplied aid under a military umbrella in support of reconstruction and state-building activities in Afghanistan and Iraq.

There is little doubt that aid flows have been affected by the "long war" on terrorism. This is not surprising: security and development goals do not always coincide. Thus, aid to Pakistan from the United States jumped almost tenfold, from USD 89 million in 2000 to USD 775 million in 2001, and that from the United Kingdom trebled, from USD 24 million in 2000 to USD 70 million in 2002. The reconstruction needs of Afghanistan and Iraq have required a shift of resources away from other programs in middle-income countries where 140 million people live in poverty.[2] Similarly, Denmark has redeployed USD 23 million of its aid towards projects in the Middle East and more than twice this amount has gone to Iraq reconstruction. These allocations might otherwise have gone to Africa (Christian Aid, 2004).

Thus far, however, the increased aid from the United States and European countries to "front-line states" of the Middle East and Asia has been made possible by expanding the overall aid budget envelope rather than by diverting funds away from aid to from low-income countries. Multilateral programs have yet to be significantly affected.[3] In other words, the main budgetary impact of 9/11 and 3/11 thus far has been an increase in special appropriations and supplemental aid budgets (Woods and research team, 2004).

In March 2005, the OECD Development Assistance Committee adjusted its strictures on the types of aid eligible for official development assistance (ODA) status, in partial compliance with the wishes of donors who wished to allocate aid funds to programs managed by the military, development training for security forces, and security sector reform assistance programs that involve working with military establishments.

Consensus was reached on the eligibility of expenditures for: (i) improved civilian oversight and democratic control over security expenditures; (ii) enhancing civil society's role in the security system; (iii) supporting measures for preventing the recruitment of child soldiers; (iv) security sector reform; (v) civilian activities for peacebuilding, conflict prevention, and conflict resolution; and (vi) controlling, preventing, and reducing the proliferation of small arms and light weapons. On the other hand, training the military in human rights and other non-military matters is not considered eligible.

Given the severe budget constraints that all industrial democracies are currently facing, further expenditure switching away from the Millennium Development Goals cannot be ruled out. Future aid flows will need to be vigilantly monitored to ensure that poverty reduction programs are not short-changed. And a further relaxation of eligibility rules, to count military-related expenditures as ODA, should be resisted, if only to maintain the integrity of ODA statistics.

B. State Fragility and Conflict

The main impetus for reorienting development assistance towards state building has been a fear of the negative impact of state failure at the periphery for the security of rich countries. Security planners have concluded that fragile states bypassed by the march of economic progress and democratic development could be tempted to provide safe havens for terrorists and criminals and threaten international stability. Afghanistan provides an illustration of the potential risks: it was successfully captured by Al Qaeda.

This shift in security doctrine is likely to have far-reaching consequences for development. It could be as significant as the reorientation that took place following the 1980s debt crisis, when market-driven policies captured the commanding heights of development policy. Since only capable and resilient states can be relied upon to maintain security and reduce poverty, the mainstream of development thinking is now acknowledging that state building matters for security as well as for development.

The State is Back

Thus, the state is back on the radar screen of development policymakers. They acknowledge that low-income countries need resilient and capable public institutions not only to grow and prosper but also to improve the prospects of international stability. The grand project of global economic integration that animated development cooperation in the 1990s is well underway insofar as well functioning economies are concerned. Fragile states represent the final frontier of economic globalization. A sharper focus on fragile states also makes sense from a security perspective: poor and rich countries alike have begun to appreciate their interdependence and the legitimacy of each others' concerns regarding poverty, insecurity, and instability.

While democratic values and human rights principles may be universal, perceptions necessarily differ as to the desirable scope of the functions of the state. Fukuyama (2004) asserts that the scope of the state may have to be traded off for its strength. For many years the geopolitical trend has been towards the weakening of states in reaction to the excesses of authoritarianism, as a result of the growth of the global market economy and because of the increased clout of the nongovernmental sector. But a withered state has turned out to be a dangerous state. It follows that, at least initially, state building by the international community will have to focus on the essential prerequisites of legitimacy, accountability, transparency, and the rule of law.

At one extreme, the state may be viewed as an association of citizens, that is, of individuals formally equal in their rights before the law and united in their recognition of the legitimacy of a single civil authority tasked with law enforcement. At the other extreme, the state may be conceived as a collective project in and of itself and citizens as mere contributors to large national undertakings. These rival and idealized conceptions of the state imply different modes of governance. Whereas the civil state produces procedural rules with no clear goals in sight, the enterprise state produces managerial and instrumental rules that focus on results.

In other words, the civil state seeks equality of *opportunity* for its citizens whereas the enterprise state aims at equality of *outcomes*. This difference means that the types and degrees of freedom afforded to individuals vary depending on the generic conception of the state. An enterprise state is more likely than a civil state to go to war against another state, since it will tend to subordinate citizens' interests to the national interest.[4] On the other hand, intra-state wars are more likely to erupt where the state is so weak that it lacks the capacity to fall into either of these categories.

The centrality of institutions for security as well as for development is ultimately the reason why the aid enterprise must reach well beyond the macroeconomic policy adjustments required by globalization. Policies that are not embedded in institutions cannot be relied upon to generate sustainable and equitable growth—as shown by the frequent failure of policy based operations narrowly designed around macroeconomic prescriptions. This kind of conditionality worked reasonably well where institutional capacity was adequate and policymakers "owned" the policy package. But in weak states and fragile governance environments, it has often generated unintended social tensions and promoted insecurity.

In authoritarian or corrupt states, deep political change and institutional reform may be needed to trigger needed social transformations. In turn, change may hinge on domestic leaders' ability to mobilize a critical mass of opinion intent on reform. External support is equally critical, though imported blueprints are widely resented.

Thus, the European neighborhood policy rewards countries that are on the path to democratic reform, but it also recognizes that democratic movements must be home-grown and adapted to local conditions, and that no standard model can be imposed from the outside, given the diversity of cultural and administrative traditions within which governance must be embedded.

Indeed, the success of the European Union's approach to state building lies in its focus on shared values of participation, cohesion, and solidarity combined with an institutional development emphasis that spans political, economic, social, and cultural domains. This combination contrasts with the narrow economic and technocratic orientation of development cooperation programs. The trading and budgetary incentives associated with EU membership are, of course, critical. But so are the comprehensiveness and adaptability of the policy-anchoring and skills-development activities that are associated with membership. The long and patient period of capacity building that precedes the accession process contrasts with the "quick fixes" and partial solutions that have characterized capacity building projects funded by aid.

Overcoming the Predicament of State Fragility

Quite apart from the ethical considerations that underlie the rationale for aid, the systemic cost of unrest at the periphery is such that the self-interest of OECD countries justifies a stronger drive toward positive engagement with weak states. Conversely, developing countries have much to gain by participating in the global quest for international stability and security, since they suffer the most from intra-state wars, international crime, and the impact of international terrorism on business cycles.

Nor is there a conflict between the recommended focus on fragile states and the overarching priority of poverty reduction. About a third of low-income countries have been classified as fragile by the World Bank. Home to about one billion people and a third of the absolute poor, they are the core of the development challenge. In these countries, malnutrition affects one out of every three people—twice as many as in other developing countries.[5] Yet, because "good policies" and good governance have been considered key criteria in aid allocation, fragile countries have often been isolated and bypassed by development aid.

Fragile states are called "difficult partners" in the OECD lexicon. But in truth, they constitute a very mixed group and their problems, while numerous and acute, differ little in character from those faced by other poor countries.[6] Fragile states require long-term engagement, politically astute treatment, and tailor-made solutions that take account of local leadership capacities. But so do other developing countries. Hence, it is not surprising that the principles that were agreed by the Development Assistance Committee (DAC) of the OECD, following the January 2005 High-level Forum on Fragile States (OECD, 2005), are strongly reminiscent of those that the DAC has long promoted for development cooperation in general.

Not all fragile states are low-income countries. Some are not even eligible for aid. The Failed States Index compiled by *Foreign Policy* and the Fund for Peace (*Foreign Policy*, 2005) covers all states that are vulnerable to violent internal conflict based on twelve economic, political, and military indicators.[7] Together these states are home to two billion people. The list identifies six countries at significant risk of failure. It includes Bosnia, Colombia, Egypt, Iraq, Iran, Lebanon, the Philippines, Russia, Saudi Arabia, Syria, Turkey, and Ukraine.

The concept of state building is still poorly defined. It normally refers to tasks undertaken after a conflict or a crisis and encompasses the creation or restoration of effective governance, the reconstruction of the economy and the society, and the promotion of a national identity. A friendly regime and the successful establishment of a self-sustaining democracy are considered part of state building. Such objectives are very difficult to achieve, especially with the inadequate resources and short-term horizons that tend to be allocated to the task.[8] Lack of a shared vision among external partners adds to the difficulties.

Following his review of nation building activities in Afghanistan, Cambodia, Mozambique, and Somalia, Jonathan Moore, former U.S. Ambassador to the United Nations, reported that the dominant factor in these human emergencies was the highly fragmented and inchoate approach of donors, international agencies, and NGOs. He noted that "different bureaus, ministries, official representatives within the same powerful member nations often represent conflicting positions on aid to needy countries," while bilateral aid programs are "frequently run in a unilateral manner that is based on nationalist interests without regard to coordination with other contributors and sometimes inconsistent with the overall recovery strategy of the recipient country" (Moore, 1996).

It is worth remembering that after World War II the reconstruction of Japan took seven years and Germany had to wait ten years to be granted full sovereignty—and these were countries where the political and institutional conditions for a revival were very favorable. Given adverse initial conditions and various resource constraints, no such success has rewarded the strenuous state building efforts in Bosnia, Cambodia, the Dominican Republic, Kosovo, Somalia, and South Vietnam (Pei and Kasper, 2003). Chaotic and insecure conditions, national resistance to external intervention, limited understanding of local conditions, faulty models of engagement, and unwillingness to stay the course underlie the setbacks experienced over the years.

The challenges of state building depend on a country's prior governance conditions, level of economic and social development, and national homogeneity. There is no shortcut to state building. Five years may be the minimum time needed for an enduring transition. Controversy about the task of state building, and institutional resistance to regarding state building as part of the core mission of defense, diplomacy, or development, have inhibited the investments needed to do a better job. Governments tend to treat each state building task as if it were the first and the last. As a result, learning from past mistakes has been modest.

Experience provides a number of lessons (Dobbins and others, 2003). Among controllable factors, the most important is the level of effort measured in time, manpower, and money. Multilateral approaches are more complex to organize and manage, but they are less burdensome for individual partners and they produce more national and regional reconciliation as well as more thorough institutional transformations. Unity of command and broad participation are compatible if the major actors share a common vision. The larger the stabilization force, the fewer the likely casualties suffered and inflicted. Neighboring states exert significant influences on outcomes. Addressing past grievances is an especially difficult and controversial feature of state building.

From Fragility to Conflict

Protection of property rights, the rule of law, a sound judicial system, and accountability and transparency of public expenditure management are central to development. Equally, law and order and the fair administration of justice are acid tests of state legitimacy. This is why the exclusion of security institutions from the purview of development cooperation has been a major weakness of traditional aid strategies. The dysfunction has been especially damaging for fragile states hemmed in by trade protection, high transport costs, and tough immigration restrictions.

Fragile states may eventually reach such isolation and suffer such disintegration that legitimate enterprises have no space left to operate, and illegal pursuits become the only profitable ones. In such environments, borders become porous, customs officials become corrupt, illegal practices become culturally acceptable, and the shadow economy becomes dominant. Ineffective border controls, lax policing, and major price differentials make smuggling profitable, facilitate the subversion of state authority through corruption, collusion, and intimidation, and create conditions that encourage the recruitment of idle and disoriented youths by extremist groups.

Such poor, fragile, debt-burdened states cannot generate fiscal resources for providing basic social services and maintaining law and order. The state gradually retreats from basic public functions and sometimes from parts of the country. Local chiefs, mafia leaders, or warlords eventually fill the political vacuum, sometimes in collusion with corrupt officials. Given the incapacity of the state to deliver services and ensure security, loyalty to the regime withers and the locus of authority shifts to minority groups, indigenous movements, ethnic or religious leaders, or criminal syndicates that are able to deliver security services to those who can pay. The state becomes fragmented and low intensity or large-scale violence eventually ensues.

Institutional weaknesses in the security sector compound the problem and lay the foundations for an expansion of parallel trading, illegal trafficking, and international crime. Based in fragile states, a wide range of criminal organizations take advantage of modern communications technologies and management methods to engage in illicit trade in agricultural, forestry, and wildlife products as well as in drugs, arms and weapons, diamonds, antiquities, stolen cars, toxic waste, and counterfeit goods. Some crime syndicates also engage in illegal trafficking of women and children to satisfy a flourishing sex trade.

Finally, the accumulation of private wealth in the midst of penury and misery creates social tension and contributes to criminality and a booming demand for private security services and property rights protection. Foreign companies, aid agencies, and voluntary organizations must also resort to private security services contracted out to specialized companies manned by former police and military personnel. Inevitably, the privatization of security services without adequate oversight by government undercuts the monopoly of violence on which the state's legitimacy ultimately rests.

Diverse Doctrines

Three grand theories have been offered about the root causes of intra-state conflict in developing countries. Sweeping in their generality, they all acknowledge the reality of global interdependence. Each has generated its own distinctive and convincing policy narrative and each contains its share of truth. But each also has limitations, so that adopting one doctrine at the exclusion of the others leads to a distorted appreciation of the realities of contemporary inter-state conflict.

First is the "clash of civilizations" thesis: this stresses the role of culture and identity politics in the genesis of war. Second is the "hegemonic" worldview, which points to dysfunctions in the global economic order that nurture breeding grounds for conflict. Third is the "neo-liberal" doctrine, which highlights the role of greed (as distinct from grievance) in triggering and sustaining violence. The basic aspects of each of these doctrines are outlined below.

Samuel P. Huntington (1993) visualizes a world where the major sources of conflict are located along the fault lines that divide civilizations. Whereas the conflicts of the past had pitted princes, nation states, and most recently ideologies (notably capitalism and communism) against one another, the stage is now set for a clash of civilizations. According to this vision, cultural differences rather than economic forces or political ideas have become the key drivers of world politics. They inflame tensions, nurture grievances, and provoke conflict both within and across states.

Huntington's thesis attributes violence between Armenians and Azeris, Palestinians and Israelis, Hindus and Muslims in the Indian subcontinent, Christian Orthodox and Muslims in Bosnia, Serbs and Albanians in Kosovo, Christians and Muslims in Cote d'Ivoire and Nigeria, Arabs and blacks in the Sudan, Russians and Muslims in Central Asia, and among the various sects in Lebanon to differences in culture and civilization. It postulates that sustained and violent contests between Western and non-Western societies are occurring because Western ideas (such as individualism, democracy, free markets.) are culturally constructed rather than universally shared and that, beyond the consumerism associated with economic progress, non-Western societies have been and will remain resistant to the spread of liberal democratic norms and human rights principles that have their roots in Western civilization.

Though highly controversial and hotly contested,[9] this narrative has had a powerful impact on public policy. The rationale for its major propositions runs as follows. First, differences between civilizations are deep, resilient, and basic: they define all human relationships and are not easily mutable since they are solidly rooted in history, culture, tradition, and religion. Second, the number and the intensity of interactions—and the likelihood of frictions—among civilizations have grown, given large-scale population movements and the advent of new transport and communications technologies. Third, the vast military and economic supremacy of the West has increased public resentment and triggered a cultural backlash that is unlikely to abate. Fourth, the stresses of globalization have increased the lure of ethnic identity, enhanced the solace of faith, and accentuated the restoration of group pride. Finally, the thickening of economic and political relationships among culturally cohesive groups (such as the European Union, East Asian countries) has increased the risk of confrontation among civilizations.

At the opposite end of the ideological spectrum, the structuralist (or hegemonic) worldview articulated by Mark Duffield conceives of conflict as the ultimate outcome of a policy of exclusion that has consigned large parts of the South to economic isolation (Duffield, 2001). From this perspective, the local wars that have come to dominate the global geography of violence are the natural consequence of formal rules that make the criminal economy of illegal trafficking in drugs, weapons, and people much more attractive than legal economic pursuits to poor and marginalized countries. The exclusion doctrine describes the global economy as a thriving system of exchange that has liberalized flows of trade, capital, and skills among OECD countries while keeping poor countries out of the system, with the result that "black holes" of decline, poverty, and breakdown have emerged in the poor regions of the world.

According to this worldview, the new global order has been enforced through rules of the game designed and policed by integrated supranational governance networks that emphasize North-North cooperation, while imposing on countries of the South a different logic that constrains their economic choices through debt burdens, fiscal rigor, and conditionality. The same logic favors private corporations and nongovernmental organizations for the provision of social and security services. The policies associated with this logic have weakened the state and downgraded the concept of national sovereignty. They have also endeavored to open up developing countries' markets, and have facilitated the control of labor costs in rich countries. They hinge on continuous and guaranteed access to oil, gas, and other natural resources by multinational corporations.

The third doctrine reflects the neo-liberal mainstream. It is articulated by Paul Collier who ascribes the rise of intra-state conflicts to microeconomic factors ("greed") rather than to political grievances or geo-economic considerations. In essence, the neo-liberal mental model perceives of warlords and terrorists as economic agents rather than as servants of coherent ideologies or champions of political agendas. These agents are simply in a business that happens to produce warfare because that is the most profitable occupation. Just as Clausewitz characterized war as an extension of politics, the neo-liberal economists depict contemporary intra-state wars as an extension of commerce: to carry out their business, warlords gain control over "lootable" resources, sell protection services, and evade, subvert, or capture the state security apparatus.

Warlords respond to economic incentives and use violence not only to pursue their strategic objectives but also to discipline their own organizations and intimidate their competitors. Warlords and terrorists only differ from crime syndicates in that their professed aim is to undermine or capture national economic and political systems, whereas criminal networks do not challenge the legally sanctioned economic system on which they prey. The modern business techniques of warlords, terrorists, and international criminals have helped to globalize and privatize violence by "de-territorializing" and "trans-nationalizing" conflict. International crime networks as well as warlords and terrorists rely on the thriving international arms business to secure the instruments of the violence trade. They take advantage of the cross-border circulation of people to facilitate recruitment and training. They make expert use of new information technologies as they connect within national territories and across national borders.

Inevitably, the policy implications of these alternative doctrines differ. The Huntington thesis emphasizes the crucial role that diplomacy and cultural exchanges play in the ideological competition that pits liberal doctrines against radical and fundamentalist movements. The Duffield model highlights the global structural causes of local violence; it implicitly points to the reform of global governance structures and power relationships as the solution. The ultimate goal would be a wholesale restructuring of the international system so as to give a human face to globalization.

By contrast, the remedies that flow from the neo-liberal model aim at tinkering with the incentives framework, for example by imposing controls on international trade and financial transactions. That model concentrates on discouraging illicit activity and promoting legitimate and productive business enterprises through improved regulatory regimes within developing countries. At the national level, neo-liberalism supports development cooperation as a vehicle for reform of security sector institutions, as a lever of economic adjustment, and as a vehicle for promoting private enterprise and social development. At the international level, it recommends tighter regulation of financial flows, certification of natural resources exports (as in the Kimberley process[10]), and military intervention as a last resort.

Though the three policy narratives reflect different ideological perspectives they are not necessarily contradictory. Thus, the Huntington thesis does not preclude a contest of civilizations through hegemonic rule setting as outlined by Duffield or through the proxies of warlords motivated by lucre as depicted by Collier. Conversely, the "structuralist" thesis is not averse to interpreting a contest of civilizations as a competitive process, with cultural artifacts and ideas used as tools of market expansion and economic domination. Finally, the neo-liberal principles can be extrapolated to illuminate intra-state conflict at the higher plane of nations and civilizations just as they do at the level of individual warlords, for example by explaining conflict in terms of maintaining privileged access to oil and other natural resources.

Towards a Synthesis

We propose an alternative conception of the relationship between conflict, security, and development that connects all three of the above explanations. First, it defines state fragility as the incapacity to manage the combined demands of security and development. Next, it explains the achievement of security and development in terms of generating a mix of voice (participation) and loyalty (authority). Through participation, policy options are defined and conflicting views reconciled. Through authority, decisions are not only made but made to stick. But for authority to be sustained over time, it must be backed by a social contract between the government and the governed.

The terms of the social contract vary from country to country. Some states maintain a narrow range of core functions (usually defense, law and order, protection of property rights, and delivery of basic social services). Others adopt a more activist role including wealth distribution and industrial policy. But all states have one thing in common: they aspire to a monopoly of violence. In return, they undertake to protect citizens from external threats and internal chaos, deliver a range of public goods, and create an enabling environment for private and voluntary enterprise.

To deliver its side of the social bargain, a state needs capacity. To overcome the social tensions that its development efforts will inevitably generate, the state also needs resilience. Without the resilience associated with legitimacy, it cannot mediate among various interest groups, settle disputes, or protect its authority. Security implies safety, stability, and reliability but it can also connote stagnation. Similarly, development promises prosperity but it also implies risk and uncertainty. Good governance strikes a judicious balance between the two. Security without development cannot meet popular expectations. Conversely, a headlong rush towards development may aggravate inequality among groups and induce conflict. Finally, where security arrangements are weak, the body politic may be disrupted and violence may erupt.

The role of the state is made clear by using Hirschman's "exit, voice, and loyalty" trilogy to examine how members of any group react when faced by a decline in public policy performance. Group members can exercise their voice option or can exit from the group (Hirschman, 1970). While Hirschman emphasizes the economic dimension of exit (as when consumers switch from brand to brand, employees resign, or workers go on strike) we choose to interpret violence as the ultimate form of exit. One remedy against violence is coercion. But coercion fuels resentment and social exclusion. The exercise of voice (defined by participation in democratic politics) helps to manage conflict without resort to violence. Over time, it is through voice and accountability that the state achieves resilience.

The implicit hypothesis is that capacity is critical to the delivery of development performance, while resilience is central to the mediation of conflict and therefore promotes security. Thus, development is integrally linked to state capacity while security is correlated with state legitimacy. Of course, failure on one front can lead to deterioration on the other. This is when deficits in capacity or resilience, or more often in both, can lead to conflict and—given other aggravating factors such as a natural disaster—to the breakdown of the monopoly of violence that defines the state. This occurred, for example, after the cyclone in East Pakistan which led to spiraling civil unrest, the eventual break-up of the nation, and the independence of Bangladesh.

Customs, rules, and social protocols determine the balance between exit (violence) and voice (resilience). They generate various degrees of loyalty, defined as the extent to which poor performance is tolerated without resorting to exit. Loyalty is strengthened by voice. Hence, freedom of expression and assembly are conducive to resilience. Conversely, the provision of human security that is made possible by the state's monopoly of violence strengthens loyalty and allows the exercise of voice within accepted social protocols. To continue the example from East Pakistan, the poor performance of the Punjabi elite (who controlled the Pakistan military regime) in disaster relief and rehabilitation fed popular resentment and strengthened the Bengali insurgency of the country's eastern wing.

The logic of state resilience is that the exercise of voice generates loyalty (the margin of tolerance for shortfalls in capacity) and makes authority responsible. Voice helps to improve performance and it provides governments with the space they need to innovate and to take judicious risks in the national interest. Within certain bounds, resilience can substitute for capacity, and capacity for resilience. The more legitimate a government, the greater the trust that citizens place in it and the greater their tolerance for shortfalls in government performance. This is why cultural identity matters. Conversely, a government that is capable of delivering security and other public services to its citizens may survive even if its legitimacy is partial.

Loyalty is a function of the degree to which citizens identify with the state. A common language, a distinctive culture, and national symbols contribute to a sense of identity. These societal features improve the efficacy of the voice option and strengthen loyalty. As a result, nationality provides state leaders with greater discretion than would be justified by a strict calculus of individual interests. Thus, nation building goes hand in hand with state building. Within limits, nationalism can substitute for both capacity and legitimacy. It is the potent "civilizational" force evoked by Huntington. It channels elemental passions and unifies the scattered energies of the population, thus adding to the margin of freedom that state leaders enjoy in promoting the state interest (and/or their own selfish interests).

On the one hand, citizenship confers privileges. On the other hand, it creates obligations that allow the state to exact sacrifices from citizens. It makes taxation possible and it requires soldiers and policemen to take personal risks (and as a last resort to offer their lives) to protect the safety of the state and its citizens. Thus, the human yearning for cultural identity is harnessed by nation-states to protect their security. Conversely, the excesses of nationalism undermine international security by promoting aggression (as in Nazi Germany), while vulnerability to intra-state security problems arises where national borders are not aligned with cultural and ethnic cleavages (as in Cote d'Ivoire, Rwanda) and triggering events or opportunistic neighbors ignite violence.

In sum, development has to do with building capacity fast enough to keep up with changes in the external environment and in popular expectations. But without the resilience conferred by legitimacy (often achieved through the glue of national identity), the increment in capabilities that is needed to maintain social cohesion may be too large for development initiatives to provide. Similarly, in a state that cannot demonstrate capacity, by providing human security and delivering services, citizens' patience wears thin. As a result, state legitimacy is undermined and conflict occurs.

This conceptual framework gives equal weight to cultural, structural, and incentive factors in explaining conflict. National, ethnic, or religious identity facilitates social cohesion by building intra-group or intra-state loyalty but it can also be tapped to foment violent conflict among groups or states (clash of civilizations). Among citizens who lack the voice option, grievances build up. As presaged by the structural doctrine, unbalanced power relations that smother voice underlie the resort to coercion and violent backlash. Finally, resort to the extreme brand of exit (violence) can be explained simply in neoclassical economic terms of greed where the incentive framework makes rebellious violence the most profitable option.

The exit-voice-loyalty model is equally applicable if the notion of human security is defined as a judicious combination of opportunity (which allows exit from, as well as access to, the benefits of citizenship), empowerment (based on freedom of assembly and other civil rights that give voice to all citizens), and security (which generates loyalty to the group and the society). At the global level too, good governance can be defined in terms of fairness of opportunity (underlying the policy coherence for development initiative), empowerment (based on adequate participation by all countries in the formulation of global policies and standards), and security (grounded in the rule of international law).

Redefining State Fragility

We now have the conceptual apparatus needed to define state fragility.

According to Leo Tolstoy, "all happy families resemble each other and each unhappy family is unhappy in its own way." Frail and failing states exhibit diverse characteristics depending on whether or not they are internationally recognized, exercise control over substantial parts of the territory and polity, possess a monopoly over the means of coercion, and are willing and able to collect taxes to benefit the citizens (Gros, 1996). Warlords rule in anarchic states such as Somalia. Official authorities in shadow states have limited control over the territory, as in Afghanistan. Anemic states such as Liberia have suffered damage from conflict and cannot deliver adequate public goods and services to their populations. Captured states such as Haiti are ruled by (and for the benefit of) narrow elites. Aborted states such as Burundi have not consolidated.

Thus the fragile states and conflict-affected countries classified by the Development Assistance Committee of the OECD as "difficult partner countries" constitute a mixed group. Since country classifications are used for strategy formulation, resource allocation, and choice of policy instruments they matter for policy coherence. These classifications are currently inconsistent both within and across donor countries.

Within the United States, policy coherence within individual agencies is achieved at the expense of incoherence across agencies. Only geopolitical considerations apply to countries that the White House classifies as "strategic" states (such as Afghanistan, Egypt, Indonesia, Iraq, Jordan, or Pakistan).[11] By contrast, the United States Agency for International Development uses a combination of socioeconomic and political criteria to distinguish "development states" from fragile states. Finally, the Millennium Challenge Account reserves its resources for countries that are committed to good governance, respectful of human rights, compliant with the rule of law, supportive of market-oriented policies, capable of sound fiscal management, and dedicated to the inclusive provision of health and education services.

Incoherence problems also arise among donor countries. For example, DFID's development-oriented model of state fragility deliberately excludes countries' political characteristics.[12] This is at odds with USAID's approach, which gives pride of place to political legitimacy criteria. Nor is there any uniformity in the country classifications proposed by think tanks and academic institutions. At the multilateral level, a typology proposed for use by the UN Development Program takes account of domestic political characteristics in its country categories while avoiding references to policy performance indicators.[13]

This approach does not match that of the World Bank, which excludes explicitly political variables from its "low-income countries under stress" (LICUS) classification and puts major emphasis on assessments of policy performance. Specifically, the World Bank's LICUS criteria give weight to macroeconomic management, the strength of institutions, and the quality of governance.[14] The criteria combine verifiable quantitative indicators with qualitative judgments. Regrettably, the detailed country-level indicators have yet to be made public.

The different policy postures imply different criteria and different country classifications.[15] For example, the World Bank's exclusion of middle-income countries from its list of "countries under stress" leaves a significant gap while UNDP's comprehensive approach does not: the latter lists Algeria, Azerbaijan, Macedonia, Saudi Arabia, Venezuela, and Yugoslavia as countries worthy of "special attention."

Comparing these classifications, we see that criteria focused on policy performance yield entirely different implications for action from those focused on security, capacity, and legitimacy that are used by the Center for Global Development:[16]

(i) Six countries ranked at the top (first two quintiles) of the CPIA ratings have a security gap according to the Center for Global Development (Senegal, Sri Lanka, Uganda, Indonesia, Nepal, Rwanda).
(ii) Three countries at the top of the CPIA ratings have a legitimacy gap (Vietnam, Pakistan, Rwanda).
(iii) Eight countries at the top of the CPIA ratings have a capacity gap (Bhutan, Burkina Faso, India, Indonesia, Mali, Mauritania, Pakistan, Senegal).
(iv) Ten countries ranked in the first three quintiles of the CPIA ratings do not meet the criteria for the U.S. Millennium Challenge Account (Albania, Bangladesh, Malawi, Moldova, Mozambique, Benin, Burkina Faso, India, Mali, Mauritania).[17]
(v) Out of thirty-four countries on the World Bank list of low-income countries under stress, seven are not on UNDP's list of countries with special development needs.
(vi) Conversely, the UNDP lists twelve low-income countries with "special needs" that are not on the World Bank's LICUS list.

Differences in approaches are to be expected: donor countries' external relations march to different drummers, and international organizations have distinct mandates. But it is difficult to visualize substantive progress being made under the aegis of the Horizontal Program of Policy Coherence of the OECD if country typologies are not harmonized and the perspectives of developing countries are not explicitly taken into account.

Developing country policymakers have not had their concerns heeded. Donors' assessments of development outcomes still do not distinguish adequately between policy performance and the initial conditions and constraints that are imposed on developing countries by history and geography (for example conflict or natural resource dependence). Aid allocations are less sensitive to recipients' needs and potentials than they are to geopolitical and commercial concerns. This hypothesis is confirmed by the literature (Roodman, 2004a).

Developing country officials are equally critical of the unilateral "branding" of low-income countries by donors and its damaging consequences for the poorest and weakest countries. They are keenly uncomfortable with the interchangeable use of such terms as "low-income countries under stress," fragile states, and "difficult partnerships." Advocacy groups, too, express skepticism about the objectivity of the ratings that donors use to allocate aid (Nancy Alexander, 2004). They argue that the UN and the international financial institutions should monitor and evaluate the impact of rich countries' policies on developing countries (Millennium Development Goal 8) as systematically as they currently monitor the progress of developing countries towards MDGs 1-7.

Fragility is a Function of Capacity and Resilience

The definition of state fragility that we propose eschews judgments about precise forms of democratic government and, unlike some other models of state fragility, it does not conflate government performance with initial conditions (about which country authorities can do little) let alone ultimate outcomes (which are the object of donor engagement). Our proposed logic of state fragility helps to connect security and development strategies by focusing on the factors that need to guide capacity building as a result of donor engagement.

Labeling a state as fragile identifies it as a state with special needs, and there is a risk that lumping all fragile states together may encourage donors to disengage prematurely or to adopt "one size fits all" approaches.

Yet, different engagement strategies are warranted towards states that have: (i) both the leadership and the means to tackle poverty reduction; (ii) the leadership but not the means; (iii) the means but not the leadership; or (iv) neither leadership nor means (Torres and Anderson, 2004).

We selected indicators that differentiate countries according to their initial and structural conditions and we assessed the effects of these factors on security and development outcomes. We included per capita income, inequality, the ratio of debt to GDP, infant mortality, malnutrition, primary products dominance, and landlockedness in the definition of initial conditions.

These variables are highly influential in determining security and development outcomes: 68 percent of countries with unfavorable initial conditions deliver poor development outcomes and (coincidentally) 68 percent of them are insecure (table 2).

Next we linked capacity, measured in terms of delivery of public goods (immunization and literacy), with development (measured in terms of the Human Development Index). Finally, we related resilience (measured by ratings of voice and accountability and political freedom) with security (measured in terms of refugee outflows and conflict incidence).[18]

Based on their structural characteristics, out of 114 low- and middle-income countries for which published data were available, 13 are rated high both on the resilience and capacity scale (not fragile); 52 are rated high on one criterion and low on the other (fragile) and 49 are rated low on both counts (very fragile). States that are rated as not fragile are twice as likely to achieve good development performance as those rated very fragile (69 percent vs. 35 percent) and twice as likely to be secure (38 percent vs. 18 percent) (Table 3).

As presaged by the theory, states that rank high on capacity but low on resilience have a better chance of achieving a high development rating than states that rank low on capacity but high on resilience (45 percent vs. 38 percent). Conversely, they have a worse chance of achieving security (35 percent vs. 67 percent) (table 4).

Dealing with commitment deficits

How then should donor countries engage in difficult environments? Lumping weak, unstable, and misgoverned countries together within a single pool is inappropriate. The anatomy of risk varies from case to case and donor countries should fit their engagement to the circumstances.

Table 2
Share of Developing Countries with Favorable or Unfavorable Endowments Achieving Security or Development

	High Development		Low Development		High Security		Low Security	
	No.	Percent	No.	Percent	No.	Percent	No.	Percent
Favorable initial conditions (44)	26	59	18	41	17	39	27	61
Unfavorable initial conditions (70)	22	32	48	68	22	32	48	68
Total (114)	48	42	66	58	39	34	75	66

Table 3
Share of Fragile and not Fragile Developing Countries Achieving Security or Development

	High Development		Low Development		High Security		Low Security	
	No.	Percent	No.	Percent	No.	Percent	No.	Percent
Somewhat fragile (52)	22	42	30	58	25	48	27	52
Very fragile (49)	17	35	32	65	9	18	40	82
Subtotal fragile (101)	39	39	62	61	34	34	67	66
Not fragile (13)	9	69	4	31	5	38	8	62
Total (114)	48	42	66	58	39	34	75	66

Table 4
Impact of Capacity and Resilience on Security and Development

	High Development		Low Development		High Security		Low Security	
	No.	Percent	No.	Percent	No.	Percent	No.	Percent
High capacity/ low resilience (31)	14	45	17	55	11	35	20	65
Low capacity/ high resilience (21)	8	38	13	62	14	67	7	33
Total (52)	22	42	30	58	25	48	27	52

More often than not, the good and the bad coexist. Where external engagement is likely to do more harm than good, benign neglect is the right choice. But before doing so, the consequences of inaction should be weighed, including the potential humanitarian consequences and spillover effects on regional and global security.

To start with, a distinction should be drawn between "difficult partnerships" and fragile states. Poor management by donors may limit aid effectiveness, as for example when numerous project implementation units are set up and burden fragile administrations. Nor should a state's fragility be equated with lack of commitment to development. There are situations such as Afghanistan's where capacities are weak but domestic leadership is legitimate and motivated. In such circumstances donor passivity is unwarranted.

Unfortunately, commitment does not translate into capacity to deliver basic services. Capacities at various levels of government should be carefully assessed and partners selected accordingly. In the short- and medium term, use of donors' ad hoc delivery systems or non-state channels may be unavoidable. However, efforts should be made to align such arrangements with state processes and agencies to the extent feasible and with a view to nurturing the legitimacy of central and local authorities. Wherever possible, capacity building assistance should be provided to facilitate an orderly transition of service delivery back to the state apparatus.

Especially problematic are instances where holders of state authority lack legitimacy or commitment to development. In such cases, regime stability should not be an overriding consideration. Government representatives should not be treated as privileged interlocutors, though contacts with judiciously selected officials should be preserved, and their willingness to reform continuously tested. Alternative partners should be sought within the civil society and the private sector. This said, outside parties should not actively seek to destabilize a regime, given the unintended results that such social engineering from the outside may produce.

Restraint in providing incentives to non-state actors is highly desirable. Shrewd use of a range of instruments that mix positive incentives with dissuasion (and in some cases sanctions) can be effective if aid, trade, and security assistance are consistently calibrated to changes in behavior. Inconsistent signals, bombastic threats, and "stop-go" postures unconnected to results on the ground should be avoided. Recognition and incentives should be conditional on performance. Aid should be used with great circumspection and with adequate safeguards, and close fiduciary oversight should be maintained. Thus, even in "low commitment" environments the country-led approach should not be jettisoned. Instead, it should be reinterpreted.

Interaction with a wide range of actors in society can nurture political will, build local capacities, and encourage dialogue between the authorities and the civil society. Long-term, coherent, proactive, and flexible country strategies are needed in fragile states even more than elsewhere. Explicit assessments of the political force field, security risks, and development opportunities should guide the design of engagement strategies. Whatever the mix of instruments, the engagement should be grounded in the human assets and institutions that are in place, and it is best to adopt an evolutionary and incremental approach that helps donors harmonize aid practices.

C. New Policy Directions

A human security paradigm implies policy emphases that take account of the anatomy of conflict and its relationship to poverty. Poor countries are much more vulnerable to conflict than rich countries. Out of 20 countries with the lowest human development ratings in 2002, 16 were in conflict or just emerging from conflict. And though most terrorists are drawn from the middle classes, the ideologies they serve do not thrive in countries that have benefited from equitable and socially inclusive development.

Chapter 3 (section B) provided some evidence about the conflict-poverty nexus. The statistical correlation between violent conflict and underdevelopment is robust even though the political, economic, and social mechanisms that connect security and development are still poorly understood. One might conclude that to invest in development is to invest in security. But not every kind of development intervention meets the security imperative. In examining the types of policy needed, the following discussion emphasizes human security priorities. It calls for fine tuning of the human development agenda rather than its wholesale restructuring.

Poverty reduction strategies should emphasize safety nets and social protection

Accelerated economic growth remains a key development priority since it is critical to poverty reduction. Achieving the Millennium Development Goal of halving poverty by 2015 would require a doubling of the growth rates achieved over the past decade. Good macroeconomic performance is necessary but it is not sufficient. Inefficient public spending may undermine much of its gains. Social development is needed as well. In particular, reduction of inequality and improved gender equity matter—about 70 percent of the poorest are women.

Brazil, with its highly unequal income distribution, must grow three times faster than Vietnam to achieve the same average income increase among the poorest fifth of the population. Human security also requires a special emphasis on strengthening social safety nets. While poor people use extraordinary ingenuity in dealing with risk, they are vulnerable to illness and injury, crime and domestic violence, loss of employment, harvest failures, and price fluctuations. Widows and divorced women are especially at risk. So are children, especially girls, when incomes drop in poor households.

Seasonal income decline is a major cause of child labor and child malnutrition. All risks are intensified by old age. Improved public expenditure management, equitable access to infrastructure and social services, and social safety nets are characteristic of pro-poor economic strategies. To succeed, such strategies require the empowerment of poor and disadvantaged people and their substantive participation in the public decisions that affect their lives. Risks can be mitigated through diversification, savings, and insurance but extreme poverty usually means a desperate need for external support.

Group-based mechanisms of risk sharing and mutual support help a great deal and public policy should encourage their spread. Trading can also stimulate diversification and risk management. But without safety nets, market liberalization can have mixed effects and hurt poor people. Ultimately, increased public intervention (through for example health insurance, old age assistance, workfare programs, social funds, microfinance facilities, and cash transfers) is the key to managing household risks, and this calls for a sound fiscal regime.

Youth unemployment raises risk of conflict

Demography has been sorely neglected in security and development policy formulation. This is because conflict and its consequences involve large, abrupt, and often surprising changes whereas demographic shifts tend to be slow, deliberate, and relatively predictable. From a human security perspective, population trends are critical since, in combination with other factors, they create the conditions that radical leaders exploit to foment unrest and violence. The development process invariably involves a demographic transition when lives lengthen and average family sizes decline. About a third of the world's countries, home to 1.5 billion people, are in the early stage of this transition, which is characterized by a youth bulge, that is, a large share of young adults in the population.

Countries at this stage of the transition are nearly 2.5 times more likely than other countries to experience a civil war. In most of them, growth is not sufficient to create enough jobs for the expanding labor force. Their unemployment rates are 3-5 times higher than the average for developing countries. Among job seekers, young adult males are least likely to find work and most likely to resort to violence in response to their deprivation. Especially where the state is weak and cannot manage social tensions, the combination of low growth and high fertility is highly combustible, especially where urbanization rates are high. The effects of youth bulges are worsened by mortality from HIV/AIDS and related diseases, which begins to strike young adults in the 20-24 year age range, jumps in the late 20s, and peaks through the 30s. Communicable diseases lead to premature deaths among key professionals such as teachers, technicians, military personnel, and police officers, and leave behind millions of under-uneducated and under-supervised youths and orphans.

Political and demographic analyses should be combined in assessing human security priorities. The State Failure Task Force funded by the

U.S. Central Intelligence Agency has established that illiberal democracies are more vulnerable to state failure than either fully democratic or authoritarian regimes, because economic liberalization in its early phases provides conditions for rapid enrichment of market-savvy minorities who may exacerbate social resentments and ethnic tensions. These vulnerabilities are amplified in countries in an early phase of the demographic transition.

The policy implications of these findings are straightforward. Population policies should be designed to accelerate the demographic transition, for example by favoring girls' education, family planning, women's rights, and gender sensitivity in other policy areas. Promotion of employment reduces the risks of conflict. Hence, economic policy should focus on providing enabling environments for rural development, small and medium enterprises, and vocational training. Trade policies, foreign direct investment, credit programs, and infrastructure development should also be geared to job creation. Emphasis on job training in deprived urban areas and community-based initiatives is especially useful as it combines the creation of social capital with the provision of jobs.

Hunger undermines human security

A critical aspect of human security is food security. Hunger lies at the intersection of poverty and conflict. The number of food emergencies has risen from about 15 a year in the 1980s to more than 30 a year since the turn of the millennium. Most of the increase has been in Africa, where the share of food emergencies attributable to human causes (violent conflict, sub-standard economic performance) has doubled over the past two decades.[19] Remarkably, East Africa is the part of the continent most affected by hunger, even though it is less vulnerable to bad weather than the Sahel. This is because hunger is more a consequence than a cause of the violent intra-state conflicts that have sprung up in frail and failed states.

Eradicating hunger is central to the vision of a world free of poverty. Despite rapid urbanization, a majority of the world's population still lives in rural areas.[20] Given the forward links from agriculture to the rest of the economy, agriculture contributes twice as much to national income than predicted by its share in GDP (de Ferranti and others, 2005). Between 1950 and 2000 world grain production more than tripled, from 590 million to more than 2,000 million tons a year. But over the past five years, grain output has been flat, while population has risen, driving down grain stocks and raising prices.

Poor nutrition is an underlying cause in more than half the cases of child mortality. Every day 17,000 children die of malnutrition. About 850 million people go to bed hungry every night. The opportunity cost of current levels of hunger and malnutrition in developing countries amounts to about USD 500 billion a year in present value terms (FAO, 2004). Overall progress towards the Millennium Development Goal of halving the number of chronically hungry people by the year 2015 has been slow and halting. In fact, the number of hungry people has risen over the latest five years for which data are available.

But there are bright spots: 30 developing countries representing half of the world's population have made major progress against crippling poverty and hunger over the past five years. There is no mystery about how they have achieved this: an average agricultural growth rate of 3.2 percent, almost one third faster than that of the average developing country. This kind of progress could be replicated across the board with appropriate food and agricultural policies and external support.

Food security requires rural development and science-based agriculture

The links between rural development and food security are complex. Hunger and malnutrition deter children from attending school and stunt their learning capacity when they do attend. Lack of rural education reduces agricultural productivity and makes children more vulnerable to extreme poverty. Managing health risks is an equally essential part of the hunger challenge. Diseases move across borders through travel, trade, migration, and refugee movements. Malnutrition also makes people more vulnerable to disease.[21] In turn, pandemics such as HIV/AIDS devastate farm production by killing young adults during their most productive years, eventually undermining the economy and threatening social stability.

Land tenure is central to human security. Lopsided land ownership in agrarian societies (such as Bolivia, Colombia, Kenya, South Africa, Zimbabwe) produces inequalities and social tensions that fuel resentment and lawlessness. Increased land values resulting from irrigation investments, mineral exploration, or forest concessions can lead to land grabs where ownership rights are tenuous and the rule of law fickle. Disputes among different ethnic groups with incompatible requirements for (and/or inequitable access to) arable land, water, forests, or fisheries tend to escalate as the natural resource gets depleted. This has been a significant factor behind local conflicts in Brazil, Cote d'Ivoire, Haiti, Mexico, Nigeria, Pakistan, the Philippines, and Rwanda. In Darfur, such violence has forced at least 1.2 million people from their homes and fields.

Loss of agricultural diversity and emerging animal diseases constitute major risks to food security and public health. Industrial agriculture gives pathogens greater opportunities to infect the food chain and ultimately human health, as in the case of avian flu. Factory farming exacerbates the rapid movement of animal diseases and food-borne infections.

Biotechnology might be able to solve problems that traditional technology cannot solve in a cost-effective fashion. Technologies exist to control the inherent risks posed by genetically modified organisms, but appropriate legislation and verification are needed to ensure the safe transfer, handling, use, and disposal of such organisms and their products, taking account of local ecological conditions following competent risk assessments, so as to avoid driving entire species to extinction.

Conceivably, biotechnology will one day allow the cost-effective production of tropical export commodities in the laboratory, replacing products that are now produced in poor countries. This would have disastrous implications for poor countries, which would require major assistance for economic diversification.

Adequate compensation for the use by the North of the indigenous genetic resources of the South is another important global policy priority. The recently approved International Treaty on Plant Genetic Resources for Food and Agriculture does not specify a clear role for governments in protecting genetic resources or contain a clear statement about farmers' rights to save and exchange seeds.

Education is the bedrock of human security

Education is an essential ingredient of peace and prosperity since it enhances human capabilities to reflect, make choices, and secure a better life. While there are instances where inflammatory material and religious intolerance have tainted school curricula, most investments in education promote social cohesion and good citizenship. Education is the key to productivity since growing economies thrive on knowledge and ideas. Equitable access to schooling reduces social and economic inequality.

Higher education is essential as a breeding ground for development leaders and managers.

Two United Nations conventions have recognized basic education as a human right. Yet 17 percent of adults cannot read or write, 20 percent of children in the 6-11 year age bracket are not in school, and 25 percent of pupils drop out before completing five years of schooling. The overall quality of schooling in the developing world is poor and tends to decline as efforts are made to increase enrollment. Most of the world's out-of-school children are in Asia and Africa.

In the least developed countries, adult illiteracy is 47 percent. Displaced populations, refugees, and disabled people are especially at risk of reaching adulthood without learning to read and write. Gender inequality is another major issue: 60 percent of the out-of-school children are girls. Yet investment in basic education for girls has very high returns. This is because women put their knowledge to work not only by securing gainful employment but also by opting for fewer children, improving family nutrition and hygiene, and enhancing the quality of child rearing.

Basic education boosts the returns to land and other assets. It is also a tool of empowerment and a source of social capital. Schools provide convenient platforms for community development interventions, feeding programs, health education classes, and immunization campaigns. Achieving worldwide primary schooling by 2015 would require a switch of less than four days' worth of military expenditures a year towards basic education. Along with increased budgetary allocations to education, education quality matters as well as improved safety and affordability of schooling, parents' oversight of school administration, and effective management of educational expenditures.

A key imbalance in the progress of globalization can be traced to the digital divide. The number of phone lines per 100 people in the least developed countries is only 3-4 percent of that in rich countries; there are more telephone lines in Tokyo than in Sub-Sahara Africa. Within developing countries, a heavy urban bias prevails—in Nepal, for example, a ratio of 100 to 1 telephone lines in cities versus the countryside. Poor countries only have 5 percent of the world's Internet hosts, and the whole of Africa has only 0.25 percent. Internet traffic between the United States and Europe is 100 times the level directed to Africa and 30 times the level directed to Latin America. Improving the connectivity and knowledge base of poor countries and making effective use of the new technologies to extend the reach of education and commerce in poor and neglected areas should have priority.

Finally, the introduction of intellectual property protection under the aegis of the World Trade Organization needs reconsideration. As noted in Chapter 2, the restriction in the flow of knowledge resulting from the Agreement on Trade-related Intellectual Property Rights will be very damaging to the poorest countries. These countries depend heavily on importing knowledge; they cannot aspire to reap the innovation benefits that intellectual property protection generates. Patent protection will raise the prices charged for medicines and other knowledge-intensive products. It will also deter the import of technologies that are badly needed to promote agricultural and industrial development.

Protection against disease is the acid test

Poor health may be the greatest threat to human security and also one that can be tackled most readily with increased financial resources. According to the World Health Organization, in 2002, communicable diseases accounted for 26 percent of all worldwide deaths, compared to 0.3 percent for conflict (WHO, 2004). Battles over infectious disease have been won (notably against smallpox) but the war continues.

Traditional diseases such as tuberculosis, cholera, and malaria have not been eradicated. Indeed, they have spread while devastating new threats such as HIV/AIDS, hepatitis C, and ebola have emerged. HIV/AIDS has become the fourth major cause of death: the devastation has only started, even though the disease has already claimed more than 20 million deaths and infected 40 million people. In Africa, life expectancy is now 47 years, compared to 62 years had there been no HIV/AIDS pandemic.

Mass air travel and vastly increased trade flows are speeding the transmission of disease and making it harder to control. In late 2002, the SARS virus jumped from animals to people in Southern China and spread to 29 countries within six months. Thankfully, the outbreak caused relatively few casualties (800 deaths) because simple measures such as surgical masks were sufficient to arrest its spread. A more easily transmitted virus could have caused many more deaths.

Prevention could avoid most of the 10.6 million deaths of children that occur annually. Vaccination for eight diseases could save 2.3 million lives a year in poor countries. Provision of clean water and sanitation would drastically improve health in poor countries. Meeting family planning needs, and providing for safe abortions and adequate antenatal care, should also have priority: complications from childbirth are the leading cause of death and disability among women in poor countries, who face a risk 38 times higher than women in rich countries. Preventable maternal death creates a million motherless children a year.

Disease and poverty are highly correlated. Poor countries account for 90 percent of diseases and only 11 percent of health spending. Per capita health spending is 800 times higher in the United States than in Niger. Research and development spending in health is skewed against the problems of the poor. And only one percent of the drugs that reach the global market are targeted to tropical diseases that account for the greatest number of casualties.

In sum, disease control and eradication will require far better coordination between rich and poor countries and far more effective health systems in fragile states. The havoc that a new and evolving strain of avian influenza (H5N1) could wreak if it were to mutate and acquire a capacity for human transmission is almost unimaginable: the United States alone could experience 80 million illnesses and 16 million deaths. The resulting pandemic would trigger highly disruptive quarantines that would severely disrupt trade, travel, and economic activity and cause a global economic depression (Garrett, 2005).

Scarcity of Natural Resources Is Not Necessarily a Source of Conflict

About 1.4 billion people in developing countries live in fragile environments. A combination of natural resource depletion and population growth has induced large-scale population movements and increased competition for access to land, water, jobs, and social services among identity groups. Competing demands over natural resources can fuel discord especially when the structure of ownership is skewed, rights to land are contested, and the claimants (for example farmers, pastoralists, ranchers, miners) belong to different ethnic groups.

Pressure on scarce natural resources is bound to increase further as climate change produces floods, droughts, and heat waves. Land disputes can be aggravated by infrastructure investment (for example for irrigation and transport) that increases land values in areas where land ownership rights are tenuous, allowing poor farmers to be displaced by rich farmers and powerful politicians. Development may also cause more intense land use and deprive nomadic communities of traditional grazing rights. By

2015, 40 percent of the projected world population will live in water-stressed countries. Worldwide, more than 400 million people face water scarcity and by 2025, 3 billion people may be short of water.

Disputes over the management of scarce natural resources such as water can lead to hostilities. But this is not always the case. Indeed, mutual dependence on a shared resource may elicit cooperation rather than violent competition in traditional societies, under modern governments, or even across borders and among adversaries (Jägerskog, 2003). This is illustrated by the peaceful sharing of international waters. The territories of 145 nations fall within international basins, and some 33 countries are located primarily within these basins (Wolf and others, 2005). History confirms that the interdependence that results from the need to share water has induced negotiated agreements and informal understandings even among bitter rivals (Jordan and Israel; Mekong riparians; Nile Basin riparians; India and Pakistan).

On the premise that communities and nations can build confidence with each other by joint efforts to improve the state and management of nature, the United Nations Environment Program, the United Nations Development Program, and the Organization for Security and Cooperation in Europe have sponsored a collaborative program involving governments, academia, and civil society. This is designed to increase cooperation within communities and across borders in Central and Eastern Europe, Central Asia, and the Southern Caucasus by assessing the interdependence of natural environment and human security, identifying environmental and conflict hot spots, disseminating the results of assessments, raising public awareness, and delivering assistance for building capacity.[22]

Abundance of natural resources is not always a curse

Exploitation of natural resources (oil, minerals, metals, diamonds, timber, and drugs) has been at stake in a quarter of 50 recent wars (Renner 2002). Illicit resource extraction has supplied warlords with resources to purchase arms and recruit combatants. The lure of easy profits has also induced military incursions by neighbors, as in the Democratic Republic of Congo. Protracted conflict over valuable resources has become a common feature of the post-Cold War environment in fragile states. Neighboring countries and private interests often play a role in these violent contests. Conversely, external intervention may hold the key to their resolution, as in Angola and Sierra Leone.

Statistically, conflict is more frequent in autocratic countries highly dependent on extractive industries. In such environments, local elites may capture the bulk of revenues, thus making domestic taxation redundant and weakening the social contract between the rulers and the ruled. But, as illustrated by now-developed countries (as well as by Botswana and Chile) there is no good reason why oil, gas, and mining resources should be a curse. They have been a blessing under governance systems able to mediate competing claims and provide a suitable enabling environment for their profitable extraction, processing, and use.

To be sure, keeping the engine of the world economy in high gear requires a steady flow of oil and minerals. Abundant natural resources in fragile states can be a source of corruption and inequality if the proceeds derived from their extraction go to enrich corrupt elites while local communities are left to bear the costs of environmental damage and social disruption. More ominously, controlling the taxes and royalties derived from natural resource extraction may allow authoritarian leaders to remain in power without regard to the needs and aspirations of their citizens. Some poorly led countries also benefit from international competition for access to oil supplies. This provides them with political leverage and shields them from international pressure regarding their human rights violations.

All of these problems are potentially soluble. The involvement of foreign companies in natural resource extraction has led to scrutiny by advocacy groups that have promoted public awareness of the links between natural resources, conflict, and corruption. The resulting public pressures have made multinational companies more sensitive to their social responsibilities. Safeguard policies have been designed to ensure that project finance by development agencies and banks is contingent on compliance with social and environmental sustainability safeguards.

Unfortunately, transparency without accountability has limits. The United Kingdom has taken the lead in inducing companies to "publish what they pay" and in encouraging poor countries' governments to disclose the allocation of their public expenditures. But it is far from clear that the Extractive Industry Transparency Initiative[23] will have more than symbolic value in the weak governance environments where it is most needed. Equally, efforts to control the marketing of diamonds, timber, and other products through registration (as in the Kimberley process) may have only a slightly positive impact on conflict prevention, given the weakness of domestic enforcement and the alternative sources of illegal gain that are available to warlords and criminals. Here again, the only durable solution lies in long-term state building, democracy development, and international cooperation on security matters.

Natural disaster prevention is an integral part of the human security agenda

Natural disasters have become more common and more serious. Twice as many were reported in the 1990s as in the 1970s.[24] They are more frequent and cause far more casualties in poor countries than in rich. More than 53 percent of natural disaster deaths occur in countries classified as having low human development, even though these countries are home to only 11 percent of the people exposed to natural hazards. Natural disasters affect poor people disproportionately since they are compelled to settle in marginal lands and cannot afford secure housing.

Thus the Asian *tsunami* threw two million people below the poverty line. Most of the directly affected people were cultivators and fishermen who eked out a living in remote and disadvantaged areas largely bypassed by development.[25] Similarly, most of the areas affected by the Kashmir earthquake of October 2005 were in remote mountainous regions that were cut off by landslides. In this tragic event, about 75,000 people died and an estimated 3.3 million were left homeless; damage was estimated at about USD 5 billion.

For individuals, nations, and institutions, crises constitute a litmus test of capacity and resilience. Asian governments have demonstrated good economic management skills and the business sector in the region is adaptable and resilient. Compared to the 1997-98 financial crisis or the SARS epidemic, the aggregate macroeconomic impact of the *tsunami* on the regional economy has been modest. The event has not created major economic uncertainty or a loss of business confidence.

The response of the international community to the *tsunami* was remarkable. Corporations, individuals, governments, and multilateral agencies pledged USD 6-7 billion in aid in an extraordinary demonstration of solidarity.[26] The loss of life from the *tsunami* was enormous (about 283,000 deaths) but it could have been many times worse. In most natural disasters, the number of injured is 3-5 times the number of deaths, but in this case, the ratios were reversed and relief officials concentrated on sanitary disposal of corpses and on distributing clean water, digging latrines, and vaccinating children. The strategy paid off.

Not all natural hazards turn into natural disasters; exposure to risk results in heavy losses and fatalities only if a society is vulnerable. In turn, vulnerability can be mitigated or in some instances completely eliminated by early warning, disaster preparedness, and skilled emergency management. Adaptive capacity that reduces the human cost of disasters is correlated with democracy and a free press. It is also a function of the quality of social services, the availability of transport infrastructure, and the size and openness of the economy.

D. Reforming aid

By now, the aid business is under severe stress. Despite recent increments in the volume of aid, the amounts are inadequate to deal with the increasingly complex and far-flung aid agenda. Official development assistance now stands at about 0.25 percent of GDP of donor countries and accounts for less than 0.8 percent of the gross national income of all developing countries, or about 4 percent of their government expenditures. For the least developed countries, inflows of official development assistance have shrunk from 12 percent to 7.5 percent of GDP while debt service is about 3 percent of GDP. Debt reduction policies are highly restrictive. Declining terms of trade have meant that capital has flowed out of rather than into Africa. Administrative costs absorb 6-7 percent of aid flows.

Untied aid accounts for only 41 percent of total aid. This means that about USD 5 billion a year is spent on needless mark-ups for goods and services. Much of the technical assistance that is funded by aid (especially involving resident experts) is perceived by recipients as expensive, donor driven, and commercially or politically motivated. Poor aid coordination and fragmentation contribute to inefficiency in aid delivery.[27,28] Finally, aid is misdirected: the least developed countries get less than 30 percent of the aid[29], and the share of aid allocated to basic social services is about half of that recommended by the United Nations. Together, these failings have led critical observers to apply a discount to the value of aid.[30]

Most development practitioners endorse the view that better aid is at least as important as more aid. But the notion that most aid is wasted is wrong. There is solid evidence that aid favors economic growth. Much of the past research on aid and growth engendered aid pessimism because it examined the impact of aid over too short a period and/or included humanitarian aid—which is negatively correlated with growth, since it is given in times of crisis. Recent work at the Center for Global Development shows that aid that is designed to have a positive impact within four years (whether in the form of budget support or the lending for infrastructure, industry, or agriculture that accounts for more than half of all aid flows) has a large and positive impact on growth (Clemens and others, 2004). In the typical aid-recipient country, every dollar of aid raises output by USD 1.64 in present value terms.

This correlation is highly significant and robust. Remarkably, it is not sensitive to the quality of policies or the level of income. The impact of aid on growth is somewhat larger where institutions are strong and/or health indicators are favorable. On the other hand, as highlighted by recent research by the International Monetary Fund (Rajan and Subramanian, 2005), the impact on growth can be reduced when aid exceeds absorptive capacities and Dutch disease sets in.

Aid instruments, methods, and skills

Assessing the quality of aid in troubled and fragile countries is tricky both because data are poor and because we do not know what would have happened without aid. But to suspend aid efforts in low-income countries that are not performing, because they labor under the handicap of poor governance and a fragmented social order, is to play a game of Russian roulette with peace and stability.

In failing and recovering states, effective aid recognizes that post-conflict reconstruction is mostly about people and institutions. It focuses on healing social wounds, building capacity, and transferring skills, and uses private and nongovernmental channels. In particular, in shadow states, special aid modalities are required to ensure effective engagement. Arguably, the Rwanda tragedy and the Darfur crisis might have been averted had aid been of sufficient scale, properly targeted and effectively managed, to enhance sustainable rural livelihoods and to reduce the social tensions around land use.

How then should aid instruments, methods, and skills be adapted to weak institutional environments? Pious mantras regarding ownership, partnership, and results orientation do not help produce results in fragile states. Investments in the security sector normally have a high priority in such environments, but steps must be taken to prevent military and police assets from being used for political repression and oppression. Large revenue-producing projects may deserve support but not in the absence of sound systems for managing public spending. Assistance for democratic elections should be promoted but not if they are likely to destabilize the society.

The project vehicle, which lost favor in the era of policy-based lending, is a highly suitable one for assisting weak states. Sachs (2005) describes "on the ground" solutions for ending poverty in poverty-stricken villages and urban neighborhoods, and he unveils a "new" approach to development policy formulation: "clinical economics." The methods he describes have merit, but they are not in fact new, since they replicate in precise detail the approaches that aid practitioners have long been using to identify development interventions suitable for external funding.

Already in 1967, Hirschman, based on his acute field observations of interventions financed by the World Bank, had identified projects as "privileged particles of development" that can have an enormous impact on society (Hirschman, 1995b). They do so, he observed, by empowering officials to embark on far-sighted development ventures, with the help of side effects (which he considered central to their justification), "trait making" characteristics (actions, admittedly hard to achieve, that would not have been adopted without the aid), and the "narrow latitudes" (constraints on errant behavior) that they induce, with a beneficial impact on public sector performance.

For social interventions that scale up promising pilot interventions, development projects (with features adapted to the risky conditions of weak states) should regain the luster they have lost. Certainly policy-based lending retains an important place in the development toolkit. But it is equally true—if still politically incorrect—that large infrastructure projects that have strategic value, and can be executed through transparent bidding procedures by autonomous project implementation units, are entirely appropriate in the tough operating environments of weak, failing, or post-conflict states.

Secure access to the natural resources required to fuel the global economy is a strategic imperative for OECD countries and now for the energy-hungry Asian giants. Regions at risk of conflict or already affected by conflict include countries with abundant oil, gas, metals, minerals, and timber resources where governance is weak or failing. Rather than assuming that natural resources constitute a curse, aid agencies ought to adopt can-do attitudes geared to better public revenue management, transparency of royalty payments, and the participation of local communities. They will thus help to improve the quality of foreign direct investment and assist poor countries to achieve sustainable development by converting natural capital efficiently into physical and human capital.

To this end, aid agencies should seek new partners and pragmatic solutions. They should maintain tough fiduciary standards when relying on government agencies in partner countries, and channel aid through private companies and NGOs while maintaining links with state agencies and processes. Partnerships with private mining and oil companies that incorporate fair royalty arrangements, transparent use of revenues, and strict implementation of social and environmental safeguards should be encouraged, in order to kick-start moribund economies and provide the revenues needed to deliver social services.

It goes without saying that the misguided aid practices of the Cold War era should not be reinstated. Instead, the capacity of aid professionals to operate effectively in conflict-prone, conflict-affected, and post-conflict countries should be dramatically enhanced. Few aid agencies are well equipped to deal with core issues of regional inequities, ethnic imbalances, and group antagonisms. The artificial wall that has been erected between economic assessment and political analysis should be dismantled.

Conditionality is often needed to provide an incentive for good performance but it should be used sparingly. Aid officials have often succumbed to the temptation of "big bang" reform packages in post-conflict situations, when governments are weak and still unrepresentative. To be sure, policy-based operations have a role to play in transferring resources, helping to strengthen or re-establish core economic ministries, and locking in basic principles of sound economic management. But these operations may exacerbate conflict and destabilize fragile governments if they involve, as they often do, shifts in resources among competing groups and if, given the law of unintended consequences, they favor one faction over the other in a conflict (Muscat, 2002).

In short, subsidy reductions, fiscal reforms, and reallocation of public expenditures can have enormous political repercussions and hence should be subjected to critical scrutiny from a conflict-prevention perspective. Finally, where states have collapsed (as in Somalia), aid agencies should accept a modified concept of sovereignty that allows their official interaction with de facto governmental entities over a period of time. The human cost of awaiting the restoration of territorial integrity may be too high. In general, aid will have to be conceived not only as an incentive for good policy performance but also as an instrument for building capacity and managing conflict.

Risks will need to be taken for peace, and the current aid consensus will need to be realigned towards a development model where institutional constraints matter as much as policy distortions, and where good governance is the *objective* of the development enterprise, rather than its precondition. This will require substantial increments of aid focused on conflict prevention, post-conflict rehabilitation and reconstruction, and security sector reform. Coordinated engagement by external actors in support of well-conceived country strategies that are "owned" by all parties is fundamental. Diplomacy should support the objectives of aid, instead of aid supporting the objectives of diplomacy.

In sum, with concern for security now a public policy imperative, new analytical thinking about aid is needed. Aid policy reform now focuses on enhancing aid efficiency, by reducing transaction costs; untying procurement; reforming technical assistance; harmonizing procurement, disbursement, and fiduciary practices; streamlining and effectively monitoring safeguard policies; consolidating aid delivery channels; and strengthening coordination. These are critical aims for the future of aid and its effectiveness, but aid efficiency is not the same as aid effectiveness. Quality aid focused on fragile states should also have a priority claim on resources since it may prevent the onset of prohibitively costly conflicts. Of course, security-oriented development cooperation in weak states will not be cheap to administer. Nor will it be readily amenable to common pool funding of country budgets by donors. Achievement of results will require adequate time and substantial resources.

Prevention is cheaper than cure

Aid should be fashioned to become an effective instrument of conflict prevention. Just as public health policy goes beyond curative measures to embrace prevention, security policy should reach out to the enabling environment within which violence breeds. The rising share of aid flows allocated to humanitarian ends and post-conflict reconstruction is a reflection of inadequate investments in conflict prevention. Some 50,000 "blue helmets" are taking part in 17 UN peacekeeping operations around the world.

According to Rotberg (2003), unless the wealthy arbiters of world security provide aid to states that are prone to failure... "the common ingredients of zero-sum leadership; ethnic, linguistic, and religious antagonisms and fears; chauvinistic ambition; economic insufficiency; and inherited fragility will continue to propel nation-states from weakness toward failure. In turn, that failure will be costly in terms of humanitarian relief and post-conflict reconstruction." Given the heavy costs of war and its aftermath, providing capacity building assistance to conflict-prone states may be risky but it is less risky than not providing it. Resources spent on conflict mediation and reconciliation represent investments in peace and prosperity. Neutral facilitation is a better option for nurturing a sustainable peace than backing the friendlier faction. Taking sides was the course tried during the Cold War; it made bloody conflicts bloodier and longer and led to higher reparation and reconstruction costs down the line.

Prudence dictates well targeted aid, not inaction, to help avoid state failure and its likely consequences: growing poverty, violent conflict, large-scale population displacement, and sanctuaries for criminal and terrorist enterprises. Aid priorities should be tailored to country circumstances to strengthen core institutions of governance and trigger restorative mechanisms for society. For example, aid can support positive leadership at the local, regional, and national levels, encourage productive links with diaspora entrepreneurs, remove transport and communications bottlenecks that isolate poor regions and communities from the national economy, assist rural development and slum improvement through grassroots initiatives and, above all, assist projects that protect or benefit economically disadvantaged or repressed ethnic groups while avoiding projects that may reinforce inequalities.

After a conflict, alternatives to reconstruction aid exist but they are unpalatable (Hamre and Sullivan, 2003). Doing nothing would not be in line with the poverty reduction mandate of aid, given that 19 of the world's 20 poorest countries are experiencing or have recently emerged from armed conflict. The "do nothing" option does not prevent the creation of terrorist sanctuaries or the likelihood of renewed conflict with its destabilizing effects on neighboring states. Quarantine involves heavy intelligence, monitoring, and interception costs but it does not remove the cause of instability. Oversight by a regional grouping helps but it can only be sustained in conjunction with reconstruction. Carving up the state among neighbors or allowing its dissolution may lead to renewed warfare or unviable and unstable units. Absorption within a larger union is appealing but it is only a realistic option for countries that border the EU and have reasonable prospects for accession.

Most violent conflicts result from a combination of precipitating and underlying causes. While the former may respond to diplomatic solutions, the latter require treatment of root or structural problems. The actions needed may range from reducing poverty, inequality, and resource scarcity to reforming governance, removing political repression, and protecting human rights. But it is futile to equate conflict prevention with the treatment of all possible economic and social ailments; doing so encourages fragmentation of efforts, while actions that should receive priority to defuse a conflict may languish.

Hence, as aid adapts to its conflict prevention role, sharp analytical distinctions will need to be drawn between structural prevention, early prevention, late prevention, conflict management, and peacebuilding. Prevention that addresses structural causes is part and parcel of development strategies to promote human security. Early prevention emerges as the best means of conflict prevention. It relies on preventive diplomacy and targeted development assistance and spares the international community a choice between respect for national sovereignty and the duty to intervene to protect the innocent.

Thus understood, conflict prevention is a chain with six major links: (i) predictive intelligence and analytical capacity, (ii) early warning system, (iii) toolbox of preventive methods, (iv) strategic framework for decision making, (v) capacity to respond, and (vi) political will to undertake preventive action (Menkhaus, 2004). The first two of these links have received extensive scrutiny. Intelligence services are being criticized both for failing to cry wolf (9/11) and for crying wolf prematurely (as in the search for weapons of mass destruction in Iraq). The reliability of intelligence data declines as the intensity of domestic power contests rises. The sheer mass of intelligence data hinders interpretation. Human intelligence is often at a premium as multiple dots are identified but remain unconnected. Predictive models predicated on systemic variables tend to predict trouble everywhere. Even the best intelligence-gathering apparatus cannot eliminate all the uncertainties.

Still, much progress has been made in building early warning capacities, and through the hard-won lessons of history a toolkit has been assembled to facilitate prevention. Equally, a variety of multi-actor models are available to help coordinate the response. With the right skills and the right incentives, preventive diplomacy can help turn spoilers into stakeholders. Conflict prevention aid can help improve governance, capacity building, and social development. It can also help to remedy social grievances and facilitate the proactive and principled involvement of non-state actors such as nongovernmental organizations and private entities. Small arms monitoring, embargoes, and targeted sanctions are also part of the arsenal, along with preventive deployment of forces as the last resort.

The weakest links in the chain are the political will to act and the strategic capacity to design a response. Advocacy, political pressure, and the promotion of a culture of prevention can nurture political will. This requires shared norms, shared definitions, and shared parameters. Equally, filling the strategic deficit in peacebuilding and conflict prevention is a fundamental priority. Conflict prevention strategies should be adapted to the local environment by involving domestic actors, adopting their terminologies, and respecting their distinctive cultural traditions. The civil society has a special role to play in changing public attitudes and facilitating reconciliation.

Post-conflict aid should heed the lessons of experience

Several lessons of experience should be applied to post-conflict rehabilitation and reconstruction aid (OECD/DAC, 1998). First, post-conflict assistance should be designed to promote four distinct goals: (i) public safety, (ii) reconciliation and justice, (iii) economic and social well being, and (iv) reform of governance. Second, integrating military, political, economic, social, and humanitarian goals is a delicate endeavor that requires a legitimate authority with good domestic leadership and generous external assistance. Acceptable security is the lynchpin of reconstruction, but healing the wounds of war through justice and reconciliation matters too. Third, effective coordination between donors and building the capacity of local agencies are more important than speedy implementation. Fourth, plans for reconstruction should be based on sound damage assessments and properly sequenced interventions that display early results and provide for the return of displaced populations and their reintegration into society.

The conversion of military assets for civilian use is an important and complex aspect of the fragile transition from war to peace (Brzoska, 2003a). Realizing a peace dividend is not straightforward. Many of the resources used for war (military installations, small arms) are of little use in peacetime. The reduction of military establishments may ease tensions and build public confidence but it may also undercut the ability to meet legitimate national security needs. Conversion of arms production enterprises to civilian purposes raises complex issues of commercial feasibility and public sector restructuring.

Sharp reductions of military spending and rapid demobilization may have the unintended effects of privatizing violence and undermining security, if unemployed soldiers turn to criminal activity in order to survive (see Chapter 5 below). Collection and disposal of weapons requires careful planning and good community relations. Recruitment of former soldiers into the police and private security forces calls for retraining programs. Reintegration of ex-combatants into the fabric of civilian society requires investments in shelter, health support, counseling, transport, registration, subsistence, training, credit facilities, referral to private sector employers, and so forth. The reinsertion of child soldiers into their families and communities requires special support programs.

Security sector reform should be mainstreamed in development programs

The concept of security sector reform is not new (Ball, 1988), but it did not gain prominence until a seminal speech by Clare Short in 1998 and it was not codified in policy statements until quite recently (DFID, 2000; 2002; 2003). Yet security sector reform is often essential to re-establish or consolidate a state's monopoly of violence. It is also central to the long-term objective of achieving democratic governance over the armed forces—an acid test of democratic reform (Brzoska, 2003b).

Despite its importance for peace and prosperity, the adoption of security sector reform as a regular feature of development aid has lagged. There is considerable skepticism about external involvement in the sovereign affairs of recipient countries. Inter-agency rivalry has intervened to hinder such initiatives in bilateral aid programs. Legal constraints (whether real or contrived) as well as political opposition by important shareholders have prevented the World Bank from becoming comprehensively involved in security sector reform, especially the military aspects.

To be sure, the evolution of aid policy towards comprehensive development frameworks (connected to the advent of debt reduction programs and poverty reduction strategies) has sharpened the focus on releasing fiscal resources to meet social expenditure targets, and this in turn has raised the pressure to reduce military spending. Equally, transparency in public spending has become an acid test of good governance.

But security sector reform has yet to assume the status of a regular sector for aid donors. This is the case even though security is the most crucial service provided by government and no assessment of public expenditure is complete without an examination of the efficacy of security services. Revealingly, respect for the dignity of poor people, and responsiveness of police officials to the needs of low-income neighborhoods, have emerged as major public demands in opinion surveys of poor people.

Current aid allocation patterns do not promote security

While aid is not the primary instrument of donor countries' engagement with fragile states, it plays an essential supporting role. The current aid allocation system short-changes fragile states and urgently needs reconsideration. It rests on three basic operational assumptions: (i) country policies cannot be changed for the better through ex ante conditionality or other forms of donor engagement; (ii) aid cannot be channeled to minimize the distorting effect of poor policies, because of fungibility and the difficulties involved in "working around" governments; (iii) policy and governance as measured by the World Bank's country policy and institutional assessment determine aid effectiveness.

All three assumptions are questionable. First, while the history of conditionality is a litany of broken promises, and standard conditions have often proved ill adapted to genuine country needs (World Bank Operations Evaluation Department, 2004b), constructive changes in policy have been made easier by judicious conditionality combined with trade inducements (as, for example, in Mexico before the agreement on NAFTA, or in Hungary and Poland before their EU accession). Similarly, businesslike aid conditions embedded in long-term development partnerships have helped many countries to reduce poverty (for example Bangladesh, Chile, Ghana, Uganda, Turkey, Vietnam) (Branson and Hanna, 2002).

Nor is aid fully fungible. It is simply incorrect to postulate that aid funds channeled through government merely release resources for other uses. This overlooks the fact that in poor, aid-dependent, fiscally pressed countries, development spending expands as aid increases and that fiduciary rules associated with project aid are specifically designed to restrain fungibility, by attesting that funds are used for the purposes intended by donors. Further, to the extent that development projects incorporate "trait-making" features (Hirschman, 1995b), aid provides genuinely additional resources.

Third, as shown by Roodman (2004a), the correlations between policy quality and aid effectiveness are weak. Indeed, statistical tests show that the positive growth consequences of aid are *more pronounced* in countries of high economic vulnerability, based on indicators that give pride of place to structural factors and human resource endowments (Guillaumont, 2005).

From an ethical perspective, then, the provision of aid to vulnerable countries has merit in that it helps to compensate them for handicaps over which they have little or no control in the short run. By contrast, linking aid flows to policy prescriptions that may not affect growth performance or proneness to conflict has no redeeming social value.

While ratings by the World Bank's independent Operations Evaluation Department confirm that projects have a poorer record in low-income countries under stress (LICUS) than in other countries, they also show that the right kind of aid can achieve good results even in a difficult policy environment. Fifty eight percent of the evaluated projects approved by the World Bank in LICUS during 1998-2002 had satisfactory outcomes. And, remarkably, the performance of private sector projects funded by the International Finance Corporation has been as good in LICUS as in other countries (Collier and Okonjo-Iweala, 2002).[31]

Conversely, through a signaling and pump priming effect, aid helps to attract private flows and voluntary sector involvement in fragile countries. It helps to create the infrastructure, partnerships, and enabling conditions that allow non-state actors to participate in development operations. These externalities are not captured by current aid allocation principles. Nor do the allocation principles take account of the potential benefits associated with aid flows that are timed to compensate for economic shocks caused by natural emergencies, major adverse movements in terms of trade, or structural vulnerability created by exposure and susceptibility to shocks (counter-cyclical aid). Nor do they acknowledge that the channels of aid delivery critically influence aid effectiveness.

Equally, ample evidence on the interaction between aid, vulnerability, and growth shows highly significant statistical correlations: aid interventions facilitate shifts in production patterns, soften the negative impact on development expenditures, and cushion the adverse effects of shocks on the economy (OECD/DAC, 2003). To this extent, deviations from the aid allocation protocol are justified, since it makes little sense to favor countries that have already reaped the benefits of economic diversification while short-changing countries that depend heavily on primary product exports.

Finally, the current aid allocation consensus is static and does not take account of the astronomical benefits of successful conflict prevention and resolution or of the risks implicit in the systematic neglect of frail and failed states.[32] The mental model underlying current aid allocation practices treats violent conflict as an exogenous variable, thus evading the need to confront the security dimension. But we know that violent conflict is a major cause of poverty and economic waste. Recent research by Paul Collier suggests that, on the average, preventing a single war would save USD 64 billion a year.[33] Therefore, aid can generate very high returns if it prevents, postpones, or reduces the incidence of conflict. This is the rationale for using a fragility index that takes account of proneness to conflict.

To be sure, economic regressions do not produce clear-cut evidence that aid either prevents or reduces conflict. This is not surprising since (i) humanitarian aid is concentrated in countries where conflicts have occurred and have an even chance of breaking out again; and (ii) until recently, aid policy had not focused on conflict prevention. Yet post-conflict aid can have a wholesome impact in preventing a return to conflict (a special case of conflict prevention).

Aid allocations should be based on risk/reward assessments rather than static models based on flawed correlations. A venture capital model of aid allocation would be more relevant to the new security and development environment than the prevailing aid allocation protocols. Using notional probabilities of outcomes, Bradford University has estimated the cost-benefit ratios of investments in conflict prevention at more than three to one for the international community and ten to one for the world as a whole. These investments are highly risky (only 58 percent of them succeed) but their average expected net values are excellent. This is because the estimated requirements for conflict prevention (aid, security support, and so on) average about USD 23 billion while a major conflict costs much more to the country concerned (an average of USD 188 billion); to its neighbors (USD 57 billion); and the international community (USD 122 billion), for a total cost of USD 367 billion.

The World Bank uses its Country Policy and Institutional Assessment system to relate aid allocations to country performance. Thirty countries are ranked in the lowest fourth and fifth quintiles of this index, which are commonly interpreted as indicating difficult environments for development cooperation. Another five countries, while not rated, are classified as low-income countries under stress. Out of these 35 countries, 15 have major or intermediate security gaps, according to the Center for Global Development. This suggests that major shifts in aid allocations would result if security needs were to receive as much weight as is currently given to the degree of poverty or the quality of policies. In fact, the use of the state fragility index for aid allocation proposed in this study would allocate USD 8.5 billion to low-income countries under stress, instead of the USD 5.5 billion they received in 1998.

E. Conclusions

Development cooperation practices need major adjustment, given the past neglect of downside risks, the high incidence of intra-state conflict, and the emerging threat of international terrorism. While multilateral solutions to security and development problems are the most appropriate, aid agencies are under strong pressure to advance bilateral geopolitical interests.

The international tensions precipitated by the Iraq conflict have undermined confidence in the "unipolar" world order and eroded public trust in the United Nations' capacity to resolve security crises. Under the pressure of events, Western military establishments are seeking to capture humanitarian functions and state building tasks. Aid "securitization" is raising concerns about diversion of resources towards the global war on terrorism at the expense of global poverty reduction. To minimize this risk, aid flows and advocacy efforts should be monitored.

Building the core capacities of the state should become a central priority of development cooperation. About a third of low-income countries show signs of fragility and constitute the core of the security and development challenge. Many of these countries are post-conflict states. External actors have tended to underestimate the time, resources, and knowledge needed for nation building. The task involves strengthening institutions that are able to mediate and resolve internal disagreements peacefully and to allocate resources in a fair and transparent way.

New policy emphases would result from a human security approach to development cooperation. Growth and poverty reduction strategies have not given sufficient priority to providing social safety nets, protecting vulnerable groups, or reducing horizontal inequalities. In countries with a youth bulge, employment programs have not secured enough resources. To respond to human security concerns, the development agenda should focus on equitable access to social services, knowledge and information technology, food security, natural resource management, and preparedness for natural disasters.

More aid and deeper debt reduction are critically needed and should be promoted in international forums. Equally, aid reform is critical to improve policy coherence for development. The problems of aid are well known but progress is hindered by diverse geopolitical agendas, the vested interests of parties such as consultants and suppliers, high coordination costs in a fragmented system, and aid agencies' reluctance to cede authority and their desire for a distinctive profile. Aid instruments need to be adapted to difficult environments. Creativity and innovation should be nurtured to find effective ways to engage with fragile states and to align aid activities to domestic processes.

In difficult environments, adaptable project instruments combined with safeguard policies should be favored and conditionality should be used with care to avoid worsening social tensions. Aid allocation protocols should be reformed to emphasize state fragility, rather than relying on indicators of governance quality that reflect initial conditions, not performance. Post-conflict activities should heed the lessons of experience.

Notes

1. Except for 2001, when it peaked over 3,000, the annual count of deaths due to international terrorist incidents did not exceed 1,000 in the period 1988-2004, according to the United States Department of State.
2. For example, Afghanistan, Iraq, and Pakistan now top the list of DFID's bilateral recipients while reductions in DFID's aid to middle-income countries may amount to GBP 100 million in 2004-05 and 2005-06.
3. Some reorientation of existing multilateral programs can be discerned. For example, the Financial Action Task Force that had been set up to combat money laundering has been mobilized to help interdict financial support to terrorist organizations.
4. Jesse Norman. Speaker at Chatham House meeting of March 9, 2005 about Philippe Sands' *Lawless World: the US, Britain and the Making and Breaking of Global Rules*. Chair: Andreas Whittam Smith.
5. Low-income, fragile states number 46-48 countries. They are home to 32-46 percent of the children who do not receive a primary education in developing countries; 41-51 percent of the children who die before their fifth birthday in developing

countries; 33-44 percent of maternal deaths in developing countries; 34-44 percent of people living with HIV/AIDS in developing countries; and 27-35 percent of people deprived of safe drinking water in developing countries.

6. Brazil, Mexico, Thailand, and South Africa are committed to democratic norms and market-based policies but many of their citizens do not benefit from basic social protections. Afghanistan, Haiti, Liberia, Sierra Leone, and Somalia are characterized by an oligopoly of violence due to state collapse. Most developing countries fall between these extremes and vast zones within them do not offer minimally adequate human rights protection, personal safety, or access to social services (examples are Cote d'Ivoire, Jamaica, Nigeria, Pakistan). Debiel and others (2005).

7. Demographic pressures, refugees and displaced persons, group grievance, human flight, uneven development, economic decline, de-legitimization of state, public services, human rights, security apparatus, factionalized elites, and external intervention.

8. A case in point is Liberia, where after eighteen months of peace there was still no electricity or running water and where the annual cost of the UN peacekeeping operation was four times the budget of the transitional government. According to George (2005), USD 59 million (the "daily burn" rate in Iraq) has not been found for a program designed to reintegrate former combatants into society despite indications that they may again take up arms as they did after a prior peace agreement broke down.

9. "We can be classified according to many competing systems of partitioning, each of which has far-reaching relevance in our lives: nationalities, locations, classes, occupations, languages, politics, and many others…The recently championed civilizational classifications have often closely followed religious divisions.…The deficiency of the thesis of 'clash of civilizations' …begins well before we get to the point of asking whether civilizations must clash." Sen (2002).

10. See <www.kimberleyprocess.com>

11. The U.S. Central Intelligence Agency uses its own criteria for identifying vulnerability to state failure. The criteria address the character of the political regime, its ethnic and religious make-up, infant mortality, trade openness, and prevalence of conflict in neighboring countries. These variables were selected through statistical regression, neural network analysis, and expert surveys rather than development policy considerations. Goldstone and others (2000).

12. DFID's model of state fragility measures (i) *Capacity*, looking at safety and security (control of external borders and internal territory, juridical statehood); political power (checks on executive powers, engagement with the population); economic management (effective public expenditure planning and management); and service delivery (more than 15 percent of GDP is raised in taxes); and (ii) *Willingness*, looking at safety and security (equitable access to security services and justice); political power (inclusion of major groups in political processes); economic management (transparency in management of revenues from natural resource extraction); and service delivery (equitable access to public services by regions and groups). By contrast, the British Government's strategy for "countries at risk of instability" is informed by security criteria that make specific reference to the characteristics of domestic political institutions and such external factors as bilateral relationships and participation in regional groupings.

13. A cooperative multilateral institution focused on capacity building, the UNDP commissioned a review of country classifications based on a needs-based approach rather than a normative policy stance. The study proposes eleven indicators of state weakness: (i) negative economic growth; (ii) natural resource dependence;

(iii) excessive debt; (iv) low human development index value; (v) severe political disruption; (vi) HIV prevalence; (vii) armed conflict incidence, (viii) literacy level of less than 50 percent; (ix) low levels of democracy; (x) corruption; and (xi) regional conflict. Out of forty-six countries that fall below four or more of these thresholds, twenty-seven are classified in the "special development needs" category. Particular mention is given to a subset of countries that meet six or more criteria.

14. The World Bank uses its Country Policy and Institutional Assessment (CPIA) index to allocate lending resources, to shape policy directions, and to establish debt relief targets. The CPIA is a synthesis of staff assessments arrayed along twenty criteria grouped into four clusters: (i) *economic management:* management of inflation and current account; fiscal policy; external debt management; quality of development program management; (ii) *structural policies:* trade policy and foreign exchange regime; financial stability and depth; banking sector efficiency and resource mobilization; competitive environment for the private sector; factor and product markets; policies and institutions for environmental sustainability; (iii) *policies for social inclusion:* gender equity; economic opportunity; equity of public resource use; building human resources and safety nets; poverty monitoring and analysis; and (iv) *public sector management and institutions:* property rights; rule-based governance; quality of budgetary and financial management; efficiency of revenue mobilization, efficiency of public expenditures; transparency, accountability and corruption of the public sector.

15. The econometric evidence about the role of good policies in aid effectiveness is mixed. Current performance-based allocation protocols do not take account of conflict prevention benefits even though these are considerable.

16. The Center for Global Development uses three criteria for defining state weakness: (i) security gap measured by the incidence of conflict during 1998-2003; (ii) capacity gap measured by immunization rates for measles and diphtheria-pertussis-tetanus; and (iii) legitimacy gap measured by voice and accountability ratings derived from World Bank Institute sources. See Center for Global Development, 2004.

17. Three of them (Benin, Mali, and Mozambique) were nonetheless selected for support by the Challenge Account.

18. The focus on structural factors is broadly consistent with the approach of Guillaumont (2005) to assessing the economic vulnerability of aid recipients as a function of country size, natural resource dependence, remoteness and landlockedness, exposure to natural disasters, variability of agricultural production, and instability of exports.

19. Conflict has prevailed in eighteen African countries more than half of the time for the past two decades. In thirteen of these countries more than a third of the population is hungry.

20. The urban population will catch up with the rural population, but not until the year 2017.

21. Paradoxically, developing countries may also have to undertake comprehensive health and nutrition programs designed to tackle rapid increases in obesity, diabetes, hypertension, and cardiovascular and other diet-related diseases connected to higher consumption of oils, meat and dairy products, and reduced dietary fiber diets. Risk management must also take account of the changing profile of hunger and malnutrition due to urbanization and the globalization of food systems. This will require adjustments in agricultural policies but also in nutrition and health strategies.

22. See <http://www.envsec.org/about.php>

23. See <http://www2.dfid.gov.uk/news/files/extractiveindustries.asp>

24. They cost an average of USD 63 billion annually.
25. In addition, foreign tourists and individuals employed by the tourism industry were affected.
26. A distinctive feature of the rescue effort was the mobilization of military assets from nine nations. The regional command center set up by the United States oversaw the largest military effort in the area since Vietnam. Seven U.S. Navy and Coast Guard ships and a U.S. submarine carrying 2,000 marines were diverted from their Persian Gulf destination to Sumatra.
27. Donor fragmentation has risen by 25 percent according to Knack and Rahman (2004). The online Development Gateway includes information on 340,000 projects. Tanzania alone receives funding from eighty donors for 7,000 projects.
28. Ninety-one countries, twenty-six donor organizations and partner countries, representatives of civil society organizations, and the private sector met in Paris on February 28-March 2, 2005. Once again, they committed their institutions and countries to continuing and increasing efforts in harmonization, alignment, and managing for results, and listed twelve indicators of progress to be measured nationally and monitored internationally. See <http://insightstage01/policydivision/teams/prs/harmonization/FINALPARISDECLARATION2005.pdf>
29. Middle-income countries that account for only 27 percent of the people living on less than one dollar a day receive 33 percent of the aid total, even though many of them have significant access to other forms of external finance.
30. A report by ActionAid International discounts the value of development assistance down to 39 percent of that reflected in the official statistics of the Development Assistance Committee (DAC) of the OECD. In response, DAC acknowledged some of ActionAid's concerns about the development effectiveness of technical assistance but did not think that the discount was soundly based and stressed that DAC had issued guidelines in 1991 to help remedy the problem. Similarly, DAC noted that the problems of tied aid, high transaction costs, and other effectiveness issues raised by ActionAid had been fully discussed by donors and partner countries at a March 2005 conference that had led to substantive agreements on mutual accountability mechanisms under the Paris declaration. Finally, DAC pointed out that DAC members had made public commitments that by 2010 could add up to at least USD 36 billion more aid than the USD 79 billion that was provided in 2004. http://www.actionaaid.org.uk/wps/content/documents/real_aid.pdf>
31. This conclusion is based on the degree of loss reserves, historic write-offs, default rates, equity investment measures, and independent ratings of development outcomes, normalized for the class of investment.
32. The opportunity cost of five years (1983-88) of civil war in Sri Lanka has been estimated at 20 percent of the country's GDP (USD 1.5 billion) (Grobar and Gnanaselvam, 1993). In Mozambique, production losses have been estimated at USD 20 billion, due to the deaths of some 1.5 million people and the displacement of about half of the population from its customary sources of livelihood (Green and Mavie, 1998). In Rwanda, Bosnia, and Lebanon, GDP fell to 46 percent, 27 percent, and 24 percent of the pre-conflict peaks (World Bank, 1998).
33. "Economics Focus: The Price of Peace," *The Economist*, April 24, 2004. Collier and Hoeffler (2000) estimate that less than USD 5 billion of peacekeeping yields nearly USD 400 billion in benefits.

5

Improving Conflict-Handling Mechanisms

> *"Politics is the process of handling demands and demands unhandled can escalate from politics to violence; conflict management that does not deal with basic causes is likely to be short-lived."*—I. William Zartman

The foregoing chapters have explored the interface between security and development. They have highlighted the strong association of poverty with conflict and identified such drivers of intra-state warfare as economic stagnation, social exclusion, horizontal inequalities, youth bulges, environmental overload, and tolerance of illegal arms sales. They underscore the need for development cooperation to focus more resources on fragile states so as to help prevent the eruption of violence. They also advocate the exploration of multi-track approaches for conflict management that would entail combining a military interface with policing, community development, and local involvement, and note that donor countries should emphasize conflict prevention in their engagement with fragile states.

Against this background, the present chapter examines the state of knowledge and provides recommendations for achieving better conflict management. Based on a review of policy and practices governing international responses to conflict in different settings (section A), section B illustrates how gaps in policy and practice, along with a failure to coordinate responses, lead to under-achievement of goals. Section C identifies the key gaps that must be filled for security and development policies to converge. It finds that despite strenuous efforts to refine conflict management approaches, current international interventions and responses are not structured or resourced to deliver timely impacts on the ground, to lay the groundwork for sustained recovery and development, or to address root causes of armed conflict. An objective review of the evidence further suggests that the most promising sources of conflict resolution ideas lie *within* regions and societies directly affected by conflict (sections D and E).

Consequently, as argued in Section F, local and regional actors should be proactively involved in the design and implementation of conflict management norms and strategies. Their conflict management capacity should be developed as an integral part of external support for conflict prevention, management, and recovery. In this context, "one size fits all" anti-terrorism efforts should not be allowed to undermine capacity development or to reverse efforts to prevent and manage conflict. Last, beyond their inevitable focus on short-term measures, international policy responses should look beyond current crises and prevailing circumstances to help construct longer-term security and development scenarios for a changed terrain.

A. Conceptual Underpinnings and Policy Responses

Although conflict management theory and practice are converging, a considerable distance remains between the two. The failure to tackle root causes exemplifies a gap between concepts and policy responses and an even larger gap between stated policy and actual practice on the ground. Before examining current international approaches to conflict management, it is important to clarify the definitions and doctrines that shape interventions in the three stages—conflict prevention, resolution, and management—that are visualized as prerequisites of development.

The Anatomy of Conflict Management

The key aim in conflict management is to reduce the violence and destruction that result from conflict. Conflict resolution reaches beyond the consequences of conflict to address root causes. Both conflict management and resolution are therefore reactive; they take place after a conflict has gone beyond a threshold of violence and destruction. By contrast, conflict prevention is proactive. It seeks to prevent violent conflict through early action by addressing underlying concerns and competing demands. Consequently, the outbreak of violent conflict indicates a lack of effective preventive action.

Conflict management includes a range of activities such as negotiation, arbitration, and adjudication at one end of the spectrum, and the use of force at the other end. Conflict resolution addresses long-term changes and reconciliation in order to modify underlying attitudes. Conflict prevention focuses on actual or potential grievances that underlie conflict and addresses demands before they escalate into a full-fledged crisis (Assefa, n.d.). For example, the prevention of inter-state conflict includes timely attempts to demarcate national borders in ways that preempt boundary disputes with neighbors.[1]

Within a state, early preventive mechanisms might entail constitutional changes and reforms of governance, as illustrated by South Africa in the immediate post-apartheid years and in Mali after the end of authoritarian rule under Mousa Traore in 1990. Conflict resolution, on the other hand, entails reconciliation to defuse the residual bitterness of long-drawn out conflicts, to assuage feelings of revenge, and to address inequalities that might be a root cause of internecine war. The goal is to bring about attitudinal change among enemies. However, differences among parties cannot be expected to be completely eliminated. As Zartman (1990) aptly points out:

> Conflict can be prevented on some occasions, and managed on others, but resolved only if the term is taken to mean satisfaction of apparent demands rather than the total satisfaction of underlying sentiments, memories, and interests.

Evolving Approaches to Conflict Management

During the Cold War, little was done to address the underlying causes of the inter-state conflicts that were dominant. International actors merely sought to modulate the conflicts to make sure they did not escalate and lead to nuclear annihilation.

Policy thinking evolved in the changed geopolitical environment of the early 1990s: with the rise in intensity of internal conflicts and a significant increase in civilian casualties[2], policymakers increasingly focused their attention on modifying such traditional approaches as conventional peacekeeping. Thus the post-Cold War period saw experiments (often triggered by international civil society) with a variety of conflict-handling mechanisms, designed to shorten conflicts and reduce the damage they caused and to prevent social tensions and low-intensity conflicts from degenerating into political upheavals with high civilian casualties. As a result, much of what was largely referred to as conflict resolution and prevention is now pursued under such terms as peacebuilding and state building.

Boutros Boutros-Ghali's *Agenda for Peace* (1992) described a conflict management cycle that includes four sequential but overlapping activities of preventive diplomacy, peacekeeping, peacemaking, and peacebuilding. He defined peacebuilding as "actions taken to identify and support structures which will tend to strengthen and solidify peace in order to avoid a relapse into conflict."

On the surface, this stylistic conflict-management cycle provides a useful distinction among activities. But realities on the ground call for different dynamics. Neither Boutros-Ghali's (1992) *Agenda for Peace*, nor Kofi Annan's *Another Agenda for Peace* (1995), envisaged that peacebuilding as described could be applied *before* the onset of violent conflict as a primary prevention mechanism, rather than just as a post-conflict activity to prevent armed conflict from recurring.

With this recognition, the concept of peacebuilding has evolved and been developed under different umbrellas, including post-conflict assistance, nation building, or reconstruction. To support the diplomatic and military activities undertaken to end hostilities and provide a secure environment for resuming humanitarian and other activities, peacebuilding now entails a parallel longer-term process to consolidate the peace in order to prevent recourse to armed conflict. It includes activities geared toward building institutions, reconciling groups and people with one another, and rebuilding the economy.

In earlier UN peacekeeping operations the vast majority of peacekeepers were military personnel who were lightly armed, used force only in situations of self-defense, and were deployed with the consent of warring factions. Now peace support operations have emerged as the most common form of conflict management, designed to intervene in deadly conflict in order to reduce human suffering and to create space for delivering humanitarian assistance. Here the role of peacekeeping forces has become murkier and more fluid, rapidly alternating from the limited use of force, including joint civilian-military operations, to the use of force as needed to respond to the situation on the ground, usually in environments where conflicting parties have little or no regard for the rules of war.

Efforts to make peace, particularly after a conflict degenerates into complex humanitarian emergencies, require several layers and combinations of activities, including diplomacy, peacekeeping, the use of force, humanitarian assistance, and peacebuilding. The latter became part of international practice following the unveiling of Boutros-Ghali's *Agenda for Peace* in 1992, as peacekeeping missions were expanded to include tasks such as protecting civilians, assisting the conduct of elections, and demobilizing and reintegrating former combatants into society. These expanded tasks were referred to as post-conflict peacebuilding.

During the 1990s, the roster of peacekeeping/peace support operations became even more complex and demanding, with a proliferation of tasks including interim administration and establishment of institutions that would take over from the UN, as was the case in Kosovo and East Timor. The complexity of the crises to which the world was responding showed that in practice, conflict management methods cannot be segregated and applied in neat sequence on the ground. Further, despite the efforts to adopt more comprehensive strategies in support of negotiated settlements, studies showed that about half of the peace agreements to end civil wars collapsed within five years of being concluded (Licklider, 1995). Today, there is still a 44 percent chance that where peace has been achieved, conflict will reignite within ten years.

What then underlies the abatement or recurrence of conflict? Either conflicting parties reach a "saturation point" or "exhaustion level" in the use of violence and realize that this method of pursuing their aims is more costly than the initial injustice for which they were seeking redress (Lederach, n.d). Alternatively, they sign peace accords and agree to pursue their conflict via non-violent means following negotiations, which build expectations that the basic issues that led to violence in the first instance will be addressed.

In many instances, violence recurs despite hard-won peace agreements because the expectation of social and economic justice has not been fulfilled. This is what Lederach calls "the justice gap" in peacebuilding. Ongoing research also indicates that there is no consensus over the precise role that external actors should play in implementing peace agreements, even though there is a clear recognition that international attention and resources are crucial for successful implementation.[3]

Policymakers have thus continued to pursue more effective ways to implement peace agreements without a threat of reversal. But in doing so, they have focused mainly on conflict management, giving little attention to early and late prevention. Part of the reason is that global policy actors were not aware of proactive peacebuilding methods at the time when intra-state conflicts proliferated and their destructiveness became apparent. Gradually, new approaches have been emerging to meet practical challenges on the ground, as illustrated later in this chapter.

The Brahimi Report and Beyond

The so-called Brahimi Report of 2000 (UN, 2000) interpreted peacebuilding as "activities undertaken on the far side of conflict to reassemble the foundations of peace and provide the tools for building on those foundations something that is more than just the absence of war." This chronological view of the responses to conflict encouraged the compartmentalization of external efforts to contain or mitigate conflicts on the ground, as elaborated below. Like earlier attempts to develop better policy responses to conflict, the work of the Brahimi panel was not mainly concerned with the need to establish closer connections between security and development, and the panel was not mandated to focus in any detail on other aspects of the continuum such as the conflict resolution and prevention activities that are now classified under the rubric of peacebuilding.

In 2001, the UN Security Council (2001) addressed the issue of sequencing by conceiving of peacebuilding as a longer-term mission that serves a preventive role both before and after conflict. Thus, peacebuilding activities could be employed to prevent the outbreak of armed conflict, to reduce the destructiveness of conflict once violence has broken out, and to end the conflict and prevent its recurrence. This concept of peacebuilding reflects a perception of conflict prevention, management, and resolution as a continuum.

In the meetings of the Utstein Group (consisting of Germany, Netherlands, Norway, and the U.K. initially, later joined by Sweden and Canada), from 1999 onwards, the focus was not on policy, but on "better implementation through better coordination, better instruments, and better use of existing instruments" (Utstein Group, 2004). The Utstein agenda highlighted eleven action points, including the need for conflict prevention and in particular, the consolidation of peace following a peace settlement.[4]

A subsequent study commissioned by the Utstein Group focused on peacebuilding and assessed the lessons of experience. Revealingly, it left out all military operational aspects, thus perpetuating the notion that security and development are two separate realities. On the other hand, the same study conceptualized peacebuilding as including the provision of security, the establishment of socioeconomic foundations of long-term peace, and the establishment of a political framework for long-term peace, reconciliation, and justice. Similarly, NATO conceived of peacebuilding as a long-term enterprise under the umbrella of peace support operations. Peacebuilding was to combine diplomatic, civil, and military means to deal with underlying causes of conflict and the longer-term needs of people (NATO 2003).

Thus, getting the security and development community to develop a collective vision for handling and preventing conflict remains a challenge. From a policy perspective, there has been a gradual shift in this direction among bilateral actors and more slowly among global multilateral actors. The policy evolution has not yet taken hold on the ground to achieve improved results. Yet the evidence shows that closer links between security and development, and better connection between actors from the two communities, are crucial for policy coherence and human security to be achieved.

The rest of this chapter examines conflict management efforts in armed conflicts that have attracted UN-led responses. It examines the handling of issues at the intersection of security and development, the challenges posed by situations where armed conflict is latent, and the evolving policy responses to the challenges that the UN and other actors face during conflict management.

B. From Policy to Practice: Gaps in the Field

Experiences in conflict management among regional and global actors alike have produced mixed results. Despite the stated ideals of long-term, people-centered approaches to conflict resolution, management, and prevention, the reality on the ground has proven highly demanding and complex. The experience continues to show a lack of attention to root causes and a "disconnect" between security and development. To bring the two fields closer together, a coherent approach to conflict handling is needed.

Multiple Actors, Mixed Results

The conflicts raging across the world have attracted different responses from a cross-section of actors including single nations, regional organizations, and global actors, particularly the UN. However, it is the responses of the UN that have produced the most prominent lessons for conflict management.

Of the ten most recent UN missions, only one was a classical "blue helmet" operation designed to keep warring parties apart (Ethiopia and Eritrea). The others combine civilian and military means and vary greatly in scope from the largest, in the Democratic Republic of Congo (DRC) (about 19,000 strong), to the smallest, in Kosovo (about 6,000 strong). Civilian missions are operating in Afghanistan and Iraq while small peacebuilding offices operate in the Central African Republic, Guinea-Bissau, and Tajikistan. The results of UN conflict management interventions have been mixed and this is why world leaders have welcomed the proposal to set up a Peacebuilding Commission.

Past UN successes include the ending of armed conflicts, in Angola, Ethiopia-Eritrea, Mozambique, and Sierra Leone. But the recurrence of armed conflict or continued threat of violence has been frequent, as in Cote d'Ivoire, DRC, and Liberia. The sustainability of new (transitional) administrations in Kosovo and East Timor is still not assured, while the hope of transformation from security to development is bleak at best in Haiti. In Cyprus, Lebanon, and Western Sahara, traditional peacekeeping and observation tasks have only managed to maintain the status quo. The most dramatic failures of military peacekeeping, which left civilian peacebuilding little chance of success, were in Bosnia, Rwanda, and Somalia.

In many cases, the post-conflict situation remains precarious, without offering much hope for a sustained move toward long-term stability and development. And most of the post-conflict countries have remained at the bottom of the human development rankings. Furthermore, the cases considered by the UN Security Council only tell part of the story of contemporary conflict around the world. Of the many conflicts not inscribed on its agenda, some have the potential to affect international and regional peace and security and could benefit from more systematic intervention, involving international action, regional mediation, and single-nation diplomatic efforts; they include those in Chechnya, Colombia, Sri Lanka, Togo, and Zimbabwe.

Regional actors, still neglected, can make a contribution that extends beyond their support of UN peacekeeping missions and peace support operations. Given their relative proximity to the conflicts and their awareness of the consequences for national and regional security, regional organizations tend to be more willing than outside parties to apply radical but effective measures to nip deadly conflict in the bud. They have become more creative in developing normative frameworks for conflict prevention, and they can provide longer-term engagement in circumstances where the UN may be diverted away by the frequently changing postures of its powerful members.

The African Union, for example, adopted the Algiers Declaration in 1999, effectively rejecting any unconstitutional takeover of power in African states. Subsequent prevention efforts by leaders of the Economic Community of West African States (ECOWAS) have sought to take early action to reverse military coups (as in Nigeria and Sao Tome) or to prevent the takeover of a state by military personnel (as in Guinea Bissau). Taking early action to prevent the escalation of armed violence serves the interests of regional actors, but the strengths of regional institutions have not yet been sufficiently harnessed to ensure more effective responses to conflicts.

Overall, regional actors have intervened in far fewer conflict situations than has the UN, and most of their interventions have been smaller, simpler, and less multifunctional than UN peace support operations. Examples include the European Union's Operation Artemis in Ituri and the African Union's intervention in Burundi. In several cases, regional operations have focused on prevention and early political response (as did ECOWAS in Guinea Bissau and Liberia in 2003), and on offering a first line of peacekeeping response before the UN arrived on the scene (as did ECOMOG—the Armed Monitoring Group of ECOWAS—in Sierra Leone from 1997-2000 and in Cote d'Ivoire and Liberia in 2003).

In cases where conflicting parties are unreceptive to peace overtures, regional organizations or coalitions led by a single state—usually a global or regional power—have shown greater willingness than UN-sponsored initiatives to employ necessary force in the bid to deal with humanitarian crises. Examples of this include the Nigerian-led ECOMOG interventions in Liberia (1990-97) and Sierra Leone (1997-2000), the South African-led intervention in Lesotho (1998), the NATO intervention in Kosovo, and Australian-led force in East Timor.

Arguably, the U.S.-led interventions in Afghanistan and Iraq cannot be described as classical conflict management situations, given the interventionist role of a coalition led by the lone superpower. Thus, they may not provide a useful template for future peacemaking. While humanitarian objectives have been mentioned, the military interventions of the United States and its allies were not initially motivated by a desire to address the deep-rooted conflicts of these societies. Instead, they responded to proven and potential threats faced by the industrial democracies—an indisputable global terrorist menace in the case of Afghanistan and a perceived threat from Iraq, which had used weapons of mass destruction against its own people and was initially believed to be stockpiling them for use against the West—an allegation thus far unproven.[5]

In both of these cases, the desire to build governance structures to address the sources of conflict in local society emerged after the military action and constituted a secondary motivation. Thus they have few lessons to offer a potential UN or regional response to civil strife in Guinea, Mauritania, Sri Lanka, Togo, or Zimbabwe. Nonetheless, they offer sobering examples of the impact of peace operations led by big nations and illustrate the risks of military action to address the global terrorist threat.[6]

Overall, recent experience shows that internal crisis attracts international attention only when all the early warning signals have been missed or ignored: when the neglect of group demands and poor governance arrangements degenerates into violence, and in some cases, when violence spills across national boundaries, with increased human suffering and attendant security challenges. In reality, peacebuilding action to prevent the onset of armed conflict is rare and even when peace support missions are deployed to address ongoing conflict or prevent its recurrence, there are significant gaps between the shorter-term security-related objectives and longer-term peacebuilding/development goals.

One of the key findings from more than a decade of responses to the outbreak of armed conflict, through a roster of tasks from diplomacy to peacebuilding, is that international action has not yet produced effective and sustainable results on the ground and that therefore the threat of recurrence of armed conflict is real in many postwar environments.

A related finding is the need for better collaboration and clearer division of labor between the UN and the regional actors most likely to offer first-hand responses to crisis in their neighborhood. Their complementary strengths have yet to be properly harnessed. The vast majority of conflict situations within states do not attract the attention of the United Nations or the great powers. Among the more than fifty civil wars that have ended since 1989, only half have attracted efforts by the UN to help address root causes through peacebuilding (Forman, 2005: 2).

One reason for the persistent failure of peacemakers to steer war-torn societies toward long-term security and development is the inadequate integration of conflict management instruments. Diplomacy, preventive deployment, peacekeeping, and peacebuilding have tended to be used sequentially whereas they should have been implemented together, as stressed by Boutros-Ghali. They have taken the form of task-oriented responses rather than a strategic approach focused on achieving outcomes.

A second explanation has to do with inadequate and half-hearted responses in pre-conflict settings. Early warning mechanisms exist but they have seldom led to prompt remedial action. Related to this is the failure to link peacemaking in conflict environments to situations in neighboring states where conflict might be imminent. As discussed below, the United Nations is slowly beginning to address this problem through regional efforts at demobilization, disarmament, and reintegration (DDR), although not noticeably through preventive diplomacy.

A third explanation is that gaps remain in programs aimed at developing the capacity of regional actors to prevent and manage conflict. Regional organizations and their benefactors are not yet operating on the basis of a joint strategic vision that marries local and regional norms and values and locally driven ideas to the sophisticated planning resources of the developed world.

The dysfunction underlying these manifestations of failed interventions is referred to as "the process-structure gap" by Lederach (n.d.). In mindset, language, and thinking, actors responding to peace may construe peace either as a process or as a definite end state. Peace is considered a process until a peace accord is signed, after which those implementing the peace plan think in bureaucratic terms that aim at translating processes into structures on the ground with sharply defined roles for different actors. In fact, peace should be seen both as a process and as a set of structures—and not a steady state.

The results of conflict management efforts would improve if peace accords were not seen as ending conflict but rather as ushering in a continuous process of relationship building while adapting to changes and real life situations on the ground. Lederach thus urges that long-term peace structures should be reconceived "such that they reflect the inherent responsiveness often present in periods of active negotiation, and avoid trappings of isolating 'peace' functions in bureaucracies implementing time-bound mandates with little capacity to adapt and change to on-the-ground real-life needs" (Lederach, n.d.).

Absence of a Coherent Longer-Term Strategic Vision

Peace implementation on the ground invariably reflects the immediate objectives and priorities of the underwriters of the peace plan. Attention has focused on attaining political stability and creating a secure environment, rather than on the longer-term goal of creating lasting conditions for sustainable security and development. In UN-led operations, the lack of strategic links between various levels of response remains a problem.

At its core are the strictures of UN Security Council mandates that envisage narrow, short-term objectives of political settlement and elections and encourage early exit. Such lack of attention to the root causes of crises (Type [i] incoherence, to use the terminology outlined in chapter 1 above) is compounded by inadequate interaction between political/security missions and the development side of the UN system (Type [ii] incoherence). Thus UN activities do not always consist of actions linked to a strategic vision shared by donor countries, international financial institutions, and nongovernmental entities (Type [iii] incoherence).

The lack of strategic focus remains even though the best practice guidelines set by the UN Secretariat clearly outline objectives in multi-dimensional operations that go well beyond establishing a secure environment (UN, 2003b). The UN has attempted to address the problem of lack of coordination between many parts of the UN system, by combining all its field presence into one country team in each location and, more recently, by deploying integrated missions, as in Liberia and Afghanistan.

Planning for multi-dimensional operations now regularly includes support for the development of national institutions that guarantee accountable governments, respectful of human rights, able to manage disputes effectively, and capable of implementing the national strategies for social and economic recovery that are a key aim of peacebuilding. Peace support operations therefore encompass a combination of peacekeeping and peacebuilding activities aimed at creating the initial conditions and national capacity needed to meet this objective. These activities include military operations to monitor agreement and create a secure environment; facilitation of political dialogue and negotiation; disarmament, demobilization, and reintegration of former combatants into society; human rights monitoring and support for a national truth and reconciliation process; facilitation and monitoring of an electoral process; and facilitation of the establishment of governance and rule-of-law institutions—which often entails training and support for national law enforcement services.

The execution of peace support operations in the field often reinforces the gaps and the absence of coordinated action. Not only do short-term mandates make it difficult to undertake longer-term planning and implementation to achieve the peacebuilding objectives highlighted above, but funding is not always guaranteed, nor is it coherent. There is still evidence of compartmentalization and territorialism in the way initiatives are funded and implemented. The responses to complex crisis environments reveal these gaps, which sometimes lead to duplication of effort in the field. This is most visibly demonstrated by separate funding appeals and forums and overlaps in planning and competing programs, particularly between the work of peacekeeping missions and agencies that existed in the field before the arrival of the missions.

Addressing Compartmentalization in Peace Support Operations

In most peace operations, attention focuses almost exclusively on the security component and on the mechanics of peacekeeping rather than on a strategic vision of the longer-term change that intervention or peace implementation is seeking to achieve (such as longer-term rehabilitation of the society and economic recovery). While the immediate priority of societies in conflict is usually a secure environment and a political commitment from conflicting parties, there is a tendency to stick to the same priorities even after local conditions justify a reorientation towards longer-term development concerns.

Part of the reason lies in the types of tasks that are assigned to the various components at the mission planning stage. UN peace support missions are typically organized to include diplomatic functions and overall peacemaking, embodied in the special representative of the Secretary-General (SRSG), who is the head of the mission and of the entire UN presence in the field. In addition to the SRSG's office, the headquarters of a UN mission include several other units and functions. To provide security, the force commander is responsible for the military operations and the police commissioner is responsible for policing functions. Other headquarters components under the SRSG include units in charge of non-military tasks that support the peace process, for example those in charge of disarmament, demobilization, and reintegration; civil affairs including the rule of law and policing; child protection; and human rights, including gender components in some cases. In recent times, missions have included advisers on gender and HIV/AIDS. The nature of peace agreements in conflict situations that have led to state collapse has also required the peace support missions to include security sector reform on their agendas (most recently in Liberia).

It is not uncommon for the headquarters of a peacekeeping mission to exist separately from other aspects of the UN presence in a country, including development and humanitarian teams that were operating well before the deployment of the peacekeeping mission. While UN country teams have become better organized and coordinated over the years and the concept of integrated missions is still being tested, there is still a tendency for various parts of the UN family to act in uncoordinated ways (Forman, 2005). The lack of coordination extends to bilateral and multilateral agencies and international nongovernmental organizations.

Thus, the "disconnect" between security and development in peace support operations is due to the compartmentalization of different elements of peacemaking and conflict management. Components of peace operations, both civil and military, have been fine-tuned and heavily professionalized, so that each element is segregated and confined to a narrow area of activity, without a strategic link to other activities.

This institutional approach does not make the most of those contingents who could contribute meaningfully to long-term development goals. The planning for military components of peace support operations, for example, focuses on achieving specific often short-term objectives such as the provision of security in specific locations, and institutional attention focuses almost exclusively on the mechanics of the military operation.

Even where the military devotes time and talent to rebuilding (for example of schools or mosques, often as part of "quick impact" projects), it rarely does so in ways that help to advance other components such as disarmament, demobilization, and reintegration. The basic purpose of such actions by military personnel in peace support operations is to win "hearts and minds" in the short run, not to promote long-term development (UN, 2003b: Chapter 1).

Likewise, civilian components of peace operations tend to focus on goals that can be achieved in the short term, even when the situation demands longer-term attention. For example, elections are focused on as a benchmark for achieving democracy, and a trigger for the early exit of peace missions. Yet there might be a strong case for ensuring a series of institutional reforms, starting in some cases with a constitutional reform agenda (as in Cote d'Ivoire and Liberia) or in other cases, shepherding transition processes over a much longer period (as in East Timor). As discussed above, however, this problem is rooted in the nature of the mandate provided by authorizing bodies, which does not give room for longer-term planning.

The costs of compartmentalization are most visible in responses to conflicts that have degenerated into humanitarian tragedy. Often a range of activities and tasks are carried out with no strategic links between key security and humanitarian/relief and developmental activities. As such, military operations carried out in these environments differ greatly from the often-preferred traditional peacekeeping ones, which are conducted with the consent of warring factions and entail minimal use of force. The military operations are robust; they may entail the use of force to achieve various short-term objectives, including the creation of safe spaces/corridors, where humanitarian aid can be administered to the affected communities, sometimes numbering hundreds of thousands of people.

Increasingly, these robust operations are performed by actors other than the UN. In Liberia and Sierra Leone, for example, Nigerian-led ECOMOG forces led enforcement operations; in Sierra Leone in 2000, the U.K. force led the counter-attack against invading rebels (Fitz-Gerald, 2004); in East Timor, Australia provided the lead in an operation authorized under Chapter VII of the UN Charter; and in Iraq and Afghanistan, the U.S. led coalition forces in counter-insurgency operations.

In such circumstances, co-coordinating military, humanitarian, and peacebuilding and developmental activities is a daunting task. Peacebuilding and developmental activities are very rare at the height of intense military operations. Achieving any link among these activities is virtually impossible when insecurity is high and civilian actors are removed from the scene. At several stages of the crisis in Liberia from 1990 to 1997, where armed groups terrorized the civilian population and waged total war on the regional force, the military was the only actor on the ground with any substantial capacity to provide humanitarian assistance.[7] This is increasingly the case in dangerous environments where civilian actors are at risk, as seen in Iraq, where the U.S. Army has been in charge of humanitarian assistance in some locations.

The coordination problem continues to occur in other types of partnerships among actors responding to conflict. This is illustrated by several situations where regional actors and individual mediators championed the diplomatic process (for example, as led by the Organization of African Unity in Ethiopia/Eritrea) and the military response (as in Burundi, Liberia, or Sierra Leone) and thereafter transferred responsibility for conflict management to a bigger actor—in most cases, the UN. Experience has shown that vital memory is lost during such transfers, for lack of systematic and continuous interaction among all actors. Social and economic recovery, for example, should form part of the strategic focus of all actors and should not be considered the sole preserve of one agency.

Maximizing the Benefits of Quick Impact Projects

Quick impact projects (QIPs), now increasingly supported by UN peace support operations, are a first step in addressing the challenge of excessive concentration on security and the mechanics of peacekeeping. They have been seen to deliver immediately visible results for local communities in Eritrea, Kosovo, and Sierra Leone, where some battalions have rebuilt local infrastructure such as schools, hospitals, and mosques.[8] While the primary focus of QIPs is on winning the hearts and minds of the local population, implementing those projects in ways that complement an overall plan such as DDR will help to deliver some of the strategic objectives on the ground.

It is important to take the needed strategic view right from the mission planning stage. In Liberia, for example, the UN Mission in Liberia was criticized by parts of the local population for building temporary demobilization sites in some counties and later dismantling them for re-erection in other counties as part of the phased approach to DDR. The locals argued that the resources for building the temporary sites could have been better applied to renovating the vocational training centers located in each county of Liberia, for use in longer-term youth reintegration efforts.[9] It might have been possible to renovate some centers as part of quick impact projects, particularly where some of the contingents were so inclined.

Two issues need considerable attention if these types of activities are to deliver the right results on the ground. First, of the fifteen peacekeeping missions overseen by the UN Department of Peacekeeping Operations in 2005/06, only six have a budget for QIPs. And the proportion of the budget of peacekeeping missions devoted to quick impact projects is often too small for these projects to achieve any significant impact on the ground.[10] Clearly QIPs are not considered relevant in some of the conventional peacekeeping missions such as those in Cyprus or Western Sahara, while in other cases (such as Ethiopia/Eritrea, Kosovo, or Sierra Leone), a transition might have been made to mainstream development work under the management of the national government or a development agency. Even so, it is conceivable that some of the international military personnel who remain in these countries could continue to assist with infrastructural development where needed.

A second issue is a lack of coordination between peacekeeping missions and other agencies on the projects funded, allowing for duplication even though the UN guidelines stipulate that peace missions should coordinate QIPs with the work of the development and humanitarian community. There is a natural tendency for peacekeeping missions to look inward, giving privileged attention to political/security concerns, rather than gravitating toward other parts of the UN community that existed on the ground before the mission.

Political and Peacebuilding Support Offices

The largely civilian tasks that form the entire focus of UN peacebuilding support offices offer potential bridges between security and development; and can contribute significantly to a strategic vision leading to sustainable development. The UN Department of Political Affairs is in charge of ten peacebuilding missions around the world, half of them in Africa.[11] The aggregate capacity in these ten peacebuilding offices consists of 436 international civilian staff; thirty-seven military and civilian police advisers and liaison officers; 1,076 local civilian personnel; and forty-two UN volunteers.[12]

The central role of these missions is to help establish legitimate states with the capacity to protect citizens, manage disputes, and ensure respect for human rights. More important, peacebuilding missions offer a chance to address underlying issues that in many cases have heightened group inequalities and a pattern of social exclusion. External parties can play a useful role in facilitating institutional reforms, including constitutional reforms to change patterns of revenue allocation and resource distribution. The role of the UN Department of Political Affairs as the focal point on peacebuilding is to facilitate a coherent response by the UN system in these post-conflict environments.

In reality, situations where peacebuilding (or peace support) missions work toward a common strategic framework, driven by the needs of the local population, are the exception rather than the norm. Only the inclusion of local ideas through creative means can bring about the desired transformation in post-conflict settings. Yet in a society divided sharply along ethnic lines or by other issues at the root of the conflict, finding a coherent local agenda can be difficult, and it is a challenge for the UN to forge such coherence through its political presence on the ground. Each post-conflict context is unique and peacebuilding agendas must creatively seek the right balance and level of relevance to local needs (Type [iv] coherence).

The Role of the Special Representative of the Secretary-General (SRSG)

The conduct of an SRSG, or in some cases simply a representative of the Secretary-General (RSG), can determine the extent to which a peace mission will succeed. The UN Secretariat outlines a profile for the SRSG/RSG, who is expected to serve as a role model, work to a high standard, lead by personal example, and observe the principles of impartiality and transparency (UN, 2003b: Chapter 1). However, it is also important for the SRSG/RSG to possess certain other attributes that can serve the strategic vision of the peace mission. The representative is expected to be diplomatically astute, with an excellent grasp of the issues of concern to the target communities, and her or his judgment should be respected by the local population, not least the conflicting parties who should have confidence in the peace process.

This is all the more important in internal conflict situations where the representative's role can be even more delicate, given the possibility that s/he may have to work with armed groups who are not recognized by the international community. It is crucial that the representative be able to take a strategic view in the implementation of the mandate and assume intellectual leadership on all aspects of peace implementation, ensuring their relevance to the situation on the ground. Thus, the choice of a representative can make all the difference.

In summary, peace operations should heed the following lessons of experience:

(i) Peace and development should be envisaged as both a process and a structure, in order to avoid the current tendency to view the peace accord as an end state, after which new processes are launched to create local structures.
(ii) Peacemakers should avoid rigid bureaucratic practices and build flexibility into the processes of implementing peace agreements, so that relationships can be built and capacity can adapt to evolving realities on the ground.
(iii) The planning of peace support operations should envisage better links and use of quick-impact projects in ways that can add value to disarmament,

demobilization, and reintegration and to other reform initiatives further down the line.
(iv) More resources should be provided for quick-impact projects so that they can have the desired impact and pave the way for achieving longer-term objectives such as reintegration and community development.
(v) The (special) representative of the Secretary-General should provide intellectual leadership for the fulfillment of all aspects of UN activities on the ground, ensuring that the strategic vision matches the needs of the communities that the UN is expected to serve.
(vi) Through the leadership provided by the (special) representative of the Secretary-General, greater emphasis should be placed on conflict transformation so that the conflicting parties are persuaded to pursue the resolution of differences via non-violent means. As such, peace missions should make better use of people with experience in conflict-transformation actions that address the root causes of conflicts.
(vii) The attention of peacebuilding support offices, which tends to focus largely on politics, should be broadened and sustained to provide the leadership and support required for national reform processes and capacity building in the security and other sectors.

C. Addressing the Conflict-to-Development Gap

The success or failure of peace support operations depends to a large extent on how well peacebuilding and civilian components are implemented. In turn, the manner of implementation partly depends on whether or not violence has recurred. Disarmament, demobilization, and reintegration (DDR), security sector reform, and the nature of international response to youth crises are three neglected areas of current conflict handling approaches.

Disarmament, Demobilization, and Reintegration

The choice of program goals is the single most important determinant of the contribution that a DDR program will make to sustainable security and development. In many cases, the planners of DDR choose objectives that fall short of what is needed to ensure a better link between security and development. As indicated above, the most common goal of these programs is the attainment of relative political stability and security—rather than the greater goal of ensuring conditions for sustainable security and development.

Chapter 4 above raised some of the strategic considerations that must shape the design and implementation of disarmament and reintegration initiatives if a successful transformation is to be made from conflict to development. For example, the transformation needs to accomplish the conversion of military assets to civilian use without undermining objective security needs. In the same vein, chapter 4 warned that sharp reductions of military spending and rapid demobilization may have the unintended consequences of privatizing violence and undermining the very security that a DDR program aims to provide. Thus the needed technical exercise must be balanced with good community relations and adequate investments in areas such as shelter, health support, counseling, transport, registration, subsistence, training, credit facilities, and referral to private sector employers.

International efforts to implement effective DDR programs confront several challenges. First is the nature of the peace agreement that precedes a DDR effort. DDR is an intensely political activity. Peacemakers need to ensure that armed groups who prospered during active hostilities do not return to the battlefield or devise ways to undermine efforts to achieve sustainable peace and development. In many internal conflict situations it has been difficult to transform former armed groups into viable political parties or entities in the post-conflict, pre-election period. Even though warring factions or armed groups may lack the support of an organized constituency, this problem is not unrelated to the pursuit of early elections and early exit by the UN and other peacemakers.

Second, there is a tendency to superimpose models of peace agreements that have succeeded in other contexts, neglecting the socioeconomic and political context in the target environment. For example, it is not uncommon to find peace agreements that include the creation of institutions such as national human rights commissions or truth and reconciliation commissions, even where traditional healing and reconciliation mechanisms might have been more effective. In Liberia, the DDR plan was clearly derived from the plan in neighboring Sierra Leone, but in the overall peace implementation the leadership of the mission was inclined to superimpose the models that had worked in the Balkans—a choice that was heavily criticized by the Liberian community.[13] It is important to ensure that models that have succeeded elsewhere are not superimposed on environments that require other methods to tap local opportunities that can make a difference on the ground, as further indicated below.

Third, the way in which a DDR plan is implemented may have a significant bearing on its outcome. Issues that often create major challenges include the identification of parties to be disarmed; the nature of the incentives and the contents of the demobilization package; the quality and relevance of reintegration programs; and the time elapsed between the demobilization and reintegration phases.

The timing of DDR is significant for several reasons. Long gaps between disarmament and demobilization or between demobilization and reintegration can lead erstwhile fighters to pursue other agendas that undermine the peace plan and process. In Sierra Leone, fighters who had been in cantonment sites waiting for their demobilization for several months (for lack of funding for reintegration support) rejoined the rebels during the invasion of January 1999. In West Africa, particularly in the Mano River area and Cote d'Ivoire, warlords have used gaps in DDR programs in neighboring states to re-recruit demobilized fighters who were not fully reintegrated into their societies.

It is important to synchronize, where possible, the timing of DDR in one country with that in another, and in particular to avoid creating huge disparities in the contents of neighboring DDR programs. In Liberia and Sierra Leone, demobilization packages included cash incentives of USD 300 per former fighter. But in neighboring Cote d'Ivoire, the DDR plan included cash incentives at least twice as large. This created a potentially lucrative alternative for young fighters in Liberia, whose sole livelihood in a neighborhood ridden by war for more than a decade had been based on the use of weapons. After a short demobilization (pre-discharge orientation) period of five days spent in cantonment sites, young ex-fighters were free to roam across borders in search of the next war. For Liberian demobilized youth, both Cote d'Ivoire and Guinea offered the next opportunity.

Thus, unless a region-wide approach is taken to DDR, and particularly the reintegration of young men and women, peace processes no matter how comprehensive may be derailed. The UN and other multilateral actors have taken steps to address this weakness in West Africa and the Great Lakes region of Africa but it is too early to assess the impact on the ground.

In West Africa, DDR coordinators have met periodically since 2004 to share experiences and devise strategies for addressing the regional challenges, particularly following a proposal to extend DDR programs into neighboring states that are not necessarily in conflict.[14] In the Great Lakes, the Multi Donor Reintegration Plan which has been in place since 2003 has encountered several challenges, not least the situation in the DRC, which makes implementation particularly difficult.

Fourth, local ownership of a DDR process is crucial. Unless creative ways are found to include local ideas for demobilization and reintegration in the design and implementation of DDR initiatives, reversals in peace processes will continue to outnumber successes. Local communities not only have better knowledge of their territory and their own situation; they have to live with the consequences of armed conflict and of failed conflict management efforts. They very often have innovative ideas for reintegration that can lead to lasting solutions. But the international institutions working in these environments often lack creative channels or the flexibility to accommodate local ideas and initiatives. This problem cuts across many internationally driven initiatives and is not limited to DDR.

Fifth and last, even with all the brightest and most innovative ideas for an effective DDR program, funding gaps can very easily derail the DDR process. More often than not, either a failure to redeem pledges from donors or a lack of commitment to longer-term reintegration and rehabilitation efforts ensures that those programs are doomed to fail and that they do not even stand much chance of meeting their shorter-term objectives set in the first instance.

Donors tend to commit to relatively cheap short-term initiatives, such as Liberia's five-day demobilization exercise. A program that provided for cantonment for at least six months would have prevented fighters from roaming across the sub-region and instead would have groomed them for a functional existence in society. Just such a proposal failed to attract the support of donors whose aid priorities lie elsewhere, given Liberia's limited geopolitical importance. This is a typical choice for development actors who shy away from innovative ideas and programs because of a lack of dedicated resources at the neglected intersection of security and development.

In West Africa, for example, an option that places ex-fighters in national youth service schemes with a focus on community development for a sustained period, as part of the regional reintegration process, may not be preferred by either donors or development actors. Yet it offers the promise of a structured approach to youth reintegration. Not only would it allow the ex-fighters' progress to be monitored and documented over a sustained period, but their talents could be directed toward implementing relevant community service programs that can offer them adequate training and apprenticeships for alternative livelihoods.

Security Sector Reform

Like DDR, reform of the security sector (SSR) is critical for sustainable security and development not just in post-conflict environments but also as a conflict prevention tool, particularly in states showing signs of collapse. Collapsed states often present the best opportunity for comprehensive reform of the security sector because they offer a chance for a complete transformation.

Just as for DDR, the strategic vision for SSR should go beyond the need to achieve immediate stabilization of the conflict environment to a people-centered agenda for security and development. Thus the key principles behind SSR are designed to address some of the issues at the root of the breakdown in governance systems that led the state to collapse in the first instance.

As pointed out in chapter 4, external aid can help withdraw the monopoly of the use of force back into the hands of the state, within the context of a longer-term objective of democratic governance. That chapter also drew attention to the origins of the concept of security sector reform, which, as pointed out by Ball and Fayemi (2004), aims at achieving: a security sector that is accountable to elected civil authorities and the establishment of oversight institutions and adheres to domestic and international law; transparency, such that information on security sector planning and budgeting is widely available; capacity of civil authorities to exercise political control, and to monitor the security sector and provide constructive input into the political debate; adequately trained, professional, and disciplined security personnel; and an environment conducive to regional and sub-regional peace and security.

In war-torn societies it is a daunting task to move the security sector from its pre-war and war-time state to a situation where these principles are applied. Such a transformation will be the result of a long-term reform process that transcends the external intervention for conflict management. Much depends on the ability of conflict managers to set the scene for this at an early stage in the peace process.

Very few peace agreements have included plans for comprehensive security sector reform. Those in Liberia and Sierra Leone are two of the exceptions. Even so, the Lome Peace accord of 1999 (for Sierra Leone) did not explicitly refer to SSR, but rather provided for rebuilding the Sierra Leone Army. The Comprehensive Peace Agreement on Liberia in 2003 refers explicitly to SSR.

Implementing SSR as part of a UN-led process and other conflict management processes is challenging. The first challenge is the lack of an agreed conceptual framework. The concept of SSR is relatively new: the term was introduced into the lexicon of conflict prevention and development only in the late 1990s, although some of the activities envisaged under SSR have long existed. The new SSR agenda conceives the security sector much more broadly than was previously accepted. It moves beyond organizations mandated to use force, including the defense forces and the police and intelligence services, to non-state security organizations such as militias and private security forces. It also includes the judicial and public safety bodies and civil oversight bodies. This broad agenda is rooted in two institutional reform goals: ensuring the establishment of oversight mechanisms that are consistent with democratic norms, and creating affordable, professional security forces. SSR and the democratization of the security sector are not just about forming skills and building capacity—they have to do with social transformation and governance reform. Thus, if the governance of the security sector is not addressed, it may be impossible to provide security for the majority of people, thus creating a dependence on non-state security groups such as ethnic militias and vigilantes.

Second, as with DDR, it is the nature of the peace agreement that often decides how and whether SSR will be successfully implemented. Two issues are relevant here. One is that many peace agreements fail to address SSR. This affects how a new government will respond to the issue; a peace agreement that includes a commitment to undertake SSR would induce leaders to adopt this core governance reform as a priority task for the post-election agenda.[15] A related issue is that the crafters of many peace agreements show a dire lack of knowledge about SSR and what it entails. As a result, peace agreements do not contain relevant details to offer guidance on how comprehensive the SSR should be. For example, while the Liberian Comprehensive Peace Agreement explicitly provides for the reform of the armed and security establishment, it does not explicitly demand the reform of oversight institutions, nor does it propose the development of a coherent national vision of security that will allow for effective governance of the security establishment.

While the presence of the UN or other multilateral actors can play an important role in pressuring local leaders to reform and offer direction on the content and scope of SSR, it has been difficult to get UN missions or other agencies to provide intellectual leadership on SSR on the ground.

The result of this is that SSR activities are undertaken in isolation, without the inclusion of all needed components, and without a connection between the components being implemented (Ball and Fayemi, 2004; OECD/DAC, 2004; Center for Democratic Control of Armed Forces, 2003, 2005). There is an urgent need to put the guidelines to work, particularly in environments where the UN is leading conflict management and rebuilding efforts. It is unfortunate that though OECD/DAC has helped to develop guidelines on security system reform, there is virtually no knowledge or understanding of these issues on the ground in peace missions where the same OECD members have contributed massively to the regeneration of war-torn societies.

The Liberia peace mission is a glaring example of UN efforts to reform the police without strategic attention to the overall SSR strategy, though it did pursue some actions in the justice sector. Neither has the current mission provided any oversight of the program aimed at rebuilding the security forces. The United States has not yet internalized the same approach to security sector reform as some of its OECD partners, in another instance of Type (iii) incoherence. In effect, the rebuilding of the Armed Forces of Liberia is being undertaken by a private security firm with no link to the key principles of civilian control and oversight mechanisms.[16]

The new OECD/DAC guidelines, which allow official development assistance to be used to support SSR, can potentially have a huge impact on the role of development actors in SSR and related programs (bearing in mind the gaps identified in chapter 4 above). But the lack of linkage between the guidelines and work on the ground threatens to hold back progress.

For a successful conflict management process, security sector reform needs to be synchronized with activities for disarmament, demobilization, and reintegration. Actors are still grappling with the need to understand the complexities of both types of initiative and their convergences and divergences. Their success or failure will determine the outcome of efforts to maintain the security-development continuum.

In the aftermath of conflict or state collapse, the defense sector attracts considerable attention. But the institutional challenge lies in connecting reforms in the defense sector to reforms in policing, justice, and intelligence that also require resources. The focus of SSR activities differs among regions; for example, those in Sub-Saharan Africa focus largely on the defense sector, while those in Latin America focus more on internal security (such as police reform). East European countries have undergone reform in a different setting. Sharing of experience across regions might provide valuable lessons to practitioners.

Last, there are real challenges for the implementation of a comprehensive SSR even when the roles of strategic actors are better coordinated. These include, for example, lack of a tradition of democratic norms and practice; lack of understanding of varied political contexts; and the need to balance the need for democratic accountability with security sector professionalism and discipline.

Dealing with Excluded Youth and Young People Affected by Armed Conflict

The concerns of disaffected and excluded youth constitute perhaps the single most prominent issue at the intersection of security and development, and one of the key issues straddling pre-conflict, conflict, and post-conflict settings. Yet peacemakers and conflict management strategies have yet to systematically address this issue.

Much attention in post-conflict environments has focused on children associated with fighting forces, who are usually under the age of eighteen. Child protection was first included as part of UN peace support operations in 1999, in the mandate of the UN Mission in Sierra Leone, and the first child protection adviser was recruited in that mission in April 2000. Since then, missions in the Democratic Republic of Congo, Angola, and Afghanistan have included child protection components. Even with this achievement, however, the two leading actors on this issue—the Office of the Special Representative of the Secretary-General for Children and Armed Conflict and UNICEF—do not always manage to coordinate their responses.

A significant gap is the continuing inattention to young people who have fallen through definitional cracks. They include, for example, those who joined armed groups as children and left as adults over eighteen, and other youth associated with fighting forces. These groups too require rehabilitation and reintegration.

More broadly, the youth problem requires a coherent approach across the board. Current trends in many parts of the developing world point to a multi-faceted youth crisis, with the surging population of young people creating pressures for jobs, education, and health, while policy responses to these issues are slow, inadequate, or non-existent. The real concerns of young people have failed to attract the attention of peacemakers, policymakers, and donors. Indeed, there is a remarkable lack of policy debate to indicate that these concerns are a priority. But numerous indicators warn that if the youth problem is not addressed in the near future it will exacerbate insecurity and stall development efforts in many developing countries, particularly across Sub-Saharan Africa where youth make up more than half the population.

On its own, a youth bulge is not necessarily a negative factor or cause for concern, particularly in countries that focus on social development and can use this resource to promote their nations' development and economic growth. Countries can boost the economy by providing good education, skills training, apprenticeship systems, and a stable labor market, as South Korea has done.

But the converse has been true in many fragile states whose conditions do not allow young people's skills to be harnessed in a positive way for development. Africa, the worst-affected continent, is home to 80 percent of the world's estimated total of 300,000 young soldiers (aged ten to twenty-four). Unemployment rates among African youth, according to the International Labor Organization, average 31 percent: the highest youth unemployment rates in the world.[17] Africa also has the lowest rates of school enrollment. Out of the world total of 133 million illiterate young people, the majority are in Sub-Saharan Africa; and out of an average of 7,000 young people a day who are newly infected with HIV/AIDS, the majority are in Sub-Saharan Africa. This is not to mention the estimated 21 million youth, already infected, who require treatment.

The political marginalization of young people increases their vulnerability and makes them more susceptible to participating in illicit sources of livelihood, including crime and armed conflict. The experience of countries such as Nigeria suggests there is a very close link between the social and economic marginalization of youth and ethnic or religious violence. Young people continue to be excluded from decision making processes that affect their lives and from formal political participation.

Youth are also marginalized in the design of poverty reduction strategies and the monitoring of the Millennium Development Goals. Peace-related matters affecting youth do not feature in most of the engagement strategies of donor countries, which tend to neglect such topics as discrimination, violence, post-trauma healing and integration, and peace education. Job creation is still regarded as less important than macroeconomic stability.

In Liberia the lack of effective policies to address the youth crisis helped to ignite and sustain the violence of the 1990s. The mobilization or voluntary participation of even small numbers of youth in armed groups can pose immediate security challenges as it has in Nigeria and Cote d'Ivoire. But the more serious, longer-term challenge to security and development is the impact of a growing population of uneducated, unskilled, unemployed, and idle youth in a context of stagnant economic growth.

Many of the victims of crime and violence perpetrated by young people are other young people. High crime rates, corruption, and inefficient administration of justice create the conditions for economic inefficiency, stagnation, or decline, which in turn exacerbate unemployment and other societal dysfunctions, thus increasing insecurity. The youth crisis is more pronounced in societies affected by armed conflict, in part because the social disruptions associated with violence can predispose youth to violence.

Furthermore, in countries attempting to recover from the effects of war, youth face the difficult challenge of replacing a way of life they have become accustomed to with a new life whose prospects are uncertain. Disarmament, demobilization, and reintegration programs implemented in post-conflict situations are often inadequate, as noted above. Although only small minorities of a country's youth typically belong to armed groups, long periods of armed conflict can militarize entire societies, posing a key part of the challenge to be addressed in the post-conflict phase.

Invariably, once the imminent danger of armed confrontation is reduced, youth tend to be neglected and marginalized. Their aspirations and concerns are rarely dealt with systematically in the context of peace agreements or during the peacebuilding and reconstruction phase. Thus, the opportunity is lost to transform the enthusiasm for peace shown during the peacekeeping phase into more sustainable foundations for peace.

Failure to deal with the political and socioeconomic aspects of reintegration can raise crime rates and create a climate of insecurity that may lead a country back to violent conflict. This was seen in Liberia, where a combination of two crucial factors led to a resumption of armed conflict: the consolidation of the political power base of a warlord, and the failure to provide viable social economic alternatives for young combatants who remained attached to the command structures of their former factions.

Better analysis of the nature of the youth crises in fragile states is needed if the transformation to longer-term security and development is to be achieved. Such studies should examine existing opportunities for empowering young people and how these can be increased in the prevailing governance environment. Effective agendas should also be sought for promoting the development of young people throughout regions, particularly those regions with a growing number of fragile states and a noticeable pattern of youth vulnerability and exclusion.

In summary, if these issues at the intersection of security and development are to be effectively addressed (particularly in post-conflict settings) in ways that can guarantee lasting peace and development, greater attention must be paid to the following:

(i) The planning of DDR should envisage creative ways to ensure the reintegration of former combatants and include strategic links with related activities including security sector reform.
(ii) The local communities in which DDR and SSR are undertaken should play an integral part in the plan for long-term reintegration. Planning and programming should be flexible enough to accommodate local ideas and proposals for reintegration. Only the mobilization of local (public and private) efforts can guarantee the successful reintegration of former combatants.
(iii) Peace negotiations and agreements should strategically address critical issues such as the transformation of armed groups into political entities and actors.
(iv) Peace agreements should specify the conditions that must be fulfilled for institutional reforms, including the need to move beyond providing training to ensuring capacity development for oversight of the security sector.
(v) Creative solutions should be found for reengaging idle, unemployed, and uneducated young people, whether or not they are former combatants. The solutions might include national service programs focusing on community development and providing for longer-term apprenticeships that can convert functional illiterates into productive members of communities.

D. The Prevention Deficit: Where Wars Are Waiting to Happen

It is often argued that conflict prevention work goes unnoticed and that only failed attempts at prevention are recognized. Yet the real prevention work is yet to be done in many fragile states that are at risk of war.

The telltale signs of state failure and vulnerability to armed conflict are all too apparent in "shadow states" whose public institutions are only a façade. Beneath the façade, one may detect indicators of impending disintegration and collapse: (i) the prevalence of armed groups other than those sanctioned by the state, including civil/ethnic militia, vigilantes, and private security groups, all which point to a state's loss of monopoly over the use of force; (ii) other "self-help" initiatives beyond the provision of private security arrangements; (iii) rampant privatization of social services, for example in education and health, with which the rich compensate for weak or nonexistent public services.

In states managing to avoid a slide into war, support for a thriving informal sector can be used to channel help to common people, even if doing so further highlights the weakness of the state. Other services may be shored up by a high level of external aid (as in Uganda or Tanzania) though at the risk of creating aid dependence and potential risks of decline if the life-support machine on which the state relies is suddenly withdrawn.

In fragile states, peacebuilding activities—security sector reform, disarmament, demobilization, and reintegration, and measures to address youth vulnerability and exclusion, all of which can be linked to a longer-term reintegration program for members of armed groups—can be conceived as conflict prevention tools. But the reality is that they are part and parcel of the long-term development effort, as highlighted in chapter 4.

Unfortunately, these approaches have yet to receive enough emphasis in multilateral programs until after a conflict has erupted and has run its deadly cycle. Conversely, bilateral and civil society actors who deal with fragile states may not provide adequate, or adequately sustained, resources to meet the needs.

The United Kingdom's support for the security sector reform program in Sierra Leone is one of the few exceptions. Even this is being delivered as part of a post-conflict assistance package. Only a change in aid allocation protocols, combined with new and much more active policies of multilateral engagement in conflict prevention focused on fragile states, will make a lasting difference.

Currently, the incentives built into the aid system encourage the initiation of conflict, in order to benefit from the vast allocation of resources that is associated with post-conflict recovery programs. It would be more cost effective to focus on conflict prevention and peacebuilding in fragile states before they slide into war or endure a complex humanitarian emergency. The various sources of bilateral and European Union assistance provided to African regional organizations suchas the African Union and the Economic Community of West African States, for building capacity for conflict prevention, would be good platforms for initiating changes in development cooperation policies consistent with the demands of conflict prevention.

As well as building the capacity of regional organizations to prevent conflict and respond to crisis, there is a need to achieve better coordination among regional organizations, the UN, and other multilateral actors. It is important to establish a clear division of labor and principles of burden sharing. But it must be stressed that claims to national sovereignty (and moral hazard considerations) remain a serious challenge to any attempt to prevent conflict.

Bilateral and multilateral actors seeking to manage and prevent conflict must find judicious entry points (other than the outbreak of armed conflict) to intervene. From this perspective, the focus of the proposed Peacebuilding Commission (UN Secretary-General, 2005) on post-conflict operations and the reluctance of many countries to give it a conflict *prevention* mandate are very unfortunate.

Despite the challenges and gaps highlighted above, conflict management processes have shown a steady improvement. Organizational learning is evident in the UN and other multilateral and bilateral organizations in pursuit of more effective methods for keeping the peace and for triggering sustainable security and development in troubled and vulnerable regions. Acceleration of this learning process would yield rich dividends.

Efforts to prevent conflict in fragile states should consider implementing some of the programs previously restricted to post-conflict environments. These include DDR, SSR, and special youth development programs. Fragile states adjacent to war-affected countries should be included in peacebuilding initiatives.

E. Reliance on Regional Actors for Conflict Management

The role of regional actors is critical to the success of conflict management, but thus far their contribution to the management of regional conflicts has received only limited recognition from international actors. UN-led interventions have received by far the most resources (though still inadequate), in more than fifty wars that have ended since the end of the Cold War. But UN peacebuilding operations have been staged only in twenty-one cases. Post-conflict situations that do not attract the United Nations hold the potential for deadly reversals. Given the limited resources, regional actors are left to pick up the pieces.

Regional actors are crucial to the sustainable success of future conflict management efforts for four major reasons. First, their proximity to the crisis makes them more inclined to respond to calls for early action.

Second, they often have a better grasp of the socio-political context in which a neighborhood crisis is unfolding. Third, through their experience of difficult neighborhood crises, regional actors, particularly African regional organizations, have developed norms and standards for preventing and managing conflict and robust approaches to dealing with violent conflict. For example, the African Union, and several sub-regional organizations including the Economic Community of West African States (ECOWAS) and the Southern African Development Community (SADC) have included in their treaties and guiding principles the right to intervene in a member state when crisis or humanitarian tragedy is imminent. This principle is similar to but more robust than the "responsibility to protect" principle that emerged after the ECOWAS approach was formulated (ICISS, 2001). Beyond bold statements and agreement on norms, some regional actors have taken daring steps to undertake conflict prevention work to halt the deterioration of situations that could have moved well beyond their conflict management ability. Examples include Nigeria in Sao Tome and Principe, and ECOWAS in Guinea-Bissau and Togo.

Fourth, some regional organizations have advanced further than the UN in their approaches to collaborating with local actors, particularly civil society groups across the region. This is the case with ECOWAS, which has formalized its involvement with West African civil society. The greatest criticism of the proposal for the Peacebuilding Commission among West African civil society actors, for example, is that it does not envisage the inclusion of civil society actors.

Regional organizations thus have a key role to play. But they also have some major weaknesses. In Africa, for example, while a number of member states have continued to contribute personnel to peacekeeping operations within and outside the continent, the capacity to deploy troops to the area of operation remains a challenge. While there is now a continental framework for peace and security, including for planning and executing peace support operations, such a framework has yet to be created for peacebuilding. This is partly because the imperative has been to respond to emergency situations that require rapid responses, and partly because African regional organizations lack sufficient capacity to provide peacebuilding support. Much of the peacebuilding work on the continent is undertaken by local civil society actors and nongovernmental organizations (largely international NGOs).

Even while short of resources, regional organizations in Africa can play a critical role by developing local and regional ideas on effective peacebuilding, which exist in abundance, into a continent-wide strategy that could provide a basis for UN and international support and give the proposed Peacebuilding Commission a highly valuable regional partner.

The UN and other development agencies can play a key role in complementing that of the regional organizations, guided by the principle of subsidiarity. The weaknesses of one can be overcome by the strengths of the other. And the success of emerging policy responses such the proposed Peacebuilding Commission calls for alliances between the UN, regional, and local actors that the European Union might also encourage and support. The trinity of diplomacy, security, and development upon which the work of the Commission should focus would be well served by combining regional strengths in diplomacy and security (such as the execution of peace operations) and the UN/international community's strengths in peacebuilding and development assistance.

The future of conflict management is burden sharing between regional, national, and global actors. Those able to respond rapidly to regional crises without Security Council constraints would do so as the UN and other international actors attend to situations on the Security Council agenda. The issue of capacity becomes all the more important in this regard. The efforts to develop the conflict management capacity of organizations in Africa, the region most affected by deadly conflict, appear to concentrate only on peace support operations, partly for the same reasons that Africans themselves have focused on this area. The EU Africa Peace Facility of 250 million is earmarked mostly for peace support operations and capacity development in this specific area.

The UN has assisted the development of planning cells at the African Union. In addition, several bilateral actors have been actively engaged in helping ECOWAS develop its capacity for peacekeeping and early warning. But focusing on capacity for peacekeeping alone, and in particular on the development of an African standby force of five regional brigades by 2010, is not enough. A more ambitious capacity building program is needed. Since security conditions are evolving and will continue to do so as more conflicts are resolved or transformed, arrangements for institution building should be flexible.

African institutions should be equipped to respond effectively to a wide range of security challenges, including lower intensity conflicts and national crises that stem from the threats and challenges discussed in this chapter. The capacity to plan and implement peacebuilding related to DDR, the reform of the security sector, and planning for better youth reintegration will very likely assume greater importance in the next decade.

F. Conclusions

If ongoing regional and global attempts to improve conflict management approaches for security and development in regions in turmoil are to have a meaningful impact on the ground, radical change must occur at several levels: in the minds of leaders within regional and global institutions, and among bilateral actors keen to make a difference.

First, most promising policy responses are the result of commitment to change among innovative leaders. Just as changed leaders produce changed institutions, improved institutions can elicit new and innovative leadership. It is crucial that decision makers in critical positions appreciate the need for a new approach and that they be committed to positive change.

Second, the decision making framework within which organizations—global and regional—respond to conflict needs to achieve a closer link between security and development. A strategic vision of the desired outcomes of conflict management must be precisely articulated and disseminated. It is important that the UN assume intellectual leadership of this process. The journey began with the Report of the Secretary-General's High-level Panel (UN, 2004) and the Secretary-General's subsequent report, *In Larger Freedom* (UN Secretary-General, 2005).[18] The bracing vision of both reports should not be abandoned despite the limited progress that was achieved at the September 2005 summit of world leaders.

Third, UN peace support operations should be refocused on a strategic vision and desired outcomes and milestones that include social and economic recovery and community reintegration. Special representatives of the Secretary-General (SRSGs) should assume leadership for the connection of security and development objectives and activities in their areas of operation. As such, the representatives must have oversight for disarmament, demobilization, and security sector reform and for economic recovery and integration programs to ensure that these all flow toward the strategic vision. The representatives must also promote and nurture strategic partnerships that will lead toward the strategic objective and collective vision.

The best candidates for SRSG positions should be selected. Member countries should press the UN to focus on a coherent strategic vision that links security and development on the ground in war-affected countries. Local and regional input should be factored into the planning of all responses to conflict, whether at UN headquarters or in the field. The Peacebuilding Commission will provide the opportunity for this, if its connection to field operations is strong. It is critically important that structures and leaders responding to conflict allow for flexibility to accommodate local ideas and initiatives within the strategic framework.

Fourth, innovative thinking is needed if peace processes are to deliver the desired goal of security and development in the long term. The area of youth reintegration and development is one where much-needed innovation must occur. Contributor nations to UN operations might play a useful role in steering the UN toward the development of reintegration programs that focus on relevant, locally-driven, long-term programs for youth development. Our proposal for national youth service programs focusing on community development is worth exploring

Fifth, the UN should provide leadership in ensuring that practice is consistent with principles, particularly in security sector reform. The UN at headquarters and in the field should take on board the OECD guiding principles and apply them coherently in the field.

Sixth, the increased focus on combating anti-terrorism poses a major challenge for efforts to transform war-torn societies as well as fragile states and to establish a closer connection between security and development. It is important that external assistance should not undermine the capacity building and democratic reforms that are needed for sustainable peace and long-term prosperity. This is especially relevant in the area of security sector reform, where there is a potential for states to hold on to (or revert to) old authoritarian modes of governance that are inimical to transparency and civilian oversight, for example by using the pretext of combating terrorism to give excessive scope to the unregulated activities of intelligence agencies and to undermine human rights.

Last, despite the challenge created by the continued insistence of states on national sovereignty and the resulting restrictions on pre-conflict peacebuilding by external organizations, it is important to ensure that the "responsibility to protect" be backed by a "readiness to help prevent" by the international community. For this kind of work, regional organizations have a distinct comparative advantage and offer the best hope for preventing more damaging and costly crises. The European Union has a distinctive role to play in helping to build their capacities.

Notes

1. Algeria's efforts to demarcate its borders with Tunisia, Niger, Mali, and Mauritania in the 1980s, and Mauritania's pursuit of a resolution of boundary problems with Mali in 1962, provide notable illustrations of such initiatives. Zartman (1990): 305.
2. Estimated at about 7-8 million deaths since 1990 (*Atlas of War and Peace*, 2003).
3. See, for example, Rothschild and Cousens (2002).
4. See "The Utstein Group Partnership," at <http://www.u4.no/about/u4partnership.cfm> and "Utstein Principles," at <http://www.u4.no/document/Utsteinprinciples.cfm>
5. A distinction may be made between the "retaliatory intervention" in Afghanistan, the Kosovo model of "containment," and the "preventive" military action illustrated by the Iraq intervention. John Mackinlay, "Participating in International Forces after 9/11" (King's College, London, working paper; mimeo).
6. Mackinlay's working paper also discusses some of the implications of the Afghanistan and Iraq operations for nations seeking to participate in international missions.
7. See Minear and Smith (forthcoming). Their chapters on Liberia and Iraq illustrate that military actors are sometimes the only actors present to perform humanitarian functions.
8. In Sierra Leone, the Bangladesh Battalion (Banbatt 6) was especially praised by locals for its support and building of a school in 2002. Mission of the United States Office of the Special Representative of the Secretary-General for Children and Armed Conflict (OSRSG) to Sierra Leone, July 2002.
9. Report on Consultations held in Liberia by the Conflict, Security, and Development Group, International Policy Institute, King's College London, and the Geneva Center for Democratic Control of Armed Forces, August 2004.
10. For example, out of a total budget of USD 478 million for the mission in Haiti (MINUSTAH) for 2005/06, 1.5 million will be spent on QIPs. In Liberia, QIPs will cost USD 1 million out of a budget of USD 722 million, the same as in Cote d'Ivoire (UNOCI), with a budget of USD 364 million as well as in Burundi (ONUB), with a budget of USD 296 million for the same period. In DRC (MONUC) the budget for QIP is USD 300,000 out of a total budget of USD 384 million; and in the Sudan (UNMIS), QIPs will cost USD 630,000 out of a total budget of USD 315 million. See UN doc. A/c.5/59/29, General Assembly, 26 April 2005.
11. UN peacebuilding missions in Africa include those in Central African Republic (since February 2000), Office of the Special Representative of the Secretary-General for the Great Lakes (since December 1997), Peacebuilding Support Office in Guinea-Bissau (since March 1999), the Political Office for Somalia (since April 1995), and the Office of the Special Representative of the Secretary-General for West Africa (since November 2001).
12. <www.un.org/peace/ppbm>
13. Authors' interviews in Liberia in July-August 2004.

14. See for example, the UN Secretary-General's Report on Sub-regional and Cross-border Issues, UN Doc. S/2004/200; and the report of the UN Security Council Mission to West Africa, UN Doc. S/2004/525.
15. Of course, such a commitment is not always foolproof, as shown by Liberia's experience in 1997, when Charles Taylor failed to adhere to a previous commitment to reform the Liberian armed forces after winning elections by a landslide.
16. Reuters, "Liberia: U.S. Hires Private Company to Train 4,000-Man Army," February 15 2005; James West, "Armed Forces of Liberia Training to Begin Soon" *Liberian Observer (Monrovia),* 19 May 2005.
17. These statistics do not include the working poor, most of whom are confined to activities in the informal sector.
18. The key proposals of the United Nations Secretary-General are for:
    - Increased aid to meet the 0.7 percent target of gross national income by 2015 or sooner;
    - Mitigating the impact of climate change through research and a more inclusive international framework following the expiration of the Kyoto Protocol in 2012;
    - A comprehensive convention against terrorism;
    - A UN Peacebuilding Commission to improve assistance to post-conflict countries;
    - Replacement of the Commission on Human Rights by a Human Rights Council;
    - Endorsement of the "responsibility to protect" to facilitate collective action against ethnic cleansing and crimes against humanity;
    - Establishment of a Democracy Fund for technical assistance;
    - Expansion of the Security Council to make it more representative; and
    - Streamlining of the UN Secretariat to make it more flexible, transparent, and accountable.

See <www.un.org/largerfreedom>

6

Development Cooperation and Human Security

> *"Globalization must be managed so that its fundamentally benign effects are assured and reinforced. Without this wise management, it is imperiled and at risk."*—Jagdish N. Bhagwati

Chapters 1 through 5 surveyed the security and development landscape and identified the pressure points of the new international order. This final chapter draws the implications for development cooperation. The overarching conclusion is simply stated: the risk-blind, aid-centered, and country-focused aid paradigm must give way to a risk-sensitive, coherent, and globally oriented development cooperation policy agenda. In what follows, we consider the rationale for change (section A); the global governance architecture (section B), the emerging trends that should inform global risk management (section C), the major drivers of global risks (section D), the implications for country assistance plans (section E), and the new policy priorities that should inform such plans (section F).

A. The Rationale for Change

The heady vision of the United Nations Charter ("to save succeeding generations from the scourge of war") has not been realized. The decline in the number of intrastate conflicts must be weighed against the persistence of regional tensions, the proliferation of weapons, the rise in international terrorist incidents, and the insecurities associated with coercive responses and military interventions. Nor is the war on global poverty being won. Progress towards the Millennium Development Goals has been halting. Inequalities within and across nations have increased.

Environmental threats have escalated. Natural disasters have become more frequent and deadly.

If the original ideals of development cooperation following the end of World War II did not generate sufficient momentum it is because they were quickly subjugated to Cold War imperatives. For three and a half decades, the industrial democracies concentrated their energies and resources on containing the Soviet Union. Once it imploded they focused on creating a global market. When the Berlin wall fell, the aid industry was conscripted in the rush towards global market integration. A major transformation of the global economic order ensued. But in the new and more demanding global economic context, few poor countries proved able to combine economic dynamism with social equity and environmental safety.

Eventually, aid priorities were adjusted to allay the humanitarian concerns of the civil society. Poverty reduction supplanted economic growth as the overarching goal of development. The neo-classical Washington consensus was "augmented" to embrace governance reforms and social equity, and a broadly based development agenda (market friendly, people friendly, and environment friendly) was adopted: the Millennium Development Goals. Unfortunately, neither the architecture of the development system nor its major instruments and practices were transformed to help implement this ambitious agenda.

The private sector and the civil society were quick to tap the opportunities offered by globalization, and restructured their operations to achieve a global reach through effective management of cross-border operations. But the aid business was slow to reform, and maintained its concentration on country assistance plans as the basic unit of account. In response to such global crises as HIV/AIDS, ramshackle organizational arrangements were cobbled together and, as described below, a bewildering number of networks emerged to fill the global governance gap. The underlying institutional and funding structure of the aid system has remained intact and the delivery system for global public goods and services has remained fragmented and under-funded.

Recently, development advocates have focused their efforts on reversing the secular decline in aid flows. While aid is critical to the economic and social prospects of the least developed countries, it has become less relevant as a resource transfer mechanism in a global context characterized by rapidly expanding trade, investment, and migration flows. Nor have the links between aid policy and the other transmission belts of globalization been tightened, despite ample evidence that trans-national threats to peace, prosperity, and environmental sustainability have multiplied. Silo thinking still permeates the development and security establishments and, at the country level, the downside risks of policy prescriptions are not always appreciated or sufficiently emphasized.

In sum, the international community has yet to draw the full implications for human security of the surge in travel, trade, and communications spawned by the new information technologies. Short-term and parochial concerns still dominate domestic politics, and international institutions do not elicit sufficient public support, so that long-term risks requiring global collective action are not attended to. It is time to change course. To be responsive to the new challenges created by the ongoing transition to a more integrated global economy, the mandate of the development enterprise should be adjusted to respond to three interrelated sets of challenges.

First, the design of global and regional programs for delivering public goods has become the new frontier of development effectiveness. The emerging world order has intensified the demand for global and regional public goods, while public "bads" are thriving on a global scale. Arms and weapons flood the international market. Vulnerable states succumb to civil strife and the resulting conflicts spill over neighboring territories. Health pandemics spread like wildfire. Given demographic trends and the demands that growth imposes on the environment, the global commons are under stress. Given the cross-border nature of the threats to peace and prosperity, development cooperation needs to break out of the "country focus" that it adopted when it was tasked to facilitate the process of globalization.

Second, the aid enterprise needs to be reformed. If aid remains critical to development it is because it has a privileged role to play in facilitating the adjustment of non-aid policies and in steering globalization in a more development friendly direction. The impact of aid is dwarfed or negated by the huge volume of cross-border transactions that globalization has boosted. Given globalization, what matters most for poverty reduction is the policies of rich countries that shape trade, investment, migration, intellectual property rights, and the environment. Hence, it stands to reason that development cooperation should reach beyond aid.

Third, policies for development cooperation need to be coordinated not only within nations but also across nations. Aid is no longer effective as a resource transfer mechanism from the rich to the poor. While the aggregate gains from globalization exceed the losses, some countries, groups, and individuals enjoy a disproportionate share of the benefits while others bear a disproportionate share of the costs. Neither the prospective volume of aid nor its current practices are geared to the redistribution challenge associated with asymmetric globalization. Humane globalization requires adjustments in the policies themselves.

For donor countries, this means that new strategies of engagement with developing countries should be designed. The strategies should be based on careful examinations of the "footprint" of non-aid policies. Such assessments are needed to define the necessary changes in rich countries' policies. The goal of this new brand of country assistance plans is to enhance the poverty reduction impact of all policies that impact on the welfare of poor countries, including international trade, private investment, migration, intellectual property rights, security, and the environment. At a minimum, rich countries' engagement with poor countries should do no harm.

In sum, the development cooperation business must reach beyond aid and across borders, and the country-focused phase of development history must give way to a new paradigm that puts equitable global development at the center of a renewed aid enterprise.

B. The Global Governance Environment

No single entity exists to coordinate national policies, redistribute resources, or deliver global public goods. Nor, given the inherent limits of human organization, could such an entity be created without impinging on national identities and individual liberties. Therefore, at this stage in history, no feasible blueprint can be drawn up for centrally managed global governance. Even modest recommendations for strengthening the multilateral system have been set aside. As a result, reform at the United Nations has been hesitant and partial, while the shareholders of the Bretton Woods institutions have not endorsed the structural changes needed to make them more legitimate and relevant to the changing needs of developing member countries (Einhorn, 2006).

Of course, the range and complexity of global issues and the diversity of interests involved in managing global governance are much too vast to be handled by multilateral institutions, however competent and legitimate. Nor can many of the functions involved in trans-national resource allocation, policy design, or public goods provision be fulfilled by states acting on their own. While states are still the most powerful actors, they must increasingly rely on regulatory means to achieve public policy objectives. Increasingly, they must devolve their peripheral responsibilities to non-state actors.

As a result, rules set and organizational incentives designed in consultation with non-state actors and public-private partnerships have multiplied and some of the policy design and implementation responsibilities of the state have instead become the responsibility of international networks that bring together representatives of the public, private, and voluntary sectors (Kaul and Conceição, 2006).

The Advent of Networks

In the new space created by globalization, networks have been setting rules for national enforcement and incentives for voluntary adoption by non-state actors. The new networks differ widely in structure and in mode of operation. Some are constituted as informal and flexible groupings led by states or industry groups with voluntary associations and knowledge organizations playing a mediating role. Others adopt formal partnership structures characterized by shared objectives, distinct accountabilities, and reciprocal obligations. Equally, outsourcing, devolution, and privatization are now common in the production and delivery of public goods whether local, national, regional, or global.

Conversely, corporate social responsibility programs are no longer simply the province of charitable giving by individual companies. Industrial associations are now designing codes of conduct, in consultation with governments and civil society representatives. Typically, professional assessment of performance against agreed environmental and social sustainability standards involves rating agencies and non-governmental organizations.

Thus, hybrid trans-national arrangements combining public and private interests and civil society organizations have sprouted and spread, whether for knowledge transfer, policy design, harmonization, implementation, verification, or evaluation. The new horizontal networks operate at various levels of government globally, within regions, or across countries that share values and interests. They arise spontaneously or result from formal or informal agreements among states. They are interconnected on a global scale through the new information technologies.

Within specialized domains of intervention, multilateral agencies are often entrusted with one or more aspects of policy design, implementation, and review and/or the associated delivery of global or regional public goods. But more often than not, they are called upon to use their convening power to create platforms for multi-sector stakeholder consultations and reciprocal lesson learning. In certain instances, they are contracted to provide information, analysis, and advice to individual states or groups of states.

The Disaggregated State

To accommodate diverse processes of international cooperation, the state has become disaggregated. Each of its components interacts with similarly situated counterparts in other countries. The network thus constituted reaches out to specialized knowledge communities as well as to private and public interest groups within and across borders. This helps to ensure coherence across countries but in turn it requires domestic mechanisms for recombining the outcomes of the diverse horizontal network interactions, so as to achieve domestic policy coherence across departmental boundaries. Such coherence is essential if the policies incubated within international horizontal networks are to acquire national ownership.

External coherence and internal incoherence have become inseparable. "Whole of government" mechanisms must be shaped to fit the political and administrative traditions of individual countries. No two "joined up" governments are alike. But the overarching objective is the same: policy coherence. Without it, the legitimacy and effectiveness of the networks themselves cannot be assured, since we live in a world of states and the responsibility for domestic governance ultimately rests with national governments. Thus, transfer of executive responsibility to supranational networks is rare. Invariably, the process of vertical policy regulation and enforcement rests with individual states. This inevitably raises issues of compliance and opportunistic behavior among states, since in the absence of a supranational hierarchy powerful enough to impose penalties free riding is rampant.

The voluntary and informal structure of most horizontal networks also brings up problems of verification in implementation, since information asymmetries tend to prevail in large groups. Typically, the tasks of collecting objective monitoring information and periodically evaluating compliance with agreed standards are carried out through peer group reviews. In addition, specialized non-governmental organizations scrutinize the performance networks and disseminate the results to the public.

The Imperative of Participation

The end result of globalization is that a state can no longer operate as an independent entity according to protocols governed by diplomacy within strictures imposed by intergovernmental organizations. Increasingly, states find themselves enmeshed within a fluid web of horizontal networks that are tasked with setting the rules of the global system. In turn, this means that to be an effective player in the new global order, a state must structure itself as a flexible bundle of policy entities equipped to interact continuously through cross-border networks made up of similarly specialized units in the public and private sectors and civil society. Exclusion from the horizontal networks that govern the processes of globalization condemns individual states to irrelevance and marginalization in an interconnected world.

For developing countries, participation in such networks is a critical need, but it is neither automatic nor cost free. It requires a critical mass of skills, access to specialized professional advice, ready access to information technology, and significant budgets for consultancy services and travel. Therefore, to level the playing field of development cooperation the first task is to provide poor countries with the wherewithal for meaningful participation, so that they can contribute their experience and protect their interests when decisions are made that affect their economic and social prospects.

How then can a humane and peaceful world order emerge? Can disaggregated states, interconnected through a maze of formal and informal networks, ensure peace, stability, protection of the environment, and security for all human beings? The answer lies in political change and development advocacy. To reform governance structures and processes, only an organic process of change responding to public opinion and building on existing networks is conceivable. The sorry fate of recent proposals by the Secretary-General of the United Nations suggests that top-down reform focused on the superstructure of international organizations is unlikely to succeed.

The Rome of global governance will not be built in a day. In time, a groundswell of public opinion combined with diplomatic efforts and patient restructuring of the current governance architecture may bear fruit. But in the meantime, partial and jerrybuilt solutions to discrete development needs will have to be sought through the design and operation of horizontal networks that share information, create knowledge, and tackle development problems one issue at a time.

Given the scale and complexity of the challenge, subsidiarity should be viewed as the fundamental principle of organizational design in the new international space. In an operating environment that lacks enforcement capacities, voluntary compliance with standards generated by consensus, arising out of participatory processes, is more likely to succeed than efforts to impose idealistic norms. With limited resources, governments will have to concentrate on the commanding heights of global policy and leave the rest to informal and formal networks. Their behavior is likely to be shaped by public attitudes to risk and uncertainty.

The Geopolitics of Risk

To assess current and future risks to human security calls for an understanding of how the geopolitical force field has evolved. The nuclear confrontation of the Cold War era kept everyone on edge but the rules of the game were clear, the strategic choices were stark, and development cooperation marched to the drums of the Cold War. Since errant behavior involved catastrophic risks, the ideological contest induced predictability in international relations and policy convergence in development cooperation. No such discipline exists today. Numerous and interacting risks have emerged, perceptions of their relative importance and severity differ, and the purpose of development cooperation has become blurred. The old certainties are gone.

Whereas geo-economics provided a framework for development cooperation in the post-Cold War era and poverty reduction eventually became the rallying cry of development advocates, geopolitics resumed its dominance once the United States declared a new "long war" against Islamic extremism. This has created fresh fault lines within traditional alliances. A groundswell of international public support for the United States swept the world following the terrorist attack of 9/11 but quickly evaporated once the Bush administration launched its global war on terrorism.

At a defining moment of history, in reaction to an unprecedented attack on proud symbols of its values and its military ascendancy, the lone military superpower reconsidered its strategic doctrine and by going it alone squandered a unique opportunity to lay the foundations of a global security order. In response to the terrorist challenge, the United States had emphasized the military dimension of its power and provoked a backlash that swelled the ranks of Islamic extremist movements, divided the Atlantic alliance, and undermined its own influence.

The U.S. is now striking a more open and sober diplomatic posture but the concentration of its foreign policy on the threat of mega-terrorism contrasts with the perceptions of European countries who view the challenge in a more nuanced way but have yet to adopt a unified posture. The result is a fragmented international system in which no single country, even the lone superpower, can claim to be in charge. The increased political clout of the populous and dynamic Asian economies, the drift to the left in Latin America, and the electoral victories of radical leaders in Iraq and Palestine contribute to perceptions of drift. The United States remains dominant militarily but it is pursuing unsound fiscal and energy policies which have contributed to instability and imbalances in the world economy.

In brief, the capacity to deal with global security challenges and threats is declining just at a time when risks are escalating. The era when a single superpower could call the shots is waning, as can be seen in the attempts by the United States to enlist Russia and even China in its efforts to block Iran's nuclear ambitions. Nor does Europe appear willing or able to fill the leadership gap, given its reluctance to exercise hard power, its limited military assets, the travails of EU enlargement, and sundry internal disputes. And the legitimacy of the United Nations is eroding, given the widespread perception that the Security Council has too narrow a power base and the world body's inability to reform its outmoded organizational structure.

Given the complex political force field described above, it is not likely that international organizations of the traditional type, composed of formal delegations of the constituent states headed by an ambassador and operating by consensus, will be able to do much more than concentrate on major security issues and operate as a convening platform for specialized international agencies and horizontal networks. Therefore, to achieve results, governance reform should concentrate on strengthening existing specialized agencies and improving the workings of horizontal networks.

For such an approach to be legitimate and effective, more balanced power sharing arrangements will have to be instituted, giving developing countries a bigger voice in the decisions that will shape global security and development trends. In parallel, capacity building services will have to be delivered to ensure that poor states can exercise their voice options so as to achieve an influence commensurate with their demographic and economic weight. Accountability, transparency, responsiveness to the needs of the poor, merit-based selection of leaders, and other requirements of sound governance should be promoted not only in international organizations but also in the formal and informal networks that now carry much of the burden of global governance.

New policy directions will also have to be promoted along lines sketched in the previous chapters. The new development cooperation agenda should ensure (i) coherence for development at the level of individual policies, within and among rich nations and in alignment with the priorities of poor developing nations; (ii) better enforcement of international human rights legislation; and (iii) high quality development programs at the country, regional, and global levels.

The institutional adaptation will not succeed unless the mounting public discontent with globalization is addressed. To be sure, the benefits of globalization should not be taken for granted and everything possible should be done to avoid a reversal of its gains and a return to the fortress mentalities of fear and protectionism. On the other hand, the sustainability of global integration depends heavily on correcting the egregious asymmetries of the current world order and effectively mitigating its downside consequences. This is why risk management and human security will have to move to the very top of the development cooperation agenda.

C. Trends in Global Risk

We live in an age of anxiety. The new risks associated with globalization are such that a human security agenda is needed to supplant development doctrines that have, for far too long: (i) ignored issues of major public concern such as law and order, peace and security, or failed states; (ii) made light of the downside risks associated with unilateral policy adjustments; and (iii) ignored the proliferation of cross-border threats and challenges that can only be tackled by broadly based international coalitions. Hence, we now turn to a description of global risk trends, starting with the risk of war.

The number of major armed conflicts rose precipitously in the aftermath of World War II. But by the mid-1970s colonial wars had fizzled out and inter-state wars became less frequent even as the number of states trebled. On the other hand, intra-state wars became embedded in the fabric of the international environment and, as a result, the number of major conflicts rose above fifty by the early 1990s. The trend was reversed following the end of the Cold War: proxy wars fizzled out and conciliation efforts by the civil society and the United Nations intensified. The total number of major conflicts now stands at twenty-nine.

Over the past half century, battle deaths have fluctuated around a downward trend, and the death rate associated with violent conflict in the 1990s was only one third of what it was in the 1970s. The decline is in part because the nature of warfare has changed. Industrial killing involving huge standing armies and heavy weapons has been supplanted by low intensity wars fought with small arms and on the cheap by paramilitary forces, militias, intelligence agencies, private military firms, and child soldiers.

But battle death statistics conceal the human damage caused by conflict-induced disease, malnutrition, large-scale population displacements, egregious human rights violations, and depletion of social capital—let alone the vast reduction in productivity and incomes that war disruption causes. Reliable data on these indirect impacts are not available. If what gets measured gets done, far better information will have to be collected and analyzed to make war history.

There is no room for complacency. The downward trends in the number of major armed conflicts and the battle casualty count are not irreversible. The human security landscape is still threatening and uncertain (Human Security Center, 2005). Sixty significant conflicts are still being waged around the world. Most of them harm civilians as much as if not more than combatants, whether as a result of ethnic cleansing techniques or as a collateral consequence of aerial bombing. Some involve gruesome rapes and molestations verging on genocide (as in Darfur). According to the International Crisis Group, ten conflict situations around the world deteriorated in April 2005 while only five improved. Many conflicts have been suppressed or contained rather than resolved.

According to the United States State Department, the number of significant international terrorist attacks has grown more than eightfold over the last two decades. In parallel, terrorist casualties have risen dramatically since the 1980s and while sophisticated metrics for this new kind of war are not available it is clear that the ideological, cultural, and political tensions that underlie the terrorist phenomenon have risen considerably since 9/11 and the war on terrorism that it provoked. Long-term worst case scenarios involving use of nuclear or biological weapons by terrorists depict catastrophic outcomes involving millions of casualties.

In a global survey commissioned by the Human Security Center of the University of British Columbia, 11 percent of the respondents had been personally attacked or threatened with violence in the prior five years and twice as many thought it likely that they would become victims of violence in the next year. More than a fourth of respondents (27 percent) saw criminal violence as the greatest threat they faced compared to 15 percent for terrorism, 13 percent for poor health and economic threats, and 12 percent for accidents and natural disasters.

The global economy has recovered since the downturn of 9/11, but worrying signs of fragility have emerged and a painful correction is in the cards since most economists believe that the world is failing to come to grips with structural shifts that demand convergence in national economic policies. Since the early 1990s, the current account of the United States has shifted from rough balance to a deficit of more than 6 percent of GDP. The dollar has depreciated. The U.S. national debt has ballooned to more than USD 8 trillion (22 percent of GDP) and, with interest rates increasing, the budgetary burden of servicing the debt has begun to escalate. For the first time since 1933 the personal savings rate of Americans has moved into negative territory. A severe crisis could be triggered by a burst in the real estate bubble or by an abrupt change in foreign savers' readiness to hold dollar assets of depreciating value.

Conversely, foreign currency reserves outside the United States have risen by USD 2 trillion since 2001. While the savings of Japan and Europe are structural and linked to demographic factors, those of developing countries largely reflect public investment restraints designed to cushion the economy from the potential impacts of global financial crises. Whatever the ultimate cause of the current imbalance and its ultimate resolution, a paradoxical situation has been allowed to take hold: the low- and middle-income countries of the world are funding unsustainable consumption levels in the United States. From a poverty reduction perspective, there could not be a more shocking example of policy incoherence.

D. The Anatomy of Global Risks

Looking ahead, global risk concerns are likely to include such hardy perennials as financial crises triggered by global economic imbalances (or oil supply disruptions), the possible mutation and dissemination of the avian flu virus, deadly terrorist attacks, or unpredictable outbreaks of violence whether in marginalized immigrant communities in Europe or against Western symbols of influence in the developing world.

Headline Risks

Combined with the unknowns of geo-economic and political trends, the global risk landscape has darkened. Specifically, 2005 was dominated by the aftermath of the *tsunami* disaster, the ravages caused by Gulf of Mexico hurricanes, and an earthquake of major proportions in a remote area of Pakistan. Late and uncoordinated responses to that disaster, as well as the surprising incompetence of United States federal and state authorities in the wake of the New Orleans flood, confirmed that the world direly needs to be better prepared for natural disasters.

Equally, the London suicide attacks of 7/7 were a stark reminder that Islamic extremism can be homegrown, while the relentless attacks of the insurgency in Iraq and the persistence of violence in Afghanistan have thrown into sharp relief the limits of coercive foreign intervention. Such "headline risks" have displaced public attention from the silent and chronic crises of underdevelopment punctuated by episodic advocacy campaigns aimed at "making poverty history." HIV/AIDS and other infectious diseases have continued their deadly spread, and long drawn out conflicts, whether in Darfur or in northern Uganda, still inflict gruesome pain and suffering on civilians, especially women and children.

Major Drivers and Underlying Causes of Risk

A host of interacting factors underlie the above risks: environmental stress, economic volatility, social exclusion, political crises, and governance dysfunctions. The most obvious and pervasive risks have to do with the economic marginalization of vast zones of the developing world in which governmental structures have been overwhelmed by the demands placed on them. Faced with civil unrest or domestic insurgencies (whether due to greed, political grievance, or horizontal inequalities), domestic authorities find themselves unable to maintain law and order on their territories. Beset by natural disasters, they must rely on often inadequate international help. Nor are such governments equipped to deal with outbreaks of contagious diseases, given the dilapidated state of their health services.

The experience of some countries illustrates the nature of global risks as simultaneously local and trans-national. Domestic insurgencies may receive generous financial help from diasporas; violence from neighboring countries may feed into domestic conflict; the perceived humiliation of a religious or ethnic community may stoke the flames of discontent and intolerance; increasingly nimble, sophisticated, and decentralized criminal networks may establish residence; and instability may result from the capture of natural resources by warlords in cahoots with private foreign interests.

Other long-term risks are insidious and very hard to manage in that they build up gradually and call for sustained mitigation measures on a worldwide basis. Climate change tops the list of such existential threats. The consensus of scientific opinion is that failure to control the emission of greenhouse gases (for example through taxes on energy use and tighter regulation of power utilities and automobile design) is likely to intensify the risk of droughts, floods, and cyclones and could inflict irreversible and far reaching ecological damage on the entire planet. Yet no international consensus about the nature and consequence of the risk and its possible remedies has yet been reached.

Trans-national threats are rooted in the connectivity of the global economic order that characterizes globalization, including a thriving illicit trade in arms, drugs, diamonds, people, and counterfeit articles; the potential for instant disease contagion made possible by mass air travel; the vulnerability of interconnected power utilities to systemic failure, or the exposure of computer networks to ever more sophisticated virus attacks and covert infiltration techniques. Policy responses have been slow to materialize not only because of the uncertainty that inevitably prevails about "over the horizon" risks (and the irrational fears they sometimes provoke) but also because the incidence and severity of potential risks vary considerably among groups and nations and collective action dilemmas intervene when it comes to deciding on remedial courses of action.

Conflicting Risk Perceptions

Freedom from fear and freedom from want are inextricably connected. In eleven countries surveyed by the Human Security Center (2005), one third of respondents believed that economic issues should be the top priority of government and another 20 percent named social issues (including poverty, health, and education). But war, crime, and terrorism together scored as the highest priority for more than one in four respondents. This means that the traditional aid agenda focused on economic and social development needs to be enhanced to cover "hard" security issues in order to be fully responsive to public concerns.

The risks associated with poverty, disease, and illiteracy are of greater concern to the public in developing countries than in developed countries (for example, 71 percent and 51 percent of Turkish and Indian respondents respectively rated economic issues as the top priority whereas only 14 percent of Canadian and 10 percent of U.K. respondents did so). Within countries, the risk perceptions of the business community differ from those of the general public. From the perspective of business executives responding to a corporate risk survey tabled for debate at the 2006 World Economic Forum, natural disasters and terrorism rank eighth and tenth in severity while risks that are of greatest public concern in poor and rich countries alike lag far behind; for example, global pandemics are in thirteenth place, and civil unrest is in sixteenth place, followed by climate change and chronic diseases.

E. Towards a New Country Engagement Framework

Given the above trends and to put the lessons of this review to work, the international community should adopt a development framework oriented towards human security. This requires building a margin of safety into all development policymaking. On the one hand, avoidance of preventable hazards is integral to good public policy. On the other hand, emotion and fear should not be allowed to sway decision making: fear is contagious, panic reactions can do more damage to public welfare than a feared event itself, and populist decision making influenced by baseless rumors can be very costly to society.

Therefore, in the tradition of deliberative democracies, development policy will require an objective assessment of the probability of harmful events, their severity, and the costs involved in alleviating their impact or preventing their occurrence altogether. This is why cost benefit analysis should become an important tool of risk management and assessment and also why the dissemination of knowledge about the threats and challenges to human security has become an ethical imperative.

Priorities should be set among risks, and selectivity achieved, on the basis of full information about the upside opportunities and the downside risks associated with alternative policy actions. Thus the proper framework for decision making is a comprehensive human security framework that combines the joint pursuit of freedom from want and freedom from fear—while ensuring that duty bearers are made responsible to deliver on their respective accountabilities to mitigate risks to public welfare and to protect the basic human rights of individuals and groups.

Public support for the UN Secretary-General's proposed construction of an "iron triangle" that connects collective security, development, and human rights has been lukewarm. There remain widespread differences in risk perceptions among the policymakers of developing countries, Europe, and the United States. The need is still urgent to forge links of understanding across the Atlantic and around the world.

Due Diligence Requires Country Assessments of Policy "Footprints"

The "footprint" metaphor from ecology also has relevance for the economic relationship between rich and poor countries. Policy coherence for development is necessary to sustain the global economic system, just as responsible energy use and conservation practices are necessary to protect the environment. But the "footprint" idea adds a precautionary element in a context where the economic prospects of all countries have become inextricably linked. Beyond "doing no harm," assessments of policy footprints would help to achieve synergies among aid and non-aid policies to accelerate economic growth and reduce poverty.

Under a planning and implementation cycle based on policy coherence for development, country assistance plans would differ from the current model by taking account of : (i) the consistency of aid and non-aid policies of the donor country (the shape of the foot); (ii) the capacity of the poor country to withstand the resulting external shocks (the impressionability of the ground); (iii) the technical complexity and political feasibility of the policy reforms (the slope and rockiness of the path); and (iv) the development rewards of the journey (the pot of gold at the end). Thus understood, the "country footprint" assessment instrument would adapt development assistance to the human security imperative.

At the center of the country-footprint assessments would be estimates of the vulnerability and exposure of individual developing countries to external influences, that would be designed to ensure that the risks and rewards of proposed external engagement are properly weighed, and to identify what complementary domestic policies the country should adopt to ensure that the external policy actions yield their full poverty reduction impact. The diagnostic process would involve many actors and should be designed with care to avoid heavy transaction costs. Ideally, the analysis of policy imprints should be conducted by the developing country upstream of the poverty reduction strategy process and should involve all internal stakeholders and external partners.

Next, a diagnostic phase would identify the specific distortions that the donor country proposes to remove or reduce (or compensate for) through policy adjustment (or targeted assistance). The larger the distortion, the greater the poverty reduction benefits associated with its removal. Following the vulnerability/exposure assessment, the diagnostic process would turn to a review of "joined up" processes that would bring to bear diverse perspectives and facilitate the identification of policy options and tradeoffs. What paths should be selected to avoid political gridlock? How should policy actions be selected and framed so that they do not work at cross purposes?

"Joined up" policies need to be publicly owned to be sustainable. Even more than traditional aid-centered country strategy processes, country footprint assessments would reach beyond the concerns and objectives of aid agencies to incorporate the perspectives and goals of a wide range of government and non-government partners. Many actors should be involved: the private sector (for example to deal with corporate social responsibility issues), the civil society (for example regarding the integration of migrants in local communities) and a wide range of government departments (for example for compensatory schemes for likely losers from a reform of the EU's Common Agricultural Policy). Next, specific policy adjustment actions should be screened to determine what policy actions should be taken in parallel by all OECD partners.

Analytically, the phases of the policy coherence for development cycle would be guided by (i) the rewards for poverty reduction embedded in potential changes of OECD policies; (ii) the distinctive incoherence characteristics of individual donor policies; (iii) the exposure and vulnerability of the developing country to policy incoherence; and (iv) the identification of desirable adjustments in aid and non-aid policies, consistent with political realities. These features would be matched to the complementary developing country actions needed to take full advantage of the external policy adjustments. In some circumstances, they would include the domestic actions within OECD countries that may be needed to generate and sustain public support for the adjustments. The consultative process and the increasingly detailed analytical exercises that take place at preparation and in the periodic reviews during implementation would mirror those of the diagnostic phase.

Ex post assessment of the poverty reduction impact of policy coherence for development requires up-to-date evaluation and research techniques. It can be a learning experience for all parties concerned. Some policy research scenarios may be selected out of a bottom-up review of policy constraints in a particular developing country. Others may be identified with reference to policy reforms already under consideration as part of the UK, the EU, or the OECD agenda.

For example, impact research may evaluate the effects of increased aid flows or trace the effects on the pilot country of, say, liberalization of agricultural imports, or the removal of export and other subsidies, or the reduction of tariffs on clothing exports to OECD countries, or the relaxation of restrictions on the temporary mobility of workers from developing to developed countries.

Country Engagement Strategies Should be Informed by Risk Assessments

Market oriented policies facilitate the integration of poor countries' economies with the global market and promote growth and poverty reduction. But they also increase the sensitivity of the country's economy and society to external policy influences. The more integrated a developing country with the global economy, the more likely it is to benefit from development cooperation. But by the same token, the more vulnerable it becomes to global economic downturns and the more deeply affected by the protectionist actions of rich countries.

Thus, the "footprint" of other countries' policies depends not only on their design but also on the characteristics of individual developing countries that they affect. Thus, when selecting the priority areas to be addressed by external engagement, it is necessary to weigh the risks associated with the individual country's vulnerability and exposure. Different combinations of vulnerability and exposure have different implications for the risks of policy incoherence for poverty reduction (table 5).

Table 5
The Vulnerability-Exposure Nexus

	A. LOW EXPOSURE	B. HIGH EXPOSURE
1. LOW VULNERABILITY	Low risk Low reward	Low risk High reward
2. HIGH VULNERABILITY	High risk Low reward	High risk High reward

The desirable path of structural change involves a gradual shift from cells A1, A2, and B2 towards cell B1. This is best achieved through capacity building measures that help to move the country from row 2 to row 1 (high to low vulnerability) combined with policy adjustments that help shift the country from column A to column B (low to high exposure).

Where leadership is highly able, and broadly based public ownership for reform exists (as in countries that have prospects of joining the European Union), a "big push" option (combining policy adjustment with capacity building) can succeed. Elsewhere, it involves high risks. The riskiest strategy involves policy adjustment followed by capacity building.

Thus, the backlash against structural adjustment in Africa can be traced to country assistance strategies that emphasized a shift from column A to column B through donor conditionality without prior institutional development. It would have been more prudent to sequence development interventions by an initial move from row 2 to row 1 followed by a shift from column A to column B.

Policy Implications

Given that only two percent of wars occur in rich countries and all ongoing conflicts are within poor countries, it is not enough to use the inter-state security policies of the past to address the security issues of today. Nor is a fragmented approach that treats violent conflict, human rights, and various facets of poverty in separate compartments likely to succeed in an interdependent world. As shown in earlier chapters, a human security agenda calls for: (i) legitimate and responsive states; (ii) acknowledgement of the primacy of the individual; (iii) respect for human rights and compliance with international law; (iv) subsidiarity (devolution of responsibility to the lowest competent level); and (v) participation (involvement of individuals and civil society groups in the decisions that affect them).

In combination with policy coherence for development tenets that ensure joined up processes of analysis and priority setting (and the assignation of duties and responsibilities through transparent governance arrangements), the human security paradigm facilitates the convergence of security and development policy formulation. It addresses the predicaments of violent conflict along with those created by poverty and deprivation. It responds to universal aspirations eloquently captured by the United Nations Secretary-General's *In Larger Freedom* report.

Operationally, the human security paradigm offers a framework for nurturing common values across the diverse constituencies that make up the security and development communities. It conforms to principles of social responsibility that have been widely adopted in the private sector and the civil society. Through well established techniques for assessing and managing risks, it addresses issues of vulnerability, prevention, protection, and control. And its implementation brings to bear the prescriptions of international law and the analytical models of the social sciences, including the new institutional economics.

This agenda complements and enriches current human development approaches. Initial steps to encourage its widespread adoption would include:

(i) Sponsoring a participatory and analytical process to formulate Millennium Security Goals that would complement the Millennium Development Goals.
(ii) Commissioning research about the impact of rich countries' policies on poor countries with emphasis on the key policies that affect the welfare of developing countries (aid, trade, migration, foreign investment, intellectual property, environment, and security).
(iii) Funding independent monitoring and evaluation of rich countries' policy performance with regard to their obligations to level the playing field of the international economy ("MDG 8 plus").
(iv) Making full use of country policy footprint assessments to mainstream human security approaches and manage the risks of development cooperation activities at the country level.

F. Human Security Priorities

Investment in Conflict Prevention

The DAC Guidelines on Poverty Reduction underline the critical importance that the poor ascribe to their security, and the first responsibility of the state is to protect its citizens. It follows that conflict prevention should be incorporated in poverty reduction strategies. From this perspective, it is paradoxical that professional assessment of military spending programs is not yet a regular feature of public expenditure reviews. Few if any traditional programs for development cooperation have sought to strengthen democratic systems that facilitate non-violent resolution of conflicts and the protection and inclusion of minorities.

Equally, security sector reform has yet to be integrated into poverty reduction strategy papers.

Working "in" and "on" conflict rather than simply "around" conflict and making peacebuilding an explicit priority of development aid is central to a human security emphasis. Any external engagement with a developing country, especially a fragile state, creates incentives as well as disincentives for peace. Because the first priority is to do no harm, the social and political risks of current and proposed external engagements need to be systematically assessed. Close involvement of developing country partners enhances such assessments.

Of course, in conflict-prone situations, aid is not always the most appropriate instrument. Other instruments should be considered and great care exercised not to reward opportunistic behavior. Thus, development assistance and other forms of recognition should be designed to favor behavioral change that will support the achievement of goals specified at the outset of country engagement. In any event, policy coherence is critical to the effectiveness of aid, and thus it makes sense for development cooperation activities in trade, finance, investment, foreign affairs, and security to be guided by a single engagement strategy coordinated closely within the entire donor community.

This focus also implies basic shifts in the scope and content of plans for country assistance. In particular, donor countries' engagement with conflict-prone poor countries should focus on helping build clean, lean, and able systems of security—in defense, policing, justice, and penal systems (and improving the capacity of relevant civilian bodies in government to manage the security forces more effectively). Also needed are efforts to nurture basic state functions, including the oversight of security systems and processes by civilian authorities.

Community-driven development, social fund programs, women's education, and gender equality initiatives, in combination with enhanced delivery of social services, provide entry points for building trust, enhancing the legitimacy of the state, and including disenfranchised youths in rewarding activities that can compete with the appeal of extremist ideologies. Stronger governance institutions, more modern financial, security, and justice systems, and the involvement of diasporas in development work and the promotion of foreign direct investment would also make valuable contributions to human security.

This implies capacity building for core government competencies, including the management of public expenditures and natural resources.

Country assistance plans have focused on macroeconomic policy reform, not on encouragement of broadly based development strategies. Yet, a focus on neglected areas and groups is essential in order to defuse the social tensions associated with horizontal inequalities. Equitable access to social services, social protection, and safety nets should also be included in human security oriented country assistance plans, as should programs for young people.

To mainstream the key priorities of the human security agenda in development cooperation activities it will be necessary to use the poverty reduction strategy process. Giving primacy to human security implies putting greater emphasis on structural stability, respect for the rule of law, human rights, and social development. Working with a human rights focus through a conflict prevention lens would ensure that duty bearers are made aware of their responsibilities. It would also provide a bridge between civil and political rights and the social, economic, and solidarity rights of the human security agenda.

Since intra-state conflicts often spill over national borders and may be caused by incursions by non-state actors from neighboring countries, conflict prevention strategies need to be enriched by a regional perspective. Indeed, certain aspects of human security are best implemented through regional organizations positioned to suppress drug trafficking, control international crime, prosecute terrorists, the regulate trade in small arms and light weapons.

Equally, to contribute to peacebuilding, development cooperation programs should emphasize regional cooperation connected to collective security, coordinated education and health protection initiatives, infrastructure development (such as transport corridors), and watershed development. Adequate capacity building assistance to regional bodies naturally flows from this precept.

Finally, unless the foreign policies of major external actors are coordinated, conflict prevention is undermined. But care must be taken not to subject human security to the foreign policy priorities of individual donor countries. The objective application of human security principles—focused on the impacts of alternative policy options on human lives—implies that broadly based poverty reduction—aiming at progress towards a world free from want as well as from fear—should remain the overriding objective of development cooperation. Narrow considerations of power politics and national interest have no place in a human security agenda focused on the individual.

This does not detract from the need to combat the catastrophic risks of violent conflict or terrorist attacks. But legitimate local actors and the civil society need to be closely involved to ensure that resources are not diverted to schemes that do not match the needs of developing countries or that override the human rights of local populations. And, as argued above, Development Assistance Committee strictures on what activities are eligible for official aid should be scrupulously observed, so that the integrity and credibility of aid reporting is preserved.

In sum, investment in conflict prevention means that donor countries should:

(i) Cultivate a culture of conflict sensitivity by ensuring that professionals working in conflict-prone areas are trained and fully cognizant of the cultural, social, political, and economic circumstances of the countries they are helping as well as adequately trained to operate effectively in conflict-prone areas. All staff should be equipped with adequate multidisciplinary skills and analytical instruments to assess regional and ethnic imbalances and political dynamics.

(ii) Carry out conflict assessments, social analysis, and risk analyses to ensure that country assistance strategies are conflict sensitive and implemented by all donor countries and government departments to guarantee policy coherence. Equally, development cooperation activities should be planned with due concern for their regional cooperation dimensions, and appropriate capacity building assistance should be provided to regional bodies to facilitate their involvement.

(iii) Develop conflict sensitivity criteria for country engagement strategies. These strategies need a realistic long-term perspective, adequate risk management safeguards, concentration of efforts on a few visible actions, involvement of reform-minded local actors, and innovative approaches that nurture the civil society and the private sector.

(iv) Manage the risks of unintended consequences (such as corruption or capture by a dominant group) that are associated with aid in conflict-prone environments. In particular, make sure that social and environmental safeguards and accurate political analysis are part of the quality assurance process for operations that are planned in conflict-prone environments.

(v) Promote domestic ownership by identifying reform-oriented interlocutors and interacting with them while formulating and implementing country assistance strategies.

New Approaches to Conflict Management

External actors sometimes intervene without considering the political and security consequences of their involvement and, as a consequence, they make matters worse. Supporting one warring party against another may energize the insurgents. Interrupting a civil conflict with an externally imposed agreement, without genuine reconciliation, may lead to a longer and more deadly war. Humanitarian assistance may be diverted or taxed by warlords. Anti-terrorism assistance may favor heavy-handed military options and invite more intense violence. Well-meaning growth-inducing investments may increase horizontal inequalities and provoke social resentment. Large-scale operations may fuel inflation, distort the exchange rate, exacerbate unequal unemployment patterns, favor local elites, and induce corruption. In brief, the goal of doing no harm means that the risks of external involvement must be weighed along with the potential rewards.

Typically, development interventions start too late. The familiar mental model of diplomacy, military intervention, conflict management, peacemaking, reconstruction, and finally development does not match the realities on the ground. Once the complex emergency is over, the humanitarian intervention is labeled a triumph. By then, the voluntary agencies that deliver services for this phase of the aid cycle are ready to move on to the next crisis. Meanwhile, the reconstruction phase and the development intervention are still at the planning stage. Yet experience has shown that the post-conflict phase should be launched at an early phase of peacekeeping, so as to accelerate the economic recovery that is needed for reintegrating combatants into society and reconfiguring political coalitions.

Conflict management interventions should take account of the lessons of experience. First, regional actors have been woefully neglected and inadequately supported. Given their relative proximity to the conflicts and the consequences for national and regional security, they tend to be more willing than outside parties to apply radical but effective measures to nip deadly conflict in the bud and to provide longer-term engagement that ensures sustainability. They may be more sensitive to early warnings of potential conflict and more willing to take account of deteriorating situations in neighboring states.

Second, peace support mandates have been too narrowly focused on short-term objectives of political settlement and elections. They have encouraged early exit without dealing with the root causes of crises. This problem has been compounded by inadequate interaction between the political/security mission and the development side of the UN system, the international financial institutions, and NGOs. Resources allocated by peacekeeping missions to quick impact projects have been too limited to achieve any significant impact. Better links to timely security sector reform and disarmament, demobilization, and reintegration operations are needed.

Third, the management of peace support operations should be fully empowered to coordinate all operations on the ground. Peacebuilding support offices should involve local stakeholders to facilitate the transformation of domestic institutions and assist in national institutional reform processes in the security system and related sectors. Planning and programming should be flexible enough to accommodate local ideas and proposals for reintegration.

Fourth, peace agreements should strategically address such critical issues as the transformation of armed groups into political entities and actors. Equally, they must move beyond training to ensure capacity development—for example for oversight of the security sector, for the engagement of idle, unemployed, and uneducated young people in development programs, and for involving fragile states adjacent to war affected countries.

Hard won lessons of experience suggest the following recommendations regarding the role of development cooperation in conflict management:

(i) Draw on knowledge gathered by peacemaking nongovernmental organizations to develop harmonized criteria of engagement (and non-engagement) that help to prevent unintended consequences in conflict situations.
(ii) Experiment with joined up approaches to military-civilian interventions in conflict situations, in ways that protect the principles of independence and non-partisanship that characterize humanitarian and development activities.
(iii) Help design and pilot new kinds of integrated operations that combine short-term rehabilitation, security sector reform, and disarmament, demobilization, and reintegration together with long-term development assistance that involves non-state actors and draws on domestic energies, local talent, and—above all—regional actors.
(iv) Encourage multilateral development organizations and international financial institutions to remain engaged in conflict-affected countries, provide economic and development management advice, and help mainstream security sector reform and military expenditure reviews in poverty reduction strategy papers and similar development planning instruments.
(v) Influence the UN to broaden the mandates of its interventions, to strengthen their links to other multilateral, regional, bilateral, and voluntary actors, and to select special representatives of the Secretary-General with care and empower them to address the full range of recovery and capacity development issues on a timely basis.

Engaging with Fragile States

The variation among failed states means that a tailor-made approach to each is critically important, but it does not preclude the elaboration of a policy that incorporates lessons of experience and helps to avoid repeating mistakes.

Engagement with fragile states has usually been motivated by past colonial links, economic interests, or a geographical location close to the donor country, rather than by objective criteria. Decisions on whether or not to engage tend to be based on opportunistic considerations of donor countries' national interest. It is to guard against such a risk that an explicit policy is needed and that it should be endorsed by the development community.

The combination of a general reluctance to invest resources in troubled countries (because they are "poor performers"), a frequent lack of agreement among donor countries about how to handle the situation, and the normal syndrome of bureaucratic risk avoidance tends to result in benign neglect that lets crises fester. By the time a major intervention becomes unavoidable it can have only limited results, at very high cost and with uncertain outcomes. When things go wrong, one or more donor countries may decide to use the exit option. This usually makes things worse, so that a new crisis erupts and the prior pattern is repeated. This stop-go sequence is usually associated with engagement strategies that focus on treating the worst symptoms of the crisis instead of addressing its root causes.

Donors' reluctance to engage enough resources in fragile states is often due to a prior judgment that fragile states are not fit for development assistance until they have had a conflict and it has been "resolved." There are several reasons for this stance. First, no policy is in place that justifies early intervention in situations characterized by high risks but also high potential gains in human security. Another reason is the mistaken notion that ownership, partnership, and results orientation are prerequisites of engagement instead of outcomes that the engagement is intended to produce. A third intellectual obstacle to the design of responsive country assistance strategies is the tendency to lump all fragile states together, despite the differences among them. The fourth and final constraint can be traced to a lack of agreed criteria as to what constitutes a fragile state, how to measure fragility, and what the operational implications of different fragility characteristics are.

To overcome these obstacles, donor countries under DAC auspices should consider adopting a policy towards fragile states that takes account of the following recommendations:

(i) Carry out risk-reward analyses based on human security principles instead of relying only on political factors in deciding whether or not to engage. Among the risks is the potential harm that may be caused by appearing to support a regime that does not protect human rights and has no interest in poverty reduction. Among the rewards may be the protection of human rights, the prevention of large-scale kidnapping of children and rape as weapons of war, the preservation of regional stability, and the prevention of major human hardship and destruction.
(ii) Intervene in de facto states (for example Somalia) without presuming that illegitimate and corrupt local authorities are entitled to act as channels for the assistance, and provide for building capacity in the civil society that may improve the chances of political participation and eventual legitimacy.
(iii) Use security sector reform and disarmament, demobilization, and reintegration interventions as potential entry points for initiating state building and economic recovery through sequenced interventions coordinated within the donor country, harmonized among donor countries, and aligned with the existing or shadow processes of the fragile state.
(iv) Focus on results in the use of private, public, or voluntary channels of assistance and direct capacity building assistance to the local community, the regional level, or the central government.
(v) Apply the lessons of policy research in designing country engagement strategies for fragile states. That is, encourage the adoption of growth oriented strategies that emphasize safety nets and social protection, accelerated demographic transition, gender equity, youth employment, food security, enhanced access to education and health services by all, and better natural resource management and natural disaster prevention.

Learning and Harmonization in the Development Community

Finally, this review has highlighted a number of constraints on the effective pursuit of security and development at the global level. For the international development community this has several implications for action:

(i) The United Nations is uniquely placed to sponsor a participatory and analytical process to unbundle the Eighth Millennium Development Goal and enrich it so that its progress can be monitored through specific performance indicators.
(ii) The OECD Development Assistance Committee is the forum of choice to promote a revision of current aid allocation formulas by the international community so that they give adequate weight to state fragility criteria and do not create "aid orphans."

(iii) The Development Assistance Committee should also encourage the harmonization and transparency of definitions of the fragile state across the development community.
(iv) The United Nations and regional organizations should be empowered, equipped, and funded to act as security providers especially in Africa, the Middle East, and the former Soviet republics.

***

The emergence of a new concern for human security marks the passage from a post-Cold War era dominated by the demands of global economic integration to a post 9/11 world characterized by volatility and insecurity. In rich and poor countries alike, citizens aspire to freedom from fear as well as freedom from want. Combining these two imperatives within a new paradigm requires changes in the objectives, instruments, and modalities of development cooperation. Unprecedented opportunities and risks arise from the interconnectedness of societies and nations. What takes place "out there"—in the borderlands of turmoil and transition of the developing world—has become intertwined with what needs to be done "right here"—within the homelands of rich countries. External affairs and domestic politics have become intertwined. To meet the aspirations of people everywhere, the humanitarian, development, and security enterprises will have to cohere.

But there are diverse paths to convergence. Some point towards centralized and coercive global governance systems controlled by the rich and privileged few. Others lead to flexible networks run democratically for the benefit of all, and these are the paths that would be traveled by those that heed the voices of the poor, the oppressed, and the victims of violence. Such a progressive alliance would seek to make globalization humane and bring together the scattered energies of like-minded citizens, politicians, policy analysts, experienced practitioners, and development activists. As their networks spread and their ranks swell, the odds of the development cooperation journey progressing towards a global society characterized by inclusion, empowerment, and devolution would improve. If so, the concepts, ideas, and lessons of experience collected in this volume might have contributed in a small way to the judicious selection of policy goals, technical instruments, and operational methods.

Notes

1. In a survey of 43,000 people in fifty-one countries commissioned by the World Economic Forum, twice as many respondents think the next generation will live in a less safe world as expect an improvement. <http://www.weforum.org>

2. A global risk survey carried out by consulting firms, an insurance company, and the Wharton School at the University of Pennsylvania displays interesting scenario-based estimates of the probability and severity of long-term risks. <www.weforum.org/global risk>
3. <http://www.swissre.com>
4. <www.oecd.org/document/1/0,2340,en_2649_34621_1885953_1_1_1_37413,00.html >
5. The creation of capacity and resilience at the central level has obvious advantages if legitimacy can be nurtured but it may involve serious risks if the leadership is venal and brutal. By contrast, nurturing social cohesion at the community level can have high value for conflict prevention if it holds reasonable prospects for "upscaling."
6. MDG 8 plus would include reform of policies towards aid, trade (including arms and weapons), the international financial architecture, foreign direct investment, migration, intellectual property rights, and the environment. It would comply with human security principles and it would complement the seven existing MDGs (extended to 2025) as well as the new Millennium Security Goals.

References

Addison, Tony, ed., 2003, *From Conflict to Recovery in Africa*. WIDER Studies in Development Economics, United Nations University, Helsinki. New York and London: Oxford University Press.

Alexander, Gerard, 2004, "The Authoritarian Illusion," *The National Interest*, no. 77, Fall.

Alexander, Nancy, 2004, "Judge and Jury: the World Bank's Scorecard for Borrowing Governments." Citizens' Network on Essential Services. < www.servicesforall.org>

Allison, Graham, 2004, *Nuclear Terrorism: The Ultimate Preventable Catastrophe*. New York: Henry Holt.

Anderson, K., J. Francois, T. Hertel, B. Hoekman, and W. Martin, 2000, "Potential Gains from Trade Reform in the New Millennium." Paper prepared for Third Annual Conference on Global Economic Analysis, held at Monash University, Australia.

Annan, Kofi, 1995, *Another Agenda for Peace*. New York, United Nations.

Arrow, K. J., 1963, *Social Choice and Individual Values*. New York: Wiley.

Assefa, Hizkias, n.d., "The Meaning of Reconciliation." European Center for Conflict Prevention. Utrecht: People Building Peace. <http://www.gppac.net/documents/pbp/part1/2.reconc.htm>

Atlas of War and Peace, 2003. London: Earthscan, and New York: Penguin.

Bacevitch, Andrew J., 2005, *The New American Militarism: How Americans are Seduced by War*. Oxford: Oxford University Press.

Bailes, Alyson J. K., 2005, "A New World Order? Current Challenges and Prescriptions," *Journal of Social Science* no. 55.

Ball, Nicole, 1988, *Security and Economy in the Third World*. Princeton, NJ: Princeton University Press.

Ball, Nicole, and Kayode Fayemi (eds.), 2004, *Security Sector Governance in Africa: A Handbook*. University of Maryland Center for Democracy and Development.

Barkawi, Taraq, 2004, "On the Pedagogy of 'Small Wars,'" *International Affairs,* vol. 80, no. 1, January.

Birdsall, Nancy, 2005, *Why Inequality Matters in a Globalizing World*, World Institute for Development Economics Research, Helsinki, October, http://www.wider.unu.edu/.

Biscop, Sven, 2005, *Power to the System: The EU, Effective Multilateralism and the UN*. Royal Institute for International Relations, Brussels. Paper presented to the First Global International Studies Conference, Istanbul, August 24-27.

Board of the Millennium Ecosystem Assessment, 2005, "Living Beyond Our Means: Natural Assets and Human Well-Being." Draft, March 30. Washington, DC.

Boutros-Ghali, Boutros, 1992, *An Agenda for Peace*. New York: United Nations.

Branson, William, and Nagy Hanna, 2002, "Conditionality and Policy Learning." In Hanna, Nagy, and Robert Picciotto, eds., *Making Development Work: Development Learning in a World of Poverty and Wealth*. New Brunswick, NJ: Transaction Publishers.

Brauer, Jurgen, 2004, "Developing Peacemaking Institutions: an Economist's Approach." In Harris, Geoff, ed., *Achieving Security in Sub-Saharan Africa: Cost Effective Alternatives to the Military.* Pretoria, South Africa: Institute of Security Studies.

Brzoska, Michael, 2003a, "Post-conflict Reconstruction of the Security Sector: The Contribution of Conversion." In Bryden, Alan, and Phipp Fluri, eds., *Security Sector Reform: Institutions, Society and Good Governance.* Baden-Baden: Nomos Verlagsgesellschaft.

_____, 2003b, *Development Donors and the Concept of Security Sector Reform*, Occasional Paper no. 4. November. Geneva: Geneva Center for the Democratic Control of Armed Forces.

Bunting, Madeleine, 2005, "Honor and Martyrdom," *Guardian*, May 14.

Burnell, Peter, 2004, "The Coherence of Democratic Peacebuilding." Paper prepared for UNU-WIDER Conference, Making Peace Work, Helsinki.

Burrows, Gideon, 2002, *The No-Nonsense Guide to the Arms Trade.* London: Verso.

Buzan, Barry, Ole Waever, and Jaap de Wilde, 1998. *Security: A New Framework of Analysis.* Boulder, CO, and London: Lynne Rienner Publishers.

Byers, Michael, 2005, "Flyweight Belligerents: Why Britain Should Give Up Its Nuclear Arsenal," *London Review of Books* vol. 27 no. 9, May.

Byman, Daniel, and Matthew Waxman, 2002, *The Dynamics of Coercion: American Foreign Policy and the Limits of Military Might.* Rand Studies in Policy Analysis. Cambridge, UK: Cambridge University Press.

Center for Democratic Control of Armed Forces (DCAF), 2003, *A Handbook on Parliamentary Oversight.* Geneva: Center for Democratic Control of Armed Forces.

Center for Global Development, 2004, "On the Brink: Weak States and U.S. National Security: Commission Report." May. <http://www.cgdev.org/index.cfm>

Chen, Shaohua, and Martin Ravallion, 2004, "How Have the World's Poor Fared Since the Early 1980s?" Washington DC, World Bank Development Research Group.

Christian Aid, 2004, *The Politics of Poverty: Aid in the New Cold War.* London: Christian Aid.

Clemens, Michael, Steven Radelet, and Rikhil Bhavnani, 2004, "Counting Chickens When They Hatch: The Short-term Effect of Aid on Growth." Working paper no. 44. Revised November. Washington, DC: Center for Global Development.

Coker, Christopher, 2004, *The Future of War: The Re-enchantment of War in the Twenty-first Century.* Malden and Oxford: Blackwell Publishing.

Collier, Paul, and Anke Hoeffler (2000), "Greed and Grievance in Civil War." Washington, DC: World Bank.

Collier, Paul, and Ngozi Okonjo-Iweala, 2002, *World Bank Group Work in Low-income Countries under Stress: A Task Force Report.* Washington, DC: World Bank.

Collier, Paul, V. L. Elliott, Havard Eggre, Anke Hoeffler, Marta Reynal Querol, and Nicholas Sambanis, 2003, *Breaking the Conflict Trap: Civil War and Development Policy.* Washington, DC. World Bank.

Commission for Africa, 2005, *Our Common Interest: An Argument.* London: Penguin Books.

Cooper, Robert, 2004, *The Breaking of Nations: Order and Chaos in the Twenty-first Century.* London: Atlantic Books.

Dasgupta, Partha, 2005, "Bottlenecks," *London Review of Books,* May 19, 2005.

de Ferranti, David, Guillermo Perry, and others, 2005, *Beyond the City: The Rural Contribution to Development.* World Bank Latin American and Caribbean Studies (Advance edition). Washington, DC: World Bank.

Debiel, Tobias, Stephan Kligebiel, Andreas Mehler, Ulrich Schneckener, 2005, *Between Ignorance and Intervention.* Policy Paper 23. Berlin: Development and Peace Foundation.

Department for International Development (DFID), 2000, *Security Sector Reform and the Management of Military Expenditures: High Risks for Donors. High Returns for Development.* London: DFID.

_____, 2002, *Understanding and Supporting Security Sector Reform*, London: DFID.

_____, 2003, *Security Sector Reform Policy Brief,* London: DFID.

Dessus, Sebastien, Kiichiro Fukasaku, and Raed Safadi, 1999, *Multilateral Tariff Liberalization and the Developing Countries.* Paris: OECD Development Center, Policy Brief No. 18.

Dobbins, James, John G. McGinn, Keith Crane, Seth G. Jones, Rollie Lal, Andrew Rathmell, Rachel Swanger, and Anga Timilsina, 2003, *America's Role in Nation Building: From Germany to Iraq.* Santa Monica, CA, and Arlington, VA: Rand.

Duffield, Mark, 2001, *Global Governance and the New Wars: The Merging of Development and Security,* London: Zed Books Ltd.

Duffield, Mark, 2006, "Human Security: Linking Development and Security in an Age of Terror." In Klingebiel, Stephan (editor), *New Interfaces between Security and Development: Changing Concepts and Approaches.* German Development Institute, Study 13, Bonn.

Dwan, Renata, and Caroline Holmqvist, 2005, "Major Armed Conflicts." Chapter 2 in *SIPRI Year Book 2005: Armaments, Disarmament and International Security.* Stockholm: SIPRI.

Einhorn, Jessica, 2006, "Reforming the World Bank: Creative Destruction," *Foreign Affairs,* January-February, vol. 85, no.1.

Eurobarometer, 2005, "Attitudes towards Development Aid." Survey commissioned by the Directorate-General, Development of the European Commission. February.

European Union (EU), 2003, *A Secure Europe in a Better World: European Security Strategy.* 12 December. Brussels.

Fitz-Gerald, Ann M., 2004, "Security Sector Reform in Sierra Leone: Global Facilitation Network for SSR." Cranfield University.

Food and Agriculture Organization, United Nations (FAO), 2004, *The State of Food Insecurity in the World 2004. Monitoring Progress towards the World Food Summit and Millennium Development Goals.* Rome: FAO.

Foreign Policy, 2005, "Foreign Policy and the Fund for Peace: The Failed States Index." *Foreign Policy,* July/August. Washington, DC.

Forman, Shepard, 2005, "Working Better Together: Implementing the High-level Panel's Recommendations on Peacebuilding." Unpublished paper, April. New York University Center on International Cooperation.

Fukuda-Parr, Sakiko, forthcoming, "International Cooperation for Human Security: A Coherent Agenda for Development and Conflict Prevention," *Kokuren Kenkyu Journal.* Tokyo, Japan.

Fukuyama, Francis, 2004, *State Building.* London: Profile Books.

Galtung, J. (1969), "Violence, Peace, and Peace Research," *Journal of Peace Research,* vol. 6 no. 3: 167-191.

Garrett, Laurie, 2005, "The Next Pandemic?" *Foreign Affairs,* vol. 84, no. 4: 3-24, July/August.

George, Rose, 2005, "Diary," *London Review of Books,* vol. 27, no. 11, June 2.

Ginsborg, Paul, 2005, *The Politics of Everyday Life: Making, Choices, Changing Lives,* Newhaven, Yale University Press.

Glasius, Marlies, and Mary Kaldor (eds.), 2005, *A Human Security Doctrine for Europe.* London: Routledge.

Global Commission on International Migration, 2005, *Migration in an Interconnected World: New Directions for Action.* New York and Geneva, October. <http://www.gcim.org/en/>

Goldstone, Jack A., Ted Robert Gurr, Barbara Harff, Marc Levy, and Monty G. Marshall, 2000, *State Failure Task Force Report: Phase III Findings.* September 30. <http://www.cidcm.umd.edu/insc/stfail/>

Green, R. H., and M. Mavie, 1998, "From Survival to Livelihood in Mozambique," *IDS Bulletin* vol. 25, no. 4.

Grimmett, Richard F., 2001, "Conventional Arms Transfers to Developing Nations," U.S. Congressional Research Service Report for Congress, August 16.

Grobar, L. M., and S. Gnanaselvam, 1993, "The Economic Effects of the Sri Lankan Civil War," *Economic Development and Cultural Change,* vol. 41, January.

Gros, Jean-Germain, 1996, "Towards a Taxonomy of Failed States in the New World Order: Decaying Somalia, Liberia, Rwanda, and Haiti," *Third World Quarterly*, vol. 17, no. 3.

Guillaumont, Patrick, 2005, "Macro Vulnerability in Low-income Countries and Aid Responses." Paper presented to World Bank's ABCDE Conference in Amsterdam. May. Clermont Ferrand: CERDI.

Hamre, J. J., and Gordon R. Sullivan, 2003, "Toward Post Conflict Reconstruction." In Lennon, Alexander T. J., ed., *The Battle for Hearts and Minds.* Cambridge, MA: Washington Quarterly Reader, MIT Press.

Harris, Sam, 2005, *The End of Faith: Religion, Terror, and the Future of Reason.* London: The Free Press.

Hilker, Lyndsay McLean, 2004, "A Comparative Analysis of Institutional Mechanisms to Promote Policy Coherence for Development. Case Study Synthesis." Room Document 7. OECD Policy Workshop. Paris. May.

Hirschman, Albert O., 1970, *Exit, Voice, and Loyalty: Responses to Decline in Firms, Organizations, and States.* Cambridge, MA: Harvard University Press.

_____, 1995a, *A Propensity to Self-Subversion.* Cambridge, MA and London: Harvard University Press,.

_____ 1995b, *Development Projects Observed* (reissued with a new preface by the author). Washington DC: Brookings.

Holzmann, Robert, and Steen Jorgensen, 2000, *Social Risk Management: A New Conceptual Framework for Social Protection and Beyond.* Social Protection Discussion Paper No. 0006. Washington, DC: The World Bank

Hufbauer, Gary Clyde, and Paul L. E. Grieco, 2005, *The United States and the World Economy.* Washington, DC: Institute for International Economics.

Human Security Center, 2005, *Human Security Report 2005: War and Peace in the 21st Century.* New York and Oxford: Oxford University Press.

Huntington, Samuel P., 1993, "The Clash of Civilizations?" *Foreign Affairs,* Summer. Washington DC.

International Commission on Intervention and State Sovereignty (ICISS), 2001. *The Responsibility to Protect: Report of the International Commission on Intervention and State Sovereignty.* Ottawa: International Development Research Center. <http://www.idrc.ac> and <http://www.iciss.ca/menu-en.asp>

International Organization for Migration (IOM), 2005, *World Migration 2005: Costs and Benefits of International Migration.* Geneva: IOM <http://www.iom.int/>

Jägerskog, Anders, 2003, *Why States Cooperate Over Shared Water: The Water Negotiations in the Jordan River Basin.* Faculty of Arts and Sciences. Linkoping: Linkoping University.

Kanbur, Ravi, and Nora Lustig, 2000, "Why is Inequality Back on the Agenda?" Background Paper for *World Development Report 2000/2001.* Washington, DC: World Bank.

Kaul, Inge, Pedro Conceição, Katell Le Goulven, and Ronald U. Mendoza (eds.), 2003, *Providing Global Public Goods: Managing Globalization.* New York: Oxford University Press and United Nations Development Program.

Kaul, Inge, and Pedro Conceição, 2006, *The New Public Finance: Responding to Global Challenges.* New York: Oxford University Press.

Kennedy, Paul, 1987, *The Rise And Fall of the Great Powers: Economic Change and Military Conflict from 1500 to 2000.* New York: Random House.

Keohane, Robert O., and Joseph S. Nye Jr., 2000, *Power and Interdependence.* Third edition. New York: Longman.

Knack, Stephen, and Aminur Rahman, 2004, "Aid Intensity, Donor Fragmentation and the Quality of Governance." Background note prepared for *World Development Report 2004.* Washington, DC: World Bank.

Knight, W. Andy, ed., 2005, *Adapting the United Nations to a Post-modern Era: Lessons Learned.* Second edition. New York, Palgrave Macmillan.

Landman, Todd, 2005, *The Scope of Human Rights: From Background Concepts to Indicators.* Human Rights Center. March. Colchester, UK: University of Essex.

Lederach, John Paul, n.d., "*Justpeace – The Challenge of the Twenty-First Century.*" *European Center for Conflict Prevention.* Utrecht: People Building Peace. <http://www.gppac.net>

Licklider, Roy, 1995, "The Consequences of Negotiated Settlements in Civil Wars, 1945-93," *American Political Science Review*, vol. 89, no. 3: 681-90.

Lynch, Dov, 2005, "The Security Dimension of the European Neighborhood Policy," *The International Spectator*, vol. XL, no. 1, January-March.

Mallaby, Sebastian, 2005, *The World's Banker: A Story of Failed States, Financial Crises, and the Wealth and Poverty of Nations.* New York: The Penguin Press.

Mansfield, Edward D., and Jack Snyder, 2004, *Electing to Fight: Why Emerging Democracies Go to War.* Cambridge, MA: MIT Press.

McGillivray, Mark, 2005, *Reshaping the International Aid Architecture.* World Institute for Development Economics Research. WIDER Angle, No. 1/2005. <http://www.wider.unu.edu>

McLean, Iain, 1987, *Public Choice: An Introduction.* Cambridge: Basil Blackwell.

Menkhaus, Ken, 2004, "Conflict Prevention and Human Security: Issues and Challenges," *Conflict, Security, and Development*, vol. 4 no. 3, December.

Miall, Hugh, Oliver Ramsbotham, and Tom Woodhouse, 1999, *Contemporary Conflict Resolution.* Reprinted in 2004. London: Polity Press.

Minear, Larry, and Hazel Smith (eds.) (forthcoming), *Humanitarian Diplomacy.* Helsinki: United Nations University Press.

Moore, Jonathan, 1996, *The UN and Complex Emergencies: Rehabilitation in Third World Transitions.* Geneva: United Nations Research Institute for Social Development (UNRISD).

Moore, Mick, 2005, "The Development of Political Underdevelopment." In Harrison, Graham, ed., *Global Encounters: International Political Economy, Development and Globalization.* New York, Palgrave Macmillan.

Muscat, Robert J., 2002, *Investing in Peace: How Development Aid Can Prevent or Promote Conflict.* Armonk, NY: M. E. Sharpe, Inc.

Naim, Moises, 2005, *Illicit: How Smugglers, Traffickers, and Copycats Are Hijacking the Global Economy.* New York: Doubleday.

National Counterterrorism Center, 2005, *A Chronology of Significant International Terrorism for 2004.* 27 April. Washington, DC: National Counterterrorism Center.

Netherlands Minister for Foreign Affairs, 2004, "Millennium Development Goal 8: Developing a Global Partnership for Development, Progress Report by the Netherlands," May.

Nicod, Marjolaine, 2004, "Institutional Approaches to Promote Policy Coherence for Development. Findings and Lessons from DAC Peer Reviews." OECD Policy Workshop on Institutional Approaches to Policy Coherence for Development. Room Document 8. May. Paris.

North Atlantic Treaty Organization (NATO), 2003, *Glossary.* <www.nato.int/docu/glossary/eng/index.htm>

Ogata, Sadako, 2005, *The Turbulent Decade: Confronting the Refugee Crises of the 1990s.* New York: W. W. Norton.

Organization for Economic Cooperation and Development (OECD), 2001, *The DAC Guidelines, Poverty Reduction,* Paris: OECD. www.oecd.org/dataoecd/47/14/2672735.pdf)

_____, 2005, *Learning and Advisory Process on Difficult Partnerships. Principles for Good International Engagement in Fragile States.* dcd(2005)8/rev2. Development Cooperation Directorate. Paris: OECD.

Organization for Economic Cooperation and Development, Development Assistance Committee (OECD/DAC), 1998, *Conflict, Peace, and Development Cooperation on the Threshold of the Twenty-first Century.* Paris: OECD.

_____, 2003, "Aid Effectiveness and Selectivity: Integrating Multiple Objectives in Aid Allocations," *DAC Journal*, vol. 4, no. 3. Paris: OECD.

_____, 2004, *Security System Reform and Governance: Policy and Good Practice.* DAC Guidelines and Reference Series. Paris: OECD.

_____, 2006, "Development Cooperation Report, 2005," *OECD Journal of Development Cooperation.* Development Cooperation Directorate, Paris: OECD.

Overseas Development Institute (ODI), 2003, *Humanitarian Action and the "Global War on Terror": a Review of Trends and Issues.* Humanitarian Policy Group Report 14. July. London: ODI.

Pape, Robert A., 2005, *Dying to Win: The Strategic Logic of Suicide Terrorism.* New York: Random House.

Patrick, Stewart, 2006, "Weak States and Global Threats: Fact or Fiction?" *The Washington Quarterly*, vol. 29, no. 2. Washington DC: Center for Strategic and International Studies.

Pearson, Graham S., and Malcolm R. Dando, 2005, *Strengthening the Biological Weapons Convention.* Review Conference Paper No. 14. The UN Secretary General's High-level Panel: Biological Weapons-related Issues. May. Department of Peace Studies. University of Bradford.

Pedroni, Peter, 2004, *A More People-oriented Globalization for the 21st Century.* James A. Baker III Institute for Public Policy, Rice University, Houston. December.

Pei, Minxin, and Sara Kasper, 2003, *Lessons from the Past: the American Record on Nation-building.* Carnegie Endowment for International Peace Brief No. 24. May. Washington, DC.

Picciotto, Robert, 2004, "Policy Coherence and Development Evaluation." Background Paper, OECD Workshop. May. Paris: OECD.

Picciotto, Robert, Charles Alao, Eka Ikpe, Martin Kimani, and Roger Slade, 2004, "Striking a New Balance: Donor Policy Coherence and Development Cooperation in Difficult Environments." Background paper commissioned by the Learning and Advisory Process on Difficult Partnerships of the Development Assistance Committee of the OECD. December 30. See also document prepared for the Senior Forum on Development Effectiveness in Fragile States, hosted by the Department for International Development of the United Kingdom London (Lancaster House). <http://www.oecd.org>

Picciotto, Robert, and Rachel Weaving, editors, 2004. *Impact of Rich Countries' Policies on Poor Countries: Towards a Level Playing Field in Development Cooperation.* New Brunswick, NJ: Transaction Publishers.

Piron, Laure-Helene, and Andy McKayu, 2004. *Aid in Difficult Environments: Rwanda Case Study.* UNU-WIDER Conference. June 4-05. Helsinki.

Pogge, Thomas, 2005, "World Poverty and Human Rights," *Ethics and International Affairs*, vol. 19, no. 1.

Pugh, Michael, and Wagehuru Pal Singh Sidhu, 2003, *The United Nations and Regional Security: Europe and Beyond.* International Peace Academy. Boulder, CO, and London: Lynne Rienner Publishers.

Rahman, Mustafizur, 2004, "Globalization, Developed Country Policies, and Market Access: Insights from the Bangladesh Experience." In Picciotto, Robert, and Rachel Weaving, eds., *Impact of Rich Countries' Policies on Poor Countries: Towards a Level Playing Field in Development Cooperation.* New Brunswick, NJ: Transaction Publishers.

Rajan, Raghuram G., and Arvind Subramanian, 2005, *What Undermines Aid's Impact on Growth?* IMF Working Paper WP/05/126, June. Washington, DC: International Monetary Fund.

Renner, Michael, 2002, *The Anatomy of Resource Wars.* Worldwatch Paper 162. Washington, DC: Worldwatch Institute.

Rieff, David, 2005, *At the Point of a Gun: Democratic Dreams and Armed Intervention.* New York, NY: Simon and Schuster.

Rodrik, Dani, 2002, *Feasible Globalizations.* NBER Working Paper No. 9129. Cambridge, MA: National Bureau of Economic Research.

Roodman, David, 2004a, *The Anarchy of Numbers: Aid, Development and Cross-country Empirics.* CGD Working Paper 32. July. Washington, DC: Center for Global Development.

_____, 2004b, *An Index of Donor Performance: 2004 Edition.* April. Washington, DC: Center for Global Development.

Roodman, David, 2005, *Production-weighted Estimates of Aggregate Protection in Rich Countries towards Developing Countries*, Center for Global Development Working Paper 66, August.

Rorty, Richard, 2004, "Post-Democracy," *London Review of Books,* April 1.

Rotberg, Robert, 2003, "The New Nature of Nation-State Failure." In Lennon, Alexander T. J., ed., *The Battle for Hearts and Minds.* Cambridge, MA: Washington Quarterly Reader, MIT Press.

Rothschild, Donald, and Elisabeth M. Cousens, 2002, *Ending Civil Wars.* Boulder, CO, and London: Lynne Rienner Publishers.

Sachs, Jeffrey D., 2005, *The End of Poverty: How We Can Make It Happen in Our Lifetime.* Foreword by Bono. London: Penguin Books.

Sachs, Jeffrey D., 2005, *Investing in Development: A Practical Plan to Achieve the Millennium Development Goals.* Report to the UN Secretary-General. New York, NY: United Nations.

Sandler, Todd, 2004, *Global Collective Action.* Cambridge, UK: Cambridge University Press.

Schelling, Thomas C., 1966, *Arms and Influence.* New Haven and London: Yale University Press.

Sebastien, Dessus, K. Fukasaku, and R. Safadi, 1999, *Multilateral Tariff Liberalization and the Developing Countries*, OECD Development Center Brief No. 18. Paris: OECD.

Sen, Amartya, 2002, *Identity and Freedom. Reordering the World.* The Foreign Policy Center. London: Mark Leonard Editions.

Siegle, Joseph T., Michael M. Weinstein, and Morton H. Halperin, 2004, "Why Democracies Excel," *Foreign Affairs*, vol. 83, no. 5, September/October.

Slaughter, Anne-Marie, 2004, *A New World Order*. Princeton, NJ: Princeton University Press.
Staines, Nicholas, 2004, *Economic Performance over the Conflict Cycle*. IMF Working Paper WP/04/95. Washington, DC: International Monetary Fund.
Stewart, Frances, 2004, "Human Development and Security," *Conflict, Security, and Development*, vol. 4, no. 3.
Stokes, Bruce, 2005, "Public Diplomacy: America is Job No. 1," *National Journal*, May 7.
Study Group on Europe's Security Capabilities, 2004, *A Human Security Doctrine for Europe: The Barcelona Report of the Study Group on Europe's Security Capabilities*. Presented to the EU High Representative for Common Foreign and Security Policy. Barcelona. September. <http://www.lse.ac.uk/Depts/global/Human/>
Sunstein, Cass R., 2005, *Laws of Fear: Beyond the Precautionary Principle*. Cambridge, UK: Cambridge University Press.
Swedish Ministry for Foreign Affairs, 2005, *Project on Fragile States: Final Report*. Stockholm: Policy Analysis Office of the Swedish Ministry for Foreign Affairs.
Tertrais, Bruno, 2005, *War Without End: the View from Abroad*. New York: The New Press.
Torres, Magui Moreno, and Michael Anderson, 2004, "Fragile States: Defining Difficult Environments for Poverty Reduction." Policy Division Working Paper. August. London: U.K. Department for International Development.
Treverton, Gregory F., and Robert Klitgaard, 2005, *Enhancing Security through Development: Probing the Connections*, ABCDE Conference Papers, 2005. Washington, DC: World Bank. <http://web.worldbank.org/WBSITE/EXTERNAL/EXTDEC/EXTAMSTERDAM/0>
United Nations (UN), 2000, *Report of the Panel on United Nations Peace Operations*. New York: United Nations. <http://www.un.org/peace/reports/peace_operations/docs>
―――, 2003a, *Human Security Now: Protecting and Empowering People*. Report of the Commission on Human Security. New York: United Nations.
―――, 2003b, *Handbook on United Nations Multi-dimensional Peacekeeping Operations*. UN Best Practices Unit, Department of Peacekeeping Operations. New York: United Nations.
―――, 2004, *A More Secure World: Our Shared Responsibility*. Report of the High-Level Panel on Threats, Challenges, and Change. New York: United Nations, A/59/565, 2 December 2004. <http://www.un.org/secureworld/report2.pdf>
United Nations Conference on Trade and Development (UNCTAD), 2004, *World Investment Report 2004: The Shift towards Services*. New York and Geneva: UNCTAD. <http://www.unctad.org/wir>
United Nations Environment Program (UNEP), 2005, *GEO Year Book 2004/5: An Overview of Our Changing Environment*. Nairobi: UNEP. <http://www.unep.org>
United Nations Secretary-General, 2005. *In Larger Freedom: Towards Development, Security, and Human Rights for All*. Report of the Secretary General of the United Nations for decision by Heads of State and Government in September 2005. New York: United Nations Department of Public Information. <http://www.un.org/largerfreedom>
United Nations Security Council (UNSC), 2001. UNSC doc. S/PRST/ 2001/5. 20 February. New York: United Nations.
United States Government, 2002, *The National Security Strategy of the United States of America*, Washington DC, The White House, September. http://www.whitehouse.gov/nsc/nsss.pdf

References

United States Government, 2006a, *Quadrennial Defense Review.* February 6. http://www.globalsecurity.org/military/library/policy/dod/qdr-2006-report.htm

United States Government, 2006b, *The National Security Strategy of the United States of America*, Washington DC. The White House, March 2006.

Utstein Group, 2004, Towards a Strategic Framework for Peacebuilding: Getting their Act Together," Overview Report of the Joint Utstein Study of Peacebuilding, Evaluation Report. January. <www.prio.no/page/Project_detail/News_details/9244/41234.html?PHPSESSID=b7c33a8cd37312a4649>

Will, George F., 2001, "The End of Our Holiday from History," *Washington Post*, September 12, 2001.

Winters, L.A., 2001, "Coherence with No 'Here': WTO Cooperation with the World Bank and the IMF," November 2001. Paper originally prepared for the CEPR/ECARES World Bank Conference on The World Trading System Post Seattle, 14-15 July 2000. <www.tulane.edu/~dnelson/PEReformConf/Winters.pdf>

Wolf, Aaron T., Annika Kramer, Alexander Carius, and Geoffrey D. Dabelko, 2005, "Water Can be a Pathway to Peace, Not War," Worldwatch Global Security Brief #5. <www.worldwatch.org/features/security/briefs/5/>

Woods, Ngaire, and research team, 2004, "*Reconciling Effective Aid and Global Security: The Emerging International Development Architecture.*" Oxford: Center for Global Governance, June.

Woodward, Susan, 1995, *Balkan Tragedy: Chaos and Dissolution after the Cold War.* Washington, DC: The Brookings Institution.

World Bank, 1998, *The World Bank's Experience with Post-Conflict Reconstruction: Synthesis.* Washington, DC: World Bank.

_____, 2002, *Global Economic Prospects and the Developing Countries 2002.* Washington, DC: World Bank.

_____, 2005a, *World Development Report 2006: Equity and Development.* Washington DC: World Bank.

_____, 2005b, *Economic Growth in the 1990s: Learning From a Decade of Reforms.* Washington, DC: World Bank.

World Bank Operations Evaluation Department (OED), 2004a, *Addressing the Challenges of Globalization: An Independent Evaluation of the World Bank's Approach to Global Programs.* Washington, DC: World Bank.

_____, 2004b, *Annual Review of Development Effectiveness: The Effectiveness of Bank Support for Policy Reform.* Washington, DC: World Bank.

World Economic Forum, 2005, *Global Governance Initiative Annual Report 2005.* World Economic Forum: Committee to Improve the State of the World. Washington DC and Geneva. <www.weforum.org>

World Health Organization (WHO), 2004, *World Health Report 2004.* Geneva: WHO.

Worldwatch Institute, 2005, *State of the World 2005: Redefining Global Security.* <http://www.worldwatch.org/pubs/sow/2005>

Worldwatch Institute, 2006, *State of the World 2006: Special Focus: China and India.* <http://www.worldwatch.org/pubs/sow/2006>

Zakaria, Fareed, 2002, "Why Muslims Hate the West and What We Can Do about It." In Leonard, Mark (ed.), *Re-ordering the World: The Long-term Implications of 11 September.* London: Foreign Policy Center.

Zartman, I. William, 1990, "Conflict Reduction: Prevention, Management, and Resolution." In Deng, Francis M., and Zartman, I. William (eds.), *Conflict Resolution in Africa*, Washington, DC: Brookings Institution.

Index

Note: Tables are designated with a t after the locator.

Afghanistan
  aid allocations to, 172, 228
  conflicts/wars, issues of, 14, 18, 74, 114, 152-154
  state classification, 168
  terrorism and, 16, 125, 133, 211-212
Africa.
  aid allocations to, 152, 153
  Commission for Africa, 98
  humanitarian issues, 10, 38, 176-180, 229, 268
    regional organizations, 44-45, 211, 217, 232-235 *See also* individual African countries/regions
African Great Lakes Region, 115
African Union, 44-45, 211, 232-233
Agenda for Peace (Boutros-Ghali), 206, 207
Agreement on Trade-related Intellectual Property Rights, 179
agriculture, 84-86, 177-178
aid allocations.
  to developing countries, 67-69, 86-90, 152-153, 172-173, 186-189
  to poor countries, 72-73, 78, 86, 186
  to weak states, 3, 75-76, 137-138, 186-189, 193-195 *See also* aid programs; donor countries
aid and security, 65-67, 193-196
"aid orphans," 267
aid policies
  effectiveness and quality of, 22-23, 57-58, 70, 185-186, 194-196
  peacebuilding and, 261-262
  strategies and, 189-191, 195-196

aid programs
  agencies/organizations, 74, 101, 107, 112, 153-154, 188
  country assistance plans, 242, 244, 261-262
  humanitarian, 51, 148, 186-189, 196, 217, 242-244
aid reform, 147-148, 185-189, 197-198, 242-244
Al Aqsa, 123
Al Qaeda, 17, 122, 125, 154
Algeria, 115, 123, 168, 211
Algiers Declaration, 211
anemic states, 167
Angola, 182, 228
Annan, Kofi, 34, 35, 130, 206
Another Agenda for Peace (Annan), 206
anti-globalization movement, 148
anti-terrorism strategy, 99-100, 122-128, 138, 142, 204, 237
anti-Western sentiment, 123
apartheid, xi
Arab-Israeli dispute, xi, 123, 125, 140
Arafat, Yasser, xi
Argentina, 87
Armed Monitoring Group of ECOWAS (ECOMOG), 211, 217
Arrow, Kenneth, 46
Asia, 11, 12, 113, 138, 153, 179, 249
"Asian Century," 113
Association of East Asian Nations (ASEAN), 44
asymmetrical warfare, 133-134, 151
Atlantic alliance, 24
"atoms for peace," 131
Australia, 45
avian flu, 178
Azerbaijan, 168

281

balance of power, 109
balance of terror, 7, 17, 109, 128-129, 248
Balkans, 26, 74, 140, 222
Bangladesh, 75-76, 165, 194
Barak, Ehud, xi
Barcelona Study Group Report, 35, 108
bio/chemical weapons, 130-132
biotechnology, 178
Bolivia, 177
border controls, 79, 80
Bosnia, 148, 157, 158
Botswana, 183
Boutros-Ghali, Boutros, 206, 207, 213
Bradford University, 196
Brahimi Report, 208-209
brain drain/gain, 94
Brazil, 129, 174, 178
Bretton Woods institutions, 244
Burundi, 115, 167, 211

Cambodia, 157, 158
Camp David, xi
Canada, 34, 35, 208
capacity building, 164-165, 169-171
captured states, 168
Caribbean Community, 44
Carter Center, 135
Center for Global Development, 28, 108, 168-170, 186, 197
Central African Republic, 210
Central Asia, 138
Chechnya, 123, 125, 210
Chemical Weapons Convention, 132
Chile, 183, 194
China, xi-xii, 11, 19, 25, 82, 84
civil rights, 50, 54. *See also* human rights
"clash of civilizations," 160-161, 166
Clausewitz, Carl von, 162
climate change, 22, 79, 82-83, 95-96, 120, 181. *See also* environmental issues
Clinton, Bill, xi, 12
Club of Madrid, 126-127, 142
Cold War, 14, 17, 109, 128-129, 147-148, 248
collateral damage, 110-115, 119, 126, 134, 205, 251
collective multilateral security system, 74
Collier, Paul, 162, 196

Colombia, 115, 121, 157, 177
Commission for Africa, 98
Commission on Human Security, 33
Commission to Africa, 98
Commonwealth of Independent States, 44
Comprehensive Test Ban treaty, 129
conflict cycle metaphor, 107
conflict management
   conflict resolution/mediation, 5, 74, 107, 204-208, 260-261
   development cooperation and, 118-119
   international community and, 225, 227, 233, 237-238, 263
   new approaches to, 263-265
   policies and practices, 203, 211
   prevention strategies, 16, 51, 72, 141-142, 189-192
   regional/local actors and, 204, 210, 212-213, 233-236 *See also* risk assessment
conflict-poverty nexus, 173-174
conflicts. See conflicts/wars
conflicts/wars
   asymmetrical warfare, 133-134, 151
   civil war, xiii, 69, 114, 116, 148, 175
   collateral damage, 110-115, 119, 126, 134, 151, 205, 251
   costs of, 24, 189-192, 196, 207, 209, 212
   insurgency, 23, 43, 114, 119, 124, 133-134
   international, 113-114
   inter-state, 15, 109-110, 112-114, 141, 205
   intra-national, 133
   intra-state, 107-108, 114-122, 141, 176, 250
   poverty-conflict association, 108, 115-119
   See also specific conflicts/wars
Cote d'Ivoire, 160, 166, 178, 210, 211, 216, 223
country assistance plans, 242, 244, 261-262
country classifications, 171t-172t, 168-169
Country Policy and Institutional Assessment System (CPIA), 197

crime
 economy of, 161, 162, 184
 illegal drugs, 21, 121
 international, 7, 20-22, 138, 159, 254
 Kimberley Process, 27-28, 163, 183
 trafficking, 77, 94, 98, 99, 121, 159

Darfur, 14, 31, 177, 186, 251, 253
debt reduction strategies, 31, 75, 148, 198
democracy, 108, 119, 124, 127, 216
Democratic People's Republic of Korea, 113
Democratic Republic of Congo (DRC), 15, 18, 114, 182, 210, 228
demographics
 mortality, 10, 175, 177, 180-181, 184
 population change, 81-82, 140-142, 243
 youth bulge, 69, 124-125, 175, 228-231
Denmark, 153
developing countries
 aid allocations to, 67-69, 86-90, 152-153, 172-174, 186-189
 conflicts/wars impact of, 9, 13-15, 68-69
 economies of, 10-11, 31, 48, 76, 87, 252, 258
 policies, 46, 66, 88-92, 148, 244, 247
 security, 42, 171-172t, 254-255
 trade, 27-28, 30, 84
 See also poor countries; weak states
Development Assistance Committee of the OECD (DAC)
 country classification by, 167-168
 development cooperation and, 157, 267-268
 Guidelines on Poverty Reduction, 260
 Journal of Development Cooperation, 47
 official development assistance (ODA), 153-154
 projected goals of, 3-4, 30, 49, 67
"developmentalization of security," 4, 8, 71-72
diasporas, 114, 140-141, 190
digital divide, 179. *See also* technology

diplomacy, 25, 133-134, 189, 206, 213
dirigiste policies, 23
disaggregated state, 246, 247
disarmament, demobilization, reintegration (DDR), 213, 218-219, 221-227, 231
disease
 in animals, 178
 avian flu, 178
 ebola, 180
 hepatitis C, 180
 HIV/AIDS, 10, 36, 175, 177, 180, 229, 242
 protection against, 7, 10, 79, 180-181
 SARS, 180, 184
 spread of, 15, 22, 83, 117, 120
disintegration of states, 108, 117-121
DNA technologies, 132
Doha, 86, 95
Dominican Republic, 158
donor countries
 aid allocations by, 57-58, 70, 156-157, 172-173
 engagement strategies of, 21, 49, 56, 76, 152, 169, 244
 "footprint" assessment, 256-258
 policy and, 46, 81, 100, 167
Duffield, Mark, 161, 162-163

East Africa, 176
East Asia, 11
East Pakistan, 165
East Timor, 45, 207, 216
Eastern Europe, 137, 228
ebola, 180
Economic Community of West African States (ECOWAS), 44-45, 211, 232-235
ecosystems, 82, 84
Egypt, 129, 157, 167
Eighth Millennium Development Goal, 100, 267
Enron, xi
enterprise states, 155
environmental issues
 agencies/programs, 95, 182
 climate change, 22, 79, 82-83, 95-96, 120, 181
 environmental rankings, 28
 natural resources, 11, 97, 181-183
 protection, 2, 65, 75, 242, 254

resource depletion, 81-84
sustainable development, 95, 96
Eritrea, 218
Ethiopia-Eritrea conflict, 14, 210, 217
ethnic cleansing, 51, 108, 251
EU Code of Conduct, 73
Europe, 25, 77, 136-137, 140. *See also* European Union (EU)
European Environment Agency, 95
European Neighborhood Policies, 54, 55, 156
European Security Strategy, 36, 139-141
European Union (EU)
 code of conduct, 73
 EU-15, 27
 European Neighborhood Policies and, 54, 55, 156
 in global politics, 35, 115, 136-142, 211
 strategies, 26, 45, 74, 156
European Union (EU) Africa Peace Facility, 235
European Union (EU) Code of Conduct, 73
Europe-Islam security and development nexus, 141
exit, voice, and loyalty model, 164-166
Extractive Industry Transparency Initiative, 183

failed states
 causes of failure, xiii, 9, 157, 225
 reconstruction of, 175-176, 186-187
 refugee flows from, 114, 115
 security and, 132-133, 142
Failed States Index, 157
Financing for Development Conference in Monterrey (Mexico), 2, 149
Finland, 27, 29, 67
fishing industry, 83, 85
food security, 176-178
"footprint" assessment, 256-258
foreign direct investment (FDI), 65, 76, 78, 88-92
Foreign Policy, 157
fragile states. *See* weak states
France, 122, 129
Fund for Peace, 157

G8, Gleneagles summit, xiv, 75
gender inequality, 2, 50, 174, 176, 179

General Agreement on Tariffs and Trade, 29
Geneva Convention, 126
geopolitical risks, 79-80, 248-255
Germany, 157-158, 166, 208
Ghana, 194
Global Commission on International Migration Report, 94-95
global economy
 commodities/resources, 83-85
 conflict, impact on, 24, 116, 120, 189-192, 196, 207, 209, 212
 consumption/production patterns, 95-96
 debt reduction strategies, 31, 75, 148, 198
 FDI and, 65, 76, 78, 88-92
 "footprint" assessment, 256-258
 growth of, 174, 184-186, 248
 imbalance in, 148, 252
 international financial system and, 50, 86-87, 195
 market, 10-11, 48, 85-86, 242
 outsourcing, 32, 245
 policies, 3, 19, 20, 71
 tariffs, 27, 29, 84-86
 unemployment, 69, 87, 124-125, 140, 175-176
 See also poverty; trade
global market. *See* global economy
global policy, 9-10, 161, 178, 207-208
global public goods, 35, 40-41, 50, 66, 75, 80, 81, 243
global risk, 252-255
global warming, 22, 82-83, 95-96, 120, 181. *See also* environmental issues
globalization
 development and, 65-67, 149, 243-244, 250
 management of, 74-75, 77-79
 networks and, 79-81, 161-162, 245-246
 opposition to, 19, 112, 148
 risks of, 20-21, 80, 250, 268
 states and, 66, 78-79, 154, 247
 technology and, 18-19, 151
 of violence, 97, 98, 162
 See also global economy
governance
 accountability and, 39-40
 global, 161, 166, 244-245, 247-250
 for security, 42-46, 122

stability and, 90, 188, 191
gross domestic product (GDP), 24-25, 115, 117
Guidelines on Poverty Reduction (DAC), 260
Guinea, 223
Guinea-Bissau, 210, 211, 234
Gulf Wars, 14, 112-113

Haiti, 168, 178
Hamas, 123
"hard" security, 33, 254
"hard" threats, 8
"hearts and minds" campaigns, 124
hegemonic world view, 112, 160-161
hepatitis C, 180
High-level Forum on Fragile States (OECD), 157
High-level Panel Report on Threats, Challenges and Change (UN), 99, 132
Hippocratic Oath, 151
Hirschman, Albert O., 105, 164-166, 187
HIV/AIDS
 death statistics, 180
 demographics/youth bulge and, 175, 177
 as global crisis, 36, 242
 in Sub-Saharan Africa, 10, 229
"holiday from history," 3, 13
Holmgren, Torgny, 1
Horizontal Program of Policy Coherence of the OECD, 169
human development index, 117
human rights
 advocacy, 7, 250
 civil rights, 50, 54
 development/security strategies and, 152
 gender inequality, 2, 50, 174, 176, 179
 human security/categories of human rights, 44t
 safeguard policies and, 49-50, 120, 127-128, 150
 violations, 15, 50-52, 106, 107, 126, 183
Human Rights Council, 52, 54
human security
 agenda, 53-55
 development cooperation and, 32-36
 economics of, 39-46
 paradigm, 8, 9, 173, 259-260
 human security/categories of human rights, 44t
Human Security Center of the University of British Columbia, 251-252
Human Security Fund, 33
Hungary, 194
Huntington, Samuel P., 160, 162, 165
Hussein, Saddam, 112

immigration, 28, 76-77, 92-95. See also migration
In Larger Freedom (report: UN Secretary-General), 54, 70, 126, 236, 260
India, xi-xii, 19, 25, 82, 113, 129, 131
India/Pakistan conflict, 113
Indonesia, 115, 119, 167
influenza, 178, 180
information technology, xi, 18-19, 151
insurgency, 23, 43, 114, 119, 124, 133-134
intellectual property, 28, 40, 76, 180
Intergovernmental Panel on Climate Change, 82-83
International Alert, 135
International Atomic Energy Agency (IAEA), 131
International Commission on Intervention and State Sovereignty (ICISS), 35
International Covenants on Economic, Social and Cultural Rights, 50
international crime, 7, 20-21, 138, 159, 254. *See also crime*
International Crisis Group, 251
International Finance Company, 195
International Labor Organization, 229
International Monetary Fund, 186
international rule of law, 26
international terrorism. See terrorism
International Treaty on Plant Genetic Resources for Food and Agriculture, 178
Internet, 19, 179
interventionism, 13, 133
intifada, xi
"invisible hand," 105
Iran
 as nuclear threat, 14, 129, 131
 status of, 121, 157
 terrorism and, 133
 war and, 112

Iraq
  long struggle of, 123-125, 149, 212
  occupation of, 114
  reconstruction efforts in, 152-153
  state disintegration, xii, 118, 157
  terrorism and, 13, 17-18, 121, 249
  UN missions in, 210
  war and, 14, 112, 197
Iraq/Iran War, 112
Ireland, 129
"iron triangle," 256
Islam, xiii, 140-141
Islamic Conference, 44
Islamic extremism, xii, 122, 125, 248
Israel, xi, 122, 123, 125, 129, 131
Ituri, 211

Jacoby, Ruth, 1
Japan, xi, 23, 131, 157
jihad, 17-18, 69, 121, 123-125, 134. See also terrorism
"joined-up" government
  cooperation and, 1, 152
  initiatives, 29-30, 46
  policy coherence and, 58, 67, 246
"joined-up" policies, 257
"joined-up" units, 18
Jordan, 167
Journal of Development Cooperation (DAC), 47

Kant, Immanuel, 31
Kashmir, 14, 121, 125, 184
Khan, A.Q., 17
Kimberley Process, 27-28, 163, 183
Korea, 113
Kosovo, 115, 158, 207, 210, 218
Kuwait, 112
Kyoto, 28, 82, 96

Latin America, 2, 129, 227-228, 249
League of Nations, 43
Lebanon, 118, 157
Lederach, 207, 213
Liberia, 18, 111, 167, 210-211, 216-218, 222-230
Liberian Comprehensive Peace Agreement, 225, 226
"low-income countries under stress" (LICUS), 121-122, 168, 195

Macedonia, 168

Machiavelli, 149
Mali, 205
malnutrition, 2, 7, 156, 174, 177
Maoism, 69, 122
Mexico, 129, 178, 194
Middle East, 12, 97, 138, 141, 153
migration, 28, 65, 76-77, 92-95, 140. See also immigration
military, 13, 23-24, 68-69, 72-73, 100, 133-134. *See also* conflicts/wars; weapons
militia, 230, 232
Millennium Challenge Account, 167
Millennium Declaration, 3, 30, 72, 149
Millennium Development Goals (MDG)
  eighth MDG, 100, 267
  obstacles to, 3, 9-10, 67, 68, 99, 149, 153-154, 177
  progress towards, 29, 54, 88, 241-242
  support for, 2, 57, 65-66, 128
Millennium Project, 68
Millennium Security Goals, 105, 260
Millennium Summit, 68
"mission-defined coalitions," 74
Moldova, 137
Monterrey (Mexico) Conference 2002, 2, 149
Moore, Jonathan, 157
mortality, 10, 175-177, 180-181, 184. *See also* collateral damage
Mozambique, 157, 210
Multi Donor Regeneration Plan, 223
multilateralism, xii, 36, 81, 244
multinational companies, 45, 50, 90
Muslim societies, 140-142. See also Islam
Myanmar, 115

9/11, xii, 13, 55, 87, 152, 153
nationalism, 164-165
natural disasters, 55, 83, 119, 184-185
natural resources, 11, 97, 181-183
"neo-liberal" doctrine, 23, 160, 162-163
Nepal, 73, 121
Netherlands, 67, 208
networks, 79-81, 161-162, 245-250
New Agenda Coalition, 129
New Zealand, 129
Nigeria, 75, 178, 211, 217, 229, 234

Index   287

non-governmental organizations (NGO), 32, 58, 107, 157, 188, 246
non-state actors
  cooperation of, 172-173, 191-192, 195, 245
  risks posed by, 16, 32, 74, 131-134, 139
non-state security groups, 226
non-territorial risk, 79
North Africa, 12
North American Free Trade Association (NAFTA), 194
North Atlantic Treaty Organization (NATO), 44, 45, 74, 115, 209
North Korea, 14, 121, 131, 134
Northern Ireland, 135
Northern Sudan, 133
Norway, 11, 67, 208
nuclear disarmament, 128-132, 139, 142
Nuclear Non-Proliferation Treaty (NPT), 128-132, 139, 142
"nuclear starter kits," 17
nuclear weapons, 14, 17, 23, 113, 128-132
Nyerere Foundation, 135

official development assistance (ODA), 153-154
Ogata, Sadako, 33
Ogata-Sen Commission on Human Security, 35
oligarchies, 137
Operation Artemis, 211
Operations Evaluation Department (World Bank), 195
Orange Revolution, 109
Organization for Economic Cooperation and Development (OECD)
  development, 27, 70
  High-level Forum on Fragile States, 157
  reform, 18, 43, 46, 47, 156
  security and, 89, 121, 227
Organization for Security and Co-operation in Europe (OSCE), 44, 73, 182
Organization of African Unity, 217
Organization of American States, 44
Oslo process, xi
outsourcing, 32, 245
Oxfam, 73

Pakistan, 125, 129, 131, 153, 165, 167, 178
Palestine, xi, 123, 125, 140, 249
pandemics, 7, 10, 36, 80, 178, 180, 243. *See also* disease; HIV/AIDS
Pareto optimality, 150
Pareto-efficient, 39, 48, 91, 151
"partnership for development," 2
patent laws, 29
peace
  accords/agreements, 213, 222, 225-226, 231, 265
  peace building objectives, 206-209, 212-219, 261-262
  peacekeeping, 26, 41, 112, 189, 206, 215, 218-219
  peacemaking, 72, 206, 212-213, 220, 222
  pluralistic society and, 41-42
  process/structure gap, 213
  research, 109-110
  support operations, 157, 189-190, 206, 214-221, 235
  support/prevention mandates, 264-265
Peacebuilding Commission (proposed), 70, 101, 118, 210, 233, 234, 237
Pew Research Center, 14
"phantom aid," 22
Philippines, 157, 178
Poland, 109, 194
policy coherence
  definition/theory of, 46-49
  for development, 69-72, 154, 169, 209, 256-257
  monitoring of, 54, 57-59, 67, 167, 246
  problem solving, 71, 72, 100-101, 259
  for security, 65-67, 72-73, 78-79, 167, 203, 209
policy of benign neglect, 70
poor countries
  aid allocations to, 72-73, 78, 86, 186
  importation of knowledge and, 180
  security for, 87, 90, 108, 161, 180, 260
  strength of, 120
populists, 92
port security, 17, 21
post-Cold War era, 22-23, 46, 149, 205, 248

post-conflict assistance, 72, 112, 188-193, 196, 216-217
post-modern conflict, 111
poverty
  global, 2, 9-11, 22, 176-177, 181, 241
  human security paradigm and, 173
  income poverty, 10, 11, 174
  in low-income countries, 69, 121-122, 168, 169, 195
  malnutrition and, 2, 7, 156, 174, 177
  policy and, 47, 66-67, 260
  poverty-conflict association, 108, 115-119
  reduction strategies, 4-5, 148, 174-175, 187, 194, 198
Poverty Guidelines (OECD/DAC), 47
poverty-conflict association, 108, 115-119
Principe, 234
private sector, 23, 32, 65, 76, 88, 100-101
private security contractors, 100-101
"problems without passports," 2, 12
"process-structure gap," 213
proliferation of weapons, 14, 98, 128-132, 138-139, 142
Proliferation Security Initiative, 130
property rights, 41, 158
protectionism, 77
public policy, secularization of, 38-39
public-private partnerships, 58

quick impact projects (QIPS), 218-219, 221

radical leftist groups, 122
rebel groups, 115
"re-enchantment of war," 151
refugee flows
  causes of, 114, 115, 148, 177
  human rights violations and, 15, 51
  status of, 50, 93
regional/local action
  challenges/benefits of, 43-46, 209-213, 224-226
  conflict management and, 204, 210, 212-213, 233-236
  organizations, 69, 100, 217, 232-236
religion, 122, 125, 133
Republic of Korea, 113

Rice, Condoleezza, 25
rich countries
  interests of, 10-11, 81, 94, 100, 151
  investments, 88-92
  trade issues, 84-86
  See also donor countries
ricin, 132
risk assessment
  analysis, 34
  catastrophic risk, 17, 37-38, 142
  engagement strategies and, 258-259
  geopolitical, 79-80, 248-255
  management and, 8, 17-18, 36-39
  policy and, 150-151
  risk sharing, 175
rogue states, 74
Roodman, 195
Rotberg, 190
rule of law, 34, 50, 155, 158
Russia, 17, 44, 130, 131, 157
Rwanda
  destabilization of, 15-16, 84, 186
  refugee flows from, 148
  violence in, 12, 108, 111, 166, 178

Sachs, 187
Sahel, 176
Sao Tome, 211, 234
Saudi Arabia, 121-123, 125, 133, 157, 168
"securitization of development," 4, 8, 51, 71-72, 71-72
security sector reform (SSR), 46, 54, 194, 225-227, 231, 237
security/development statistics, 171t-172t
Sen, Amartya, 33
shadow states, 167, 186, 231-232
Shared Responsibility Bill, 29-31
Short, Clare, 193
Sierra Leone
  external intervention, 183, 210, 211, 217
  recovery projects in, 218, 222, 223, 225, 228
  risks to, 18, 109
Slovenia, 129
Smith, Adam, 7, 105
social responsibility programs, 245
"soft security," 33
Somalia, 12, 133, 157, 158, 167, 188
South Africa, 44, 177, 205, 211, 234

South African Development Community (SADC), 44, 234
South America. *See* individual countries
South Asia, 12, 138
South Caucasus countries, 137
South Korea, 229
South Vietnam, 158
Soviet Union (former), 3, 12, 23, 129, 133
Spain, 35, 108, 122-123, 126-127, 142, 153
Sri Lanka, 121, 122, 210
State Failure Task Force, 175-176
states
    categories of, 74, 78, 155, 167, 186-187, 231-232. *See also* failed states; weak states
    fragility defined, 171t, 168-170
    development of, 171-173
    disaggregated, 246, 247
    disintegration of, 108, 117-121, 157
    exit, voice, and loyalty model, 164-166
    globalization and, 66, 78-79, 154, 247
    monopoly on force/violence, 40, 160, 193, 225, 232
    nationalism and, 164-165
    post-conflict assistance, 216-217
    security of, 4, 154-160, 165
    sovereignty, 42-43
    state building, 56, 78, 152, 154-158, 165, 197
    state-centric doctrines, 4, 45, 109
    See also developing countries; poor countries
Stockholm International Peace Research Institute, 109-110
structural/cultural violence, 106
Sub-Saharan Africa, 10, 12, 76, 179, 227, 229
Sudan, 15, 98, 115, 125
sudden acute respiratory syndrome (SARS), 180, 184
suicide bombers, 18, 122, 126, 134
Sweden, xii, 1, 29-31, 67, 129
Sweden's Shared Responsibility bill, 1
Swedish Parliament, 29-30
Syria, 157

3/11(Madrid train bombings), 153
Taiwan, 113
Tajikistan, 210

Taliban, 108, 122
Tanzania, 11
tariffs, 27, 29, 84-86
technology
    biotechnology, 178
    DNA technologies, 132
    information technology, xi, 18-19, 151
    nuclear technologies, 129, 142
    weapon technology, 97
terrorism
    Afghanistan and, 125, 133, 211-212
    Al Aqsa, 123
    Al Qaeda, 17, 122, 125, 154
    anti-terrorism strategy, 99-100, 122-128, 138, 142, 204, 237
    balance of terror, 7, 17, 109, 128-129, 248
    as global security risk, 13, 128, 173
    Iraq and, 121, 123, 125, 249
    Islamic, xii, xiii, 124
    jihad, 17-18, 69, 121, 123-125, 134
    rule of law and, 127
    suicide bombers, 18, 122, 126, 134
    Taliban, 108, 122
    trans-national, 7, 55, 121
    war on terrorism, 25, 57, 73, 112, 152, 248, 248-249
threat assessment, 8-9
"tied aid," 22
Togo, 210, 234
Tolstoy, Leo, 167
trade, xv, 20-21, 27-29, 76-78, 84-86
trafficking. See crime
trans-national terrorism, 7, 55, 121
transparency, 42, 47, 71, 155, 158, 183
Traore, Mousa, 205
Turkey
    EU and, 125, 140
    status of, 26, 115, 157, 194
    terrorism and, 122-123

Uganda, 73, 194, 253
Ukraine, 109, 157
unemployment, 69, 87, 124-125, 140, 175-176
United Kingdom Department for International Development (DFID), 167
United Kingdom (UK), 18, 67, 129, 183, 208, 232
United Nations (UN)
    Charter, 3, 50, 241

Children's Fund (UNICEF), 228
Commission on Human Rights, 127
Conference on Trade and Development, 89
Convention Relating to the Status of Refugees, 93
Department of Peacekeeping Operations, 218-219
Department of Political Affairs, 219
Development Program, 33, 168, 182
Eighth Millennium Development Goal and, 100, 267
Environment Program, 182
High Commission for Human Rights, 52
High-level Panel, 126-127, 236
High-level Panel Report on Threats, Challenges and Change, 99, 132
leadership and, 237, 249
management and, 16, 55-56, 100, 152
missions, 209-211, 215-216, 218-221, 226-228
peacekeeping operations, 189, 206, 218-219
Secretariat, 214
Security Council, 208, 210, 214
strategic vision and, 212-215, 235
Summit (2005), 52-53, 70, 75
See also Millennium Development Goals (MDG); United Nations (UN) Secretary-General

United Nations (UN) Secretary-General
B. Boutros-Ghali, 206, 207
"iron triangle" proposal, 256
K. Annan, 34, 35, 130, 206
In Larger Freedom proposals, 54, 70, 126, 236, 260
special representative of (SRSG), 220-221, 228, 236-237
United States (US)
2006 Quadrennial Defense Review, 15, 16
Agency for International Development, 167
Central Intelligence Agency, 176
foreign policy, xi, 15, 28, 96, 129, 152, 167
government of, 13, 23, 24-25
"holiday from history," 3, 13
international status, 12, 24, 77, 149
military, 23-24, 68, 112, 211
National Counterterrorism Center, 122
State Department, 251
terrorism and, 15-17, 24, 122, 152, 248-249
Universal Declaration of Human Rights, 50
University of British Colombia Human Security Center, 35
Uruguay, 89
Uruguay Round Agreement on Trade-related Investment Measures (TRIMS), 89
Utstein Group, 208-209

Venezuela, 168
Vietnam, 174, 194
violence
costs of, 24, 68, 107, 111, 190-192, 196
globalization of, 97, 98, 162
state monopoly on, 40, 160, 193, 225, 232
structural/cultural, 106
voluntary organizations, 19, 74, 80, 135, 148
vulnerability-exposure nexus, 258t, 259

war. *See* conflicts/wars
"war after the war," 18, 112
war on terrorism, 25, 57, 73, 112, 152, 248-249
warfare, 131-134, 151, 251. See conflicts/wars
warlords, 162, 167
wars. *See* conflicts/wars
Warsaw Pact, 97
weak states
aid allocations to, 3, 75-76, 137-138, 186-189, 193-195
capacity building in, 169-170
conflict prevention in, 231, 233
digital divide in, 179
fragility defined, 171t, 167-170
as global security risks, 13, 15-16, 121-122
globalization of, 66, 78-79, 154
human risk in, 9, 120, 123, 147, 156, 228-229
"iron triangle" and, 117-120
natural resources in, 183-184

policy and, 65-67, 69-72, 78, 266-267
poverty-conflict association and, 108-109
security of, 132-133, 154-160
security/development and, 157-158, 171t-172t, 203
weapons proliferation and, 98, 138-139
See also developing countries; poor countries
weapons
  balance of terror, 7, 14, 17, 128-129, 248
  bio/chemical weapons, 130-132
  non-nuclear ratifying countries, 129
  nuclear, 113, 129, 130, 131
  "nuclear starter kits,," 17
  proliferation of, 14, 98, 128-132, 138-139, 142
  purchase, 72-73
  technology, 97, 129, 142
  trade, 96-98
  WMD, 17, 113, 129, 130, 131
weapons of mass destruction (WMD), 17, 113, 129, 130, 131
welfare state, 78

West Africa, 44-45, 115, 211, 223-224, 232-235
West Bank, 125
Westphalia Treaties, 109
"whole of government" approach, 21, 31, 49, 58, 100, 246
World Bank, 12, 85, 121-122, 168, 193-195
World Health Organization (WHO), 180
World Resources Institute, 82
World Trade Organization (WTO), 76, 89, 180
World War II, 133, 147, 250
Worldwatch, 35

youth
  children, 177, 179, 228
  marginalization of, 228-233
  reintegration of, 237
  unemployment, 69, 124-125, 140, 175-176
Yugoslavia (former), 108, 115, 118, 168

Zimbabwe, 177, 210